THE MILLION DOLLAR Quartet

JERRY LEE, CARL, ELVIS & JOHNNY

Stephen Miller

OMNIBUS PRESS

London / New York / Paris / Sydney / Copenhagen / Berlin / Madrid / Tokyo

Exclusive Distributors
Music Sales Limited,
14/15 Berners Street,
London, W1T 3LJ.

Music Sales Corporation
180 Madison Avenue, 24th Floor,
New York,
NY 10016,
USA.

Macmillan Distribution Services,
56 Parkwest Drive
Derrimut, Vic 3030,
Australia.

Every effort has been made to trace the copyright holders of the photographs in this book but one or
two were unreachable. We would be grateful if the photographers concerned would contact us.

Typeset by Phoenix Photosetting, Chatham, Kent
Printed in the EU

A catalogue record for this book is available from the British Library.

Visit Omnibus Press on the web at www.omnibuspress.com

Contents

Introduction

December 4, 1956, a day when a group of musicians got together for an impromptu jam session at Sun Studio in Union Avenue, Memphis, Tennessee, fell during a time of great change in the western world. Memories of World War Two were starting to fade from everyday consciousness as new tensions emerged, not least as a result of the Cold War between the USSR and the West. However, despite momentous events in the world of international politics – the Suez Crisis, the suppression of the Hungarian uprising and the war on the Korean peninsula – there were big social changes afoot too; and the younger generation was at the forefront.

As the West started to recover from the massive impact war had on everyday life, people could start to relax a little bit. There was more freedom to think about the ordinary pleasures of life – and it was young people in particular who demanded levels of personal enjoyment and fulfilment that most of their parents had only been able to dream about.

By the mid-fifties around one third of the American population was under 15 years of age. Teenagers were fast becoming a distinct demographic group, and were increasingly resistant to the notion that they should be seen and not heard. As peace became established and they started to acquire economic pull, they were looking for fun and inspiration tailored to their own tastes and preferences. Popular music was an area of particular interest and increasing numbers of youngsters were no longer prepared to accept slightly pepped up versions of the pop music their parents liked. They were looking for their own heroes and as the peace held and the American economy prospered they began to have the means to achieve their goals.

It was their good fortune that a number of exceptionally talented – though musically untrained – individuals were keen to give them exactly what they wanted. Chief amongst them was Elvis Presley; but there were plenty more where he came from including Johnny Cash, Jerry Lee Lewis and Carl Perkins. These four natural talents all came from a comparatively small geographical area in the southern states of Mississippi, Arkansas, Louisiana and Tennessee. Their rural upbringings had all been coloured by similar palettes made up of music, religion and poverty.

The organic development of music in these areas, with its rich mix of styles which flowed across racial boundaries – blues, country, gospel, rhythm and blues, pop and more – resulted in the kind of dramatic flowering of new and exciting sounds seen only occasionally before or since. The quartet were in the vanguard of those artists who came up with the very best of them; individual songs and musical styles which have become firmly imprinted on the music of the world ever since. Ecstatic young people welcomed them – worshipped them some might say – as an answer to their prayers. Aside from the straightforward feelgood factor of the music, writer Robert Hilburn detected another reason for its widespread appeal. The success of artists like the Million Dollar Quartet was an affirmation of the American dream following times of hardship; anybody, however humble, with hard work and determination could be successful and make a difference. "Rock 'n' roll was the promise of a better day," wrote Hilburn, "and the best artists spread that message with an almost missionary zeal."

However, no matter how great the musical gifts each member of what would come to be known as the Million Dollar Quartet possessed, they needed someone to get them known.

Sam Phillips was a man with a vision. In a way that few people can, he proved himself able to raise his head above the musical melee going on all around him and follow that vision single mindedly. He was searching for a way to capture the visceral groove of the countless vibrant sounds, particularly those coming from black artists he heard in and around Memphis. He wanted to capture the immediacy and energy of it all in a two-minute song – and then get it across to the largest possible number of people. He was sure he knew what the public wanted, before they fully realised it themselves, and that if he could just get the right formula, they would flock to buy his records in large numbers and make money for him. He loved the music but he was also a businessman. His theory proved to be correct – although even he could not have imagined the tsunami-like force he would unleash.

Elvis was the big breakthrough although Sam, in a remarkable period of two years or so, deployed his considerable talents to launch the careers of several other major figures including the other members of the Million Dollar Quartet. He was largely responsible for some of the most memorable pieces of popular music ever recorded, including 'That's All Right (Mama)', 'Whole Lot Of Shakin' Going On', 'Blue Suede Shoes' and 'I Walk The Line'.

Singer and producer Rodney Crowell was a young boy during this magical era. Even though he was brought up in Texas, the exciting sounds coming out of Memphis reached him too. In his 2001 autobiographical song 'Telephone Road' he brilliantly captured the febrile atmosphere of the times.

Magnolia Garden bandstand on the very front row
Johnny Cash, Carl Perkins and the Killer putting on a show
Six years old and just barely off my daddy's knee
When those rockabilly rebels
Sent the Devil running right through me

What all four members of the quartet loved above all else was to get together with their friends and make music; and that is precisely what they did on December 4, 1956. It was a chance get together made possible, like so much else, by the sharp thinking of Sam Phillips. It is unlikely that four artists of their calibre could enjoy such a carefree session nowadays – the lawyers and money men would want to set it up in advance, secure all the commercial angles and lay down the law on what songs would be played. Back in the early days of rock 'n' roll this kind of business-oriented infrastructure was embryonic – particularly in the southern states – and so when Elvis cruised past Sun studio and decided to go in and see what was happening that afternoon, anything was possible. Although informal jam sessions were not uncommon, the presence of Elvis, already an established star, made this one extra special.

It was ironic that while conservative elements in society held Elvis and other rising stars responsible for a major decline in the morals of the nation, they were in fact, underneath their flamboyant exteriors, patriotic young men who were respectful of tradition, particularly when it came to music, and deeply religious. Indeed when Elvis, Johnny, Jerry Lee and Carl started jamming that day they spontaneously hit on religious songs as well as some pop standards their parents would have approved of. They wanted to make their mark but they certainly did not want to foment a social revolution. Nevertheless, they did make a major contribution to a tide of radical change in social and sexual mores which swept across the western world in the years following their little gathering in Memphis.

However of far greater importance was what they gave to the world of popular music. Virtually every artist of any significance who has followed in their wake would claim at least one of them as an influence – they carried a wide variety of styles in their musical genes, added a lot more of their own and then passed them all on to the world.

"Million Dollar Quartet" has remained a powerful name; it was the obvious choice for a successful musical based on the jam session which made it all the way to Broadway. Perhaps even now some Hollywood producer is looking at the possibility of a movie. The studio on Union Avenue has been restored and is now a national monument where, for a few dollars, you can stand on the spot where Elvis recorded his very first song. Interest in the lives and music of the principals, especially Elvis Presley and Johnny Cash, continues unabated to the present day and shows no sign of letting up any time soon. Floyd Mutrux, who had the original idea for the stage musical, talks of a "continuing journey".

When the quartet sparked up their little session in 1956 it is fortunate for posterity that some of what they did was recorded. Good fortune also saw to it that the tapes survived years of being stuck in boxes at the back of various cupboards, were found before becoming irreparably damaged by the passage of time, and were then expertly restored before being made available to the public at large. By the time all of this happened Elvis was dead and the careers of the remaining members of the quartet were mere shadows of their glory days. However what the recordings bring vividly to life, in a remarkable piece of musical archaeology, is a priceless fly-on-the-wall glimpse of the very origins of modern popular music.

To set the scene for the session itself there are essays on each of the principals involved, which detail the personal journeys each took before arriving at Sun Studio on December 4, 1956.

1.

Sam Phillips

On the principle that cream always rises to the top, it is arguable that Elvis Presley, Johnny Cash, Jerry Lee Lewis and Carl Perkins were always going to achieve great things. This might be true but the fact remains that in the early days, all were, to say the least, inexperienced in the ways of the music industry. They believed they had a skill, some kind of gift even, but they were young men from poor backgrounds who, on their own, might well have achieved local success but not much more. Elvis Presley, shy and self-effacing, might simply have turned away from the music industry altogether and remained a truck driver who entertained family and friends now and then – a course of action that would most likely have ensured a longer and happier life.

Like many other young people with a musical talent, all four wanted to sing and play music and make some money. But whilst all of them became very attractive to the music industry establishment, none fitted any kind of conventional mould at the outset of their careers and they were only ever going to achieve an initial breakthrough with the assistance of some unusual kind of musical maverick. Most of the major record labels were based in large cities far from the southern states of America and their executives tended to be dismissive of what they regarded as the unsophisticated music of the poor white folks. Similarly they did not have much regard for the kind of bluesy music (often loosely referred to as race music) performed by black artists.

Broadly speaking these were the kinds of music that the four young men who would become the Million Dollar Quartet played. For music with this kind of provenance and feel to gain recognition there would have to be a significant shift in public attitudes; and this would only happen through the medium of an outsider, an original thinker, someone with an ability to recognise special talent and present it in a form that resonated with, and was acceptable to, the public at large; someone who was able to give people what they wanted even before they realised they wanted it. Sam Phillips was one such man.

The youngest of eight children, Samuel Cornelius Phillips was born on January 5, 1923 in the small rural town of Florence, Alabama. His father was a cotton farmer who worked an area of land extending to about 300 acres which he rented from the local land owner. Though not able to afford much in the way of luxuries the family was reasonably comfortable until the stock market crash of 1929. Sam's father lost most of the savings he had built up; it would be years before he recovered from this blow. As a result the older children had to work in the fields, picking cotton. It was very hard work for adults let alone teenagers. Sometimes they had to pull heavy sacks full of cotton in unforgiving hot and humid conditions.

In the fields it was normal for Sam to work alongside black people. No doubt this contributed to the fact that in his family there was no particular animosity towards such people, no feeling that they were their social inferiors. This was very far from typical in the southern states of America in the first half of the twentieth century where racial segregation and contemptuous attitudes were the norm.

It would surely have been hard for the young Sam Phillips to look down on people whose music he admired so much. The blues and gospel music he heard in the fields touched something deep inside him. He instinctively recognised that it had its origins in years of suffering and oppression but also, in the case of gospel, a hope that with religious faith, it was always possible that better times lay ahead. For him such powerfully emotional music went to the heart of what it was to be human. Similarly, he loved the music favoured by the poor white sharecroppers – simple country, or hillbilly, music which recounted heartfelt stories of hard times, love and religious faith. He realised that such music offered ordinary, often inarticulate people a means of expressing in simple terms the most profound human emotions. From a young age he tuned in to the regular radio broadcasts from the *Grand Ole Opry* in Nashville, Tennessee, the spiritual home of country music. This mixture of genres provided him with the foundations of the electrifying musical styles he would unleash on the world in later years.

It was not surprising that Sam's early passion for music led to a desire to make music himself. He played several instruments in his school band including the sousaphone and the drums. However, according to his own assessment, he was not a particularly gifted player; he did however discover a gift for inspiring others and became the conductor of the band. "I could always see the people that did have talent, and get it out of them." He came to understand that he had a gift for recognising where people's strengths lay, and encouraging them to create the best music they were capable of.

Although it was not obvious at the time, events in Sam's life were conspiring to qualify him for his life's work. At 17, he conducted a band concert for the American Legion which was broadcast on a small radio station and this in turn led to work as a radio announcer. He presented a half-hour programme called *Hymn Time* and particularly enjoyed the religious songs performed by trios and quartets of black or white singers.

At this stage Sam had aspirations to become a lawyer. He was drawn to the idea of defending people at the bottom of the social scale who found themselves on the wrong side of the law and who lacked the money and communication skills to argue their case. Such dreams were shattered with the early death of his father in 1942; there would be no money to pursue such ambitions. Sam left school and took what jobs he could to supplement the family income. For a time he worked for an undertaker and claimed later that this experience was very helpful in developing sensitivity and people skills – vital in the studio when dealing with wayward and volatile artistic temperaments. Whilst helping to support his family in this way Sam also bolstered his studio skills by taking correspondence courses in engineering and science from the Alabama Polytechnic Institute.

After gaining more broadcasting experience with another radio job in Nashville, Sam secured a position in Memphis at radio station WREC which was based in the Peabody hotel, a famous local landmark. He moved to the city in 1945 trying to ignore many routine racist comments relating to the number of "niggers" in the city. He did not share such views but because they were so prevalent at the time, he did not go out of his way to challenge them. His interests lay in music, not social crusading – he was quite happy to leave that to others. Sam gained invaluable experience at WREC; he was involved in various areas of the station's work such as creating sound effects and pre-recording programmes on to 16-inch acetate tapes, which were then broadcast at a later date. He also had the opportunity of listening to a wide variety of music including jazz, blues, pop and religious music and was a regular at the legendary Home of the Blues record shop. He loved the musical melting pot he found in Memphis.

Sam loved much of the music he heard in the city performed by black artists, particularly rhythm and blues and gospel, and soon developed ambitions to get it heard by a much wider audience. He had a strong hunch that many white people secretly listened to and appreciated the black music coming out of night clubs and small radio stations. He felt a great warmth towards black people and empathised with the unequal struggles he knew many had endured for years. Above all though, he was motivated by his passion for the music that such hardship had inspired – every shade of blues music. His ambitions were not entirely altruistic though – he believed that there was a large market for the music and that his promotion of it could make him money.

Sam resolved to open his own recording studio. However he had a wife and two young sons to support and so he knew he had to keep his job at WREC for the time being, and work on the new venture in his spare time.

Towards the end of 1949 he leased a small shop unit at 706 Union Avenue, Memphis, for a monthly rent of $150; the Memphis Recording Service was born. The name was displayed in neon lights in front of Venetian blinds. Sam was principally interested in recording music by black artists but he was also aware that to generate income he would have to spread the net wider. The tag line of the new business was, "We Record Anything – Anywhere – Anytime" – his business card also included the addendum: "A complete service to fill every recording need". It was true; in the early days his work included weddings, community events and political speeches.

Sam was the sole proprietor of the new business but from the start he was supported by Marion Keisker, a colleague from WREC. A divorcee in her early thirties, her strengths lay in the efficient organisation and administration of the studio; in addition she was not above helping with practical tasks such as putting up blinds. She was also attracted to Sam, regarding him as "beautiful... but still with that country rawness. He was slim and had those incredible eyes". Others noted that Sam was always very particular about his appearance; he was invariably smartly dressed and well groomed.

He arranged the premises as best he could in the limited space available. There was a small reception area, a control room and a studio which measured approximately 20 feet by 30 feet. With very little money behind him he could only afford the most basic equipment; but it was a labour of love and he was prepared to invest his time and his money to make it happen. It was a tribute to his engineering skills that he created such a good sound, and as it turned out the primitive nature of the studio gear undoubtedly contributed to the distinctively raw and sparse sound which would forever be associated with the studio. His first recording console was nothing more than a Presto five-input mixer board. It had four microphone ports; there was a fifth port that had a switch, which, when flicked one way activated the microphone; flicking it the other way enabled recordings to be played back. In addition there were two reel to reel tape recorders. This equipment was portable so that Sam could either make recordings in the studio or at a customer's preferred location. In 1950 magnetic tape was by no means universal and Sam initially recorded a lot of material onto 16-inch acetate discs at 78 rpm. Creating master discs was a laborious process involving the use of a Presto 6-N lathe which was connected to a turntable. By the end of 1951 Sam had switched to the more user-friendly magnetic tapes. As time went on and finances allowed, he gradually upgraded the equipment in the studio. He replaced his portable mixing board with an RCA 76-D radio console which allowed for the mixing of six microphones at once; he also acquired a couple of Ampex 350 tape decks. Microphones were upgraded from basic Shure and ElectroVoice models to RCA 77s which as engineer Jack Clement later pointed out was a "big deal" for him.

Sam followed his instincts when recording music; there was no rule book. A particular feature he favoured was the use of echo to fill out the sound. Music that was transferred to tape was a combination of the sounds the musicians were making plus the same sounds momentarily delayed. Sam was then able to play around with the timing via the mixer board to achieve the kind of enlivening effect he was looking for to enhance the appeal of the music of particular artists. The sound he wanted was also achieved through a minimalist approach to the number of instruments used. Sam always tried to work on the principle that less is more.

Sam approached artists he had come to know through his work at WREC and evolved the idea of leasing master tapes of their songs to established record labels. From the start he encouraged artists to record the songs they liked in the way that they liked to perform them – his role was to help them get the best out of such material. In this way he was different from the major labels where producers often got artists to perform selected songs in ways that they (the producers) reckoned would be most likely to achieve commercial success. Sam's initial recordings featured basic blues and boogie numbers as well as the occasional novelty recording such as 'Shorty The Barber' by Charlie Burse on which he used an actual pair of barber's scissors to achieve the right sound effect.

Sam was aware of the tensions between black and white people and that suspicion and prejudice worked both ways. He tended to sympathise with black artists, conscious that performing their songs in the studio could be particularly difficult; as he saw it they were, "trying to play, looking at some white dude behind a window, and they've been kicked around all their life". In the Memphis of the fifties such empathy was not common and indeed Sam himself experienced contempt by association as a result of his work with so many black artists. Sam's son Knox recalled visiting his father in the studio when he was a child. After observing him working closely with black musicians he would then leave the studio and go shopping with his mother in central Memphis where he would see "whites only" signs. He found this jarring contrast both striking and confusing.

Sam had the ability to recognise talent; and he wanted the real thing – i.e. what the artist played at home, not what they thought a white producer might want to hear. He was acutely aware that performing well in the cold artificial confines of a studio was difficult, not least because most of his artists were used to being energised by enthusiastic live audiences. One of his particular skills was to understand such issues and to help singers get into the right frame of mind – through encouragement, praise, allowing sufficient time, whisky, whatever it took to produce the best possible performances of the music they loved. As part of this process Sam tried to be as sensitive as possible to the foibles and idiosyncrasies of his artists; although not a naturally patient man he was capable of deploying people skills in the studio to get the right result.

Sam did his best to ensure that the sound quality of his recordings was as good as it could be; however he was less bothered about perfection when it came to the artists' performances of songs. If the emotional feel of the song was right, he was not bothered if the bass player was late coming in or the singer was briefly out of tune. It was all very different from the smoother, mainstream country sounds being produced in Nashville, let alone the sugary pop songs by the likes of Teresa Brewer and Tony Bennett.

When he was in the control room he was heavily involved in and excited by the creative process – even if at times this meant doing very little other than waiting for the right sounds to emerge and then letting the artists know when they did. "You're getting close," he would say when he sensed a singer was starting to get the best out of a song. He always encouraged his musicians to do things the way they wanted but he knew the sound he was looking for and when he believed they had got it right he would leap out of the control room, fired up, enthusiastically telling everyone that the song was going to be a "rolling stone" (a hit).

Sam did not impose time limits on sessions; he was happy for the artists to keep playing songs until they got it right. Many commented on the fact that there was no clock in the studio – a standard piece of equipment in other studios where the principle that time is money was strictly applied. The process could be exhausting, with sessions lasting late into the night. Sam was very hands on – moving microphones around, cajoling, encouraging and laying down the law in his own quite stubborn way about how a particular song should be delivered. He went to great lengths to make it possible for artists to perform songs as if they were performing live – he did not want them to feel inhibited by having to adjust their natural style of playing to fit in with the confining environment of the studio.

When he was sure he was right he had a tendency to stop listening to the artist's own views. An example of this was Johnny Cash's 1956 hit song 'I Walk The Line'. Conceived by Cash as a slowish love ballad, Sam nonetheless got him to record another, uptempo version which he released as a single. Cash was mightily displeased but the song was a major hit and so Sam's instincts were proved correct. That said he could get things badly wrong as well. For instance he failed to see that Roy Orbison's extraordinary vocal gift lent itself particularly well to intensely emotional power ballads and repeatedly tried to get him to sing uptempo blues-inflected songs.

At the start of the fifties Sam was making very little money and struggled to pay the rent and Marion Keisker's monthly salary of $100. He was still working almost exclusively with black artists and could have been forgiven for wondering if his desire to give them the chance to make their music available to a wider audience was doomed to commercial failure. Things looked up in 1951 when, as a result of a deal with Modern Records, which was keen to release "race" material, he produced five singles by the then little known BB (which possibly stood for Blues Boy) King for its subsidiary label RPM Records. Sam's preferred format for singles was invariably uptempo on one side with a slower number on the other. For him the whole point of singles was two or three minutes of musical immediacy; throughout his career he was never an enthusiast for LPs — always preferring the sprint to the marathon.

Thereafter Sam hooked up with Ike Turner, then working as a DJ in Clarksdale, Mississippi, the self-styled "King of the Piano". Sam recorded a pulsating rhythm and blues number called 'Rocket 88' by Ike's band with a great performance from the young singer Jackie Brenston. He sent an acetate copy of the song to the recently formed label Chess Records, whose owners Phil and Leonard Chess liked what they heard. They released the song which soon reached the top spot in the rhythm and blues chart. The song is one of a number of contenders for the title of the first ever rock 'n' roll record. The success of the song gave Sam a breathing space from the financial pressures of running the studio.

More and more work came his way and since he was still fitting his studio work around his "proper" job at WREC he regularly found himself working 18-hour days. Something had to give. Sam was hospitalised twice with what were described as nervous breakdowns and it has been reported that during his hospital stays he received electric shock treatment. He realised that something had to change and so he quit his job at WREC.

The success of 'Rocket 88' created more pressure for Sam; Chess wanted a follow-up but internal problems in Ike Turner's band meant that they were unable to produce another song any time soon. Sam even resorted to the unsuccessful device of recording a song by another artist and pretending that he was Jackie Brenston.

Sam had the privilege of working with Chester Burnett, better known as Howlin' Wolf. Of him Sam said rather grandiosely, "This is where the soul of man never dies." He epitomised the raw emotional singing which Sam valued so highly. He recorded a number of songs but found himself in disputes involving RPM Records and Chess, which were in large part attributable to his habit of reaching and trying to rely on verbal agreements with people he did business with.

Ever since he had started the Memphis Recording Service in 1950, a considerable number of small labels had started up in the Memphis area. This fact, taken along with the ongoing disputes with his business partners, led Sam to the reluctant conclusion that he should start his own label.

The Sun label, which operated out of the studio premises in Union Avenue, came into existence in 1952, the first release being in April of that year. 'Drivin' Slow'/'Flat Tire', written and performed by saxophone player Johnny London, sank without trace. To add to Sam's woes he was threatened with legal action by a recording company in New Mexico which claimed it had the exclusive right to use the "Sun" name. Sam's chronic financial (or "liquidity" as he preferred to call them) problems continued, threatening to sink the whole enterprise. He was fortunate to receive assistance from Jim Bulleit, a switched-on local businessman with considerable experience of the music industry. He was able to help Sam with all the areas in which he lacked experience such as finance, copyright and distribution, all of which distracted him from what he really loved doing – making music in the studio.

This took a lot of pressure off Sam but his brand of raw, black rhythm and blues was still not producing commercial success. A breakthrough came with the release of 'Bear Cat' by Rufus Thomas in March 1953. The song, written by Sam, was a light-hearted riposte to the then current hit single 'Hound Dog' by Big Mama Thornton (which would later be covered by Elvis Presley). It provided Sun with its first major hit but yet again brought problems in its wake. Sam wrote the lyrics but the melody was the same as that of 'Hound

Dog'. Legal action followed which resulted in Sam having to pay a percentage of the royalties to the composers. Rufus Thomas went on to achieve greater success in the sixties on the Stax label notably with 'Walking The Dog' and 'Funky Chicken'.

Sam was always keen to discover new talent and listened to lots of aspiring artists, but it was Jim Bulleit who came up with one of their more unusual prospects. The Prisonaires had been in the Tennessee state prison in Nashville since 1943. The five members sang close-harmony gospel songs. Sam realised that – to say the least – they had an unusual selling point. After overcoming a great deal of bureaucratic hassle the group eventually recorded a session under armed guard. Their single, 'Just Walkin' In The Rain', sold 50,000 copies but subsequent releases, following a familiar pattern at Sun, fared much less well.

Sam continued to record a variety of artists, mainly but not exclusively black. By the start of 1954 though, none had delivered any significant commercial success. Sam had two major factors working against him. The public taste was gradually moving away from the pure and raw rhythm and blues styles which he preferred. More importantly though, racial prejudice was still a powerful force in Memphis, and the southern states generally. He came across it routinely in his daily work; it was a part of the landscape which he felt powerless to oppose. He had a great sense of frustration; if only he could find a way of packaging the feel and spirit of his music in a way that white people would accept.

Perhaps as a result of the race issue, Sam did start to record a number of white country artists including Earl Peterson, "Michigan's Singing Cowboy". Like the others he achieved nothing more than minor local success and his involvement with Sun was short lived. This was the pattern for many small labels that sprang up in the fifties catering for local demand but, as with Sun, lacking the financial resources to distribute their material to wider markets. Sam did what he could, personally delivering records to DJs and distributors within a driveable radius of Memphis. At times he also encouraged the artists themselves to promote their material, advising them to look out for antennae when they were out and about, indicating the presence of radio stations, where they might drop off a copy of their latest single.

Up until this point the story of Sun resembled that of many other small studios now lost in the mists of time. Everything changed in the summer of 1953. Elvis Presley, mumblingly shy, walked into 706 Union Avenue wanting to record a song for his beloved mother, Gladys. Cost: $3.98 plus tax. He took a seat and waited until the studio was free. Marion Keisker did note one thing that set him apart from other young men who passed through the studio – his appearance. It was clear that with his carefully oiled hair and taste in striking clothes – black and pink being a favoured match – Elvis wanted to look different. He recorded two songs, a 1948 pop hit, 'My Happiness', and a ballad, 'That's When Your Heartaches Begin'. Sam recalled that Elvis lacked confidence. Something in his insecure demeanour brought to mind many of the black artists he had worked with over the years. Marion noted Elvis' name (which she spelt wrongly) with the brief assessment: "Good ballad singer. Hold."

Elvis became a regular visitor to 706 Union Avenue over the next 10 months or so and, partly because of his voice, partly because of his striking dress sense, he did make an impression on Sam. Eventually he decided to try him out in the studio but the first efforts were not promising. Elvis clearly had a good voice and Sam did detect something of the emotional power that enriched the music of many black artists; but nothing he sang made Sam think he had anything with that special spark he was looking for. However, in conversation with his friend Scotty Moore, who played guitar for a country band called the Starlite Wranglers, Sam made it clear that he thought this unknown kid Elvis had some kind of potential. Scotty and bass player Bill Black were less impressed when they had an informal session with Elvis soon afterwards.

However they did all go into the studio with Sam in June 1954. Despite everybody's best efforts, nothing really gelled. After several fruitless attempts at some well-known songs of the day such as 'Harbor Lights' and 'I Love You Because', nothing seemed to be working. It was Elvis himself who started playing around with a song called 'That's All Right (Mama)', a minor hit for blues singer Arthur "Big Boy" Crudup some years before. Sam quickly detected a rhythm and an essential feel which somehow captured the raw spirit, the joyful exhilaration, the infectious energy which he wanted – and which he sensed would have huge appeal for large numbers of young people eager for a musical magic they could call their own.

It has often been said that Sam Phillips longed to find "a white boy who could sing like a negro", although he himself later denied using this form of words. It may be that what he was really looking for was a form of music that took the vital essences of the best of black and white music; in any event he felt that with Elvis he might just have found what he was looking for.

He played a recording of the song to local DJ Dewey Phillips – a brother only in the sense of their shared musical tastes and ability to think outside the box – and watched as his normally voluble friend mutely took in the awesome power of the song. The next night Dewey played it repeatedly on his show; "That'll flat git it," he proclaimed afterwards. The switchboard went into meltdown as listeners phoned in to find out where they could get a copy. Frantic efforts were made to come up with a B-side – a speeded up version of Bill Monroe's 'Blue Moon of Kentucky' was eventually chosen. Sam was adamant that Elvis' material needed to "have a beat" for it to inspire the large young audience he was targeting. He always maintained that if Elvis had been allowed to follow his penchant for ballads and religious music he might have become a successful singer in a gospel quartet but not much more.

Things moved fast and for a time Sam paid little attention to anyone but Elvis. The young singer started appearing in public and, despite debilitating pre-show nerves, quickly learned that he was able to drive audiences delirious with a shake of his hips. It was clear from the start that Elvis was the answer to the unrequited yearnings of countless young and some not so young fans. Sam drove thousands of miles delivering copies of the debut single to DJs and trying to get jukebox suppliers and distributors interested; he was determined that Elvis was not just going to be a Memphis phenomenon.

Elvis was causing such a stir that Sam was able to secure a place for him on the stage of the very conservative *Grand Ole Opry*, the traditional bastion of country music. His reception was much less enthusiastic there, little more than polite – but there was a momentum building which was unstoppable. Ironically it was performers like Elvis who would effectively wipe out the careers of many of the traditional country singers who looked down on him.

Sam worked like a demon with Elvis to ensure that follow-up singles were released as quickly as possible. First came 'I Don't Care If The Sun Don't Shine' and then on Elvis's 20th birthday, January 8, 1955, his third single, 'Milkcow Blues Boogie', was released. A local DJ and promoter, Bob Neal, ensured that Elvis continually appeared at gigs. The fans could not get enough of him – though at this stage of things his performances lacked professional finesse. Whilst he was rapidly developing stage moves which would soon captivate audiences worldwide, he offended some with loud burps, bad language and a habit of spitting his chewing gum out into the fired-up crowd.

In the course of his hectic schedule, Elvis came to the attention of Tom Parker, a promoter who had accorded himself the bogus title of "Colonel". With a background in the worlds of vaudeville and circus, Parker understood all about giving the people what they wanted; and he was as hard as nails. He quickly saw Elvis' potential and made it clear to those in the singer's orbit that for this potential to be exploited to the full, a small regional label like Sun would have to be replaced by one of the majors; and even at this early stage some of the big players up north were getting wind of the fact that something out of the ordinary was happening down south. It was not long before Sam was in a kind of phoney war over the sale of Elvis' contract.

Despite Elvis' success, Sun was still struggling financially. Sam had to come up with much of the money involved in pressing records, paying union fees, placing advertisements and much more long before he received income from the distributors who ordered records from him. Though it pained him to think of losing a successful artist after so many years of searching for one, Sam really did need money – and Elvis just might be the answer to all his financial stresses and strains; it really did merit serious consideration.

Meanwhile, Sam continued to work with Elvis in the studio and for his fourth and fifth singles, 'I'm Left, You're Right, She's Gone' and 'Mystery Train' (his last for Sun), Sam, following his producer's instinct, introduced drums to emphasise the beat. Drums were then added to Elvis' stage show in order to generate yet more excitement for his growing army of fans.

It became increasingly clear that Tom Parker was determined to become Elvis' manager – though he did have to obtain agreement from his parents, Vernon and Gladys, since Elvis was still underage. He eventually won them round – and to all intents and purposes became the man with control over most aspects of Elvis' career – with all sorts of promises about the great things he could achieve for their boy. Soon he was negotiating with the major record labels while Sam looked on impotently from the sidelines.

While these events swirled around Sam, he was doing his best to concentrate on another project which represented the fulfilment of a long held ambition – the creation of a radio station (WHER) whose staff was almost entirely female. An important element of his character was an instinctive support for the underdog – he had always done his best to support black artists but was also aware that a form of discrimination operated against women in the world of broadcasting. That said, it was also a case of identifying a gap in the market which he believed could make him money. WHER duly took to the airwaves and continued to broadcast until the early seventies, although in 1966 some male announcers were introduced.

Sam eventually conceded defeat on Elvis when Tom Parker persuaded RCA to accept a price for his contract which Sam thought they would probably turn down: $35,000 for the contract plus $5,000 for back royalties owed to Elvis. Many have subsequently said that Sam's decision was one of the worst blunders in the history of popular music. In fact it was a very respectable deal. It had become clear that Sam, for whom bankruptcy was a possibility, could not provide the kind of national reach that Elvis needed and anyway, the money he received was more than had ever been paid for a recording artist previously. Even Frankie Laine – who unlike Elvis was already an established star – had only attracted $25,000.

Elvis was with Sun for a mere 18 months. In that time, in large part as a result of Sam's musical vision and studio expertise, he produced some of the most exhilarating and exuberant popular music ever laid down; many believe that despite the millions that were pumped into his subsequent recordings he was never able to recapture the scintillating, stripped down sound of his time with Sun – a sound that by 1955 was starting to be referred to as rock 'n' roll.

Although Sam had inevitably devoted a large part of his time to Elvis, he did listen to and develop other artists. Despite his personal preference for a rougher rhythm and blues sound he did work with a number of country artists as well. Though he achieved little success with many, he sought to introduce a more upbeat uptempo feel to the usual parameters of country music and in this way contributed to the style that would soon be called rockabilly.

An artist who was later dubbed the King of Rockabilly, Carl Perkins, enjoyed spectacular success with Sam at the start of his recording career. Like many other artists, Carl had been drawn to Sun as a result of the success of Elvis and the pure uptempo sound – "hopped up country" as Carl put it – of much of Sun's output. Carl and his brothers, Jay (guitar) and Clayton (bass), had learned and honed their musical skills in the rough and earthy environment of honky-tonks around Jackson, Mississippi.

Sam was busy when Carl and his brothers first turned up at the studio but Carl persuaded him to listen to the Perkins Brothers Band. With his well developed instinct for assessing artists he quickly told Carl that he, rather than his brother Jay, who had been a frontman up until then, was the one who had something special. Sam released several singles by Carl and soon radio stations were regularly featuring his music; its frenetic rhythms and uncluttered twangy guitar sounds driven by slap bass went down particularly well with younger fans. Carl soon became a name around Memphis but, like other Sun artists, came to realise that Sam often did not provide proper financial accounting. Although in many ways a man of integrity, Sam also regularly got artists such as Carl to sign over the rights to songs to his own publishing company; often the artists – naïve in the business aspects of the music world – did not realise that they were signing away the rights to potential income.

Another Sun artist, Johnny Cash, suggested an idea for a song to Carl. It was based on an incident that occurred when Johnny had been in the Air Force in Germany. He was friendly with a soldier who warned people not get his fancy shoes dirty. This germ of an idea became the most famous rockabilly anthem of them all, 'Blue Suede Shoes'. The song soon became a massive hit far beyond the Memphis area. Carl's fee for performances increased dramatically and he shared bills with Elvis and Johnny Cash; there were even some occasions when some fans called for Carl to return to the stage during Elvis' set.

There was a moment when Sam really thought he might have found a credible successor to Elvis. But Carl was no Elvis; he was a more talented musician, he could write songs but he did not have the looks or the personal magic. Not only that but his burgeoning career came to an abrupt stop when he was involved in a serious car crash in March 1956 on his way to what might well have been a major breakthrough appearance on Perry Como's television show.

Unbeknown to Carl, Sam had been planning to surprise him on air with a gold disc for 500,000 sales of 'Blue Suede Shoes'. It was a cruel twist of fate which effectively ended the rapidly rising career trajectory Carl was then on.

Sam was never drawn to country music the way he had been to the rawer delights of rhythm and blues. He had however been brought up with religious music and had always liked it. However when Johnny Cash talked his way into an audition saying he wanted to sing spiritual music, Sam told him bluntly there wasn't enough money in it. Disappointed but undeterred Cash tried out some of his own songs. Sam quickly recognised exceptional qualities in Johnny's singing and writing and before long – having got him to change his name from John to the more youth-friendly Johnny – he was releasing singles which met with immediate success, though only on a regional level initially. However, national and international recognition would soon follow.

By the winter of 1956, Sam Phillips had been fighting to keep his musical vision alive for nearly seven years. In the process he had discovered and nurtured a small number of artists with the rarest of gifts; artists who carried within them many of the crucial components of the DNA of the popular music which blossomed forth in their wake. It is a remarkable fact that they all sprang from a small geographical area within a fairly small radius of the musical melting pot known as Memphis, Tennessee. They all owed their crucial initial breakthroughs to Sam Phillips. He was one of a handful of key players who mixed a range of ingredients in his personal laboratory and sparked a sound and indeed a cultural movement which has been burning like wildfire ever since.

2.

Carl Perkins

All members of the Million Dollar Quartet – unlike many modern era country stars – had genuinely poor upbringings, none more so than Carl Perkins. Born on April 9, 1932 in Tiptonville, Tennessee, Carl was brought up in a three-room shack by his god-fearing parents, poor sharecroppers who struggled to make a living from picking cotton. He shared a room – and a bed – with his two brothers, Jay and Clayton. He first went to school at the age of six and in the same year started work in the cotton fields where people worked from "can till can't". Despite his tender years, Carl had to fill a burlap sack with cotton – over 60 pounds in weight when full – every day he worked. The physical exertion this involved was only part of the challenge; the soft white cotton bolls grew inside tough outer shells which meant that nasty cuts and scratches were unavoidable.

The Perkins family was the only white sharecropping family in Tiptonville. The fact that young Carl regularly found himself in the company of black people meant that he learned to regard their company as normal. In addition, from an early age it introduced him to the kind of music that would be highly influential on his own career. In the cotton fields he met an older man called John who played passionate blues and gospel songs on a battered old acoustic guitar when the day's work was finished. Sometimes, when the work was hard and the sun unrelenting, people sang songs to lift their spirits. Carl regularly heard spiritual numbers like 'Down By The Riverside' – and so it was hardly surprising that years later he was able to sing and play it spontaneously during the Million Dollar Quartet session; it was in his soul.

Carl quickly felt drawn to the magic of such music. He was soon listening to the *Grand Ole Opry* on radio station WSM in Nashville. He absorbed the music of many of the artists who helped to lay the foundations for the country music of the modern age – Jimmie Rodgers, The Carter Family, Roy Acuff. He was also very taken by the pulsating rhythm and searing vocals of Bill Monroe, the creator of bluegrass. Later, but still before he had reached his teenage years, Carl listened to radio stations that featured blues artists such as Big Bill Broonzy and T-Bone Walker; he was entranced by them all.

However, he was not long content to be a passive listener. He wanted to *play* music. Buying a guitar was out of the question but his father, Buck Perkins, knocked up a crude instrument from an old broom handle and a small box. Not long afterwards Carl was given an old acoustic guitar and his friend from the fields, John, became his teacher. Initially Carl struggled to master even the basic chords but his desire to play overcame the physical challenges of pressing down the right strings on the fret board. Broken strings were something of a disaster because there was no money to buy new ones. He simply had to tie them together as best he could but this added to his technical abilities. He might not be able to hit a particular note because of a knot where a string had been tied; instead he learned to bend the string in order to achieve the desired note. Such challenges did not discourage Carl and indeed added to his dexterity and the distinctive musical sounds he was able to achieve. From early on he dreamt of a career in music, of even appearing on the hallowed stage of the *Grand Ole Opry* – an aspiration his brother Jay mocked; he was quite happy with the prospect of becoming a truck driver.

Carl soon became aware that blacks were treated differently from whites in society. There were separate water fountains and though Carl might go to see a film with a black friend they could not sit in the same section of the cinema. Whilst Carl instinctively empathised with his black friends – who seemed to be even worse off than him, the poverty of his own situation was brought home by visits to a better-off cousin whose house had modern facilities such as plumbing and electricity.

Carl's childhood was hard in other ways; his father was a strict disciplinarian who sometimes enforced rules with a leather strap; when he was the worse for drink his liberal use of his belt seemed to happen for no fair or logical reason. That said, the fundamental family bonds were strong and Carl never felt that the family was in any danger of breaking apart.

When it came to music, Carl was like a sponge, enthusiastically soaking up a wide range of styles. He particularly liked the western swing of Bob Wills; with his backing group the Texas Playboys, Wills travelled all over America in a state of the art tour bus. It was a major event when they rolled into town. They invariably played to wildly enthusiastic audiences. His uptempo music incorporated a wide variety of musical styles; blues and country were a key element but so were some more exotic sounds such as Cajun, jazz, mariachi and Dixieland.

In the thirties, honky-tonk music was becoming increasingly popular. In a way it was the blues music of the white rural working class. It was generally played in very rough and ready bars, honky-tonks (or just "tonks") equipped with the absolute basics – tables, chairs, a counter where drinks were served and not much else. People congregated in these convivial dens on Friday and Saturday night to let their hair down after the gruelling demands of their working week. The bands usually consisted of three, four or five musicians playing guitar, dobro, bass, steel guitar and possibly drums. There were no proper stages or facilities for the musicians who often played at one end of the room; and there was little protection for them when fights broke out and the bottles started flying. Like blues music, honky-tonk spoke of the daily concerns of the people who listened to it – infidelity, drinking, work problems; each song was imbued with varying degrees of raw emotion. The playing and singing were often basic, never sophisticated or prettified but usually heartfelt; the men who played in the bands came from the same place as the audiences they entertained.

Alongside his passion for listening to as much music as possible, Carl was unstoppable in his desire to improve his guitar technique. However, by the age of 11 or so his hands were not yet fully developed; instead of waiting until they were, he worked out ways to achieve sounds on the guitar that resembled the things he liked in the music he listened to on the radio. For instance, unable to play barre chords (which involve holding down all six strings with one finger in a straight line while playing other notes with the remaining three fingers) Carl manipulated his thumb round the neck of the guitar to play the bottom two strings while playing the remaining four strings with his other fingers. In this way he started to develop the ability to play rhythm and single notes at the same time – an important element in the guitar style he would later develop.

Carl's mother, Louise, often a lone voice in support of his efforts to play his favourite instrument, recognised his burgeoning talent. She got him to play guitar when the family regularly sang gospel songs such as 'What A Friend We Have In Jesus' at the end of the week. For his part the music was more important than the religion; he was just happy to seize any opportunity to play.

With the increasing prevalence of mechanised farm equipment, the demand for sharecroppers picking cotton all day diminished. Bowing to the inevitable, Buck Perkins moved his family to Madison County where he hoped to get a job with better pay and conditions. However his poor health meant this was not possible and so the family's impoverished living conditions continued. Like many other youngsters, and with no opposition from his parents, Carl left school at the end of the eighth grade to look for a job and contribute to the family's income. He secured regular work at a dairy, doing whatever jobs were needed – milking, delivering and so on in a small community called Malesus. The work was much less demanding than the cotton fields and Carl vowed that whatever else he did in life, he would never again pick cotton.

In his early teen years Carl developed an ability to write songs – very basic at first – but he had already grasped the structure of straightforward country songs. He also proved himself able to write lyrics based on his observations of life as he was growing up. Such songs often had a romantic element even though by this time Carl had not yet been initiated into such areas of life. By the age of 14 he had written a number of songs, one of which, 'Movie Magg', would later give him a minor hit.

Taking a lead from Carl, Jay Perkins started playing guitar and was soon able to lay down a rock steady strummed rhythm. He it was who suggested the idea of the pair forming a group, the Perkins Brothers. He took Carl to a local honky-tonk called the Cotton Boll, near the town of Jackson, Mississippi, and persuaded the owner to give the embryonic band a chance to play for the customers. The fact that Carl was seven years under the legal age required to cross the threshold of such establishments was overlooked – as far as the proprietor was concerned the sole test of their suitability for the work was the amount of booze that was sold while they played. Before long they were appearing regularly in another joint called the Sand

Ditch and others followed over the next few years as they built up a fanbase around Jackson.

The experience of playing in honky-tonks proved to be a steep learning curve for Carl and Jay. It was a terrific opportunity to hone their playing and singing and get to feel comfortable performing in public. The brothers did uptempo versions of hits by leading artists of the day such as 'Walking The Floor Over You' by Ernest Tubb, "The Texas Troubadour", whose distinctive grating baritone voice had recently catapulted him to stardom. In addition they featured numbers by established figures on the country music scene such as Bill Monroe and Roy Acuff.

The initiation into the very adult world of honky-tonks toughened the boys up in ways that understandably alarmed their mother, Louise; any concerned parent would have been right to be worried. Serious fights involving knives, guns, or anything that came easily to hand like a bar-room stool, and which often resulted in the spilling of blood, were the norm at the weekends. People worked long hours, often in physically harsh conditions, and by the end of the week were keen to release their stored-up tension and resentment. Arguments over women were often the catalyst for fights – even if it was just some drunken man imagining that some other drunken man had glanced at his girlfriend the wrong way. The intensity of the fighting was all the greater because many of the customers drank illegal home-brewed liquor supplied to the honky-tonk owners by countless bootleggers. This so called moonshine was far more potent than ordinary whisky. It held a particular appeal for many of the customers who were seeking alcoholic oblivion in the shortest possible time.

In cases where the fights spread and involved more people – just like chaotic bar-room fights in western movies – bottles and chairs flew through the air and the musicians had to duck and dive to avoid being hit. To make things safer for the performers, and to ensure that they kept on playing, proprietors would often rig up some chicken wire in front of them. As Carl sardonically pointed out however – after witnessing a young woman shoot a man dead with a pearl-handled pistol – chicken wire couldn't save them from flying bullets. Carl and the other musicians who entertained the tanked-up crowds had to learn to look after themselves. Whilst it was Carl's instinct to avoid fights there were times when this was not possible and he quickly learned that if he did get into a situation where going outside for a fight was inevitable, the golden rule was to attack first and go in hard.

Carl quickly developed a taste for cigarettes, whisky and beer – despite protestations from his mother who couldn't understand why her son was not put off by his father's hard-drinking ways. He loved the heady feeling of liberation that came over him as the alcohol hit the mark – and there was no shortage of the stuff for him to drink because although the earnings were not great, the liquor was free. The effect on his performances was electric. He would jump in the air, jive around, shout encouragement to Jay, twist, shake and sweat profusely. It was clear to everybody that he was in his element. His confidence grew and he rapidly developed the ability to fire up and entertain an audience. Carl also started to exploit the appeal that performers inevitably have to some female fans and partook freely of what was on offer.

Musically, Carl pushed the boundaries of the music that was usually played in the honky-tonks. He did play country songs like other artists but he added energy and a pumped up beat that reflected aspects of the music he had learned in his younger years, in particular blues and gospel songs.

When he had accumulated enough money, he entered a hire purchase agreement to buy a Harmony electric guitar which added another, more modern, dimension to the Perkins Brothers' sound. However Carl felt that the sound created by two guitars was incomplete – he wanted a fuller band sound which meant the addition of a rhythm section. He talked his younger brother, Clayton, into learning bass and soon he was providing a basic but effective slap-click sound that beefed up the band's output and really made Carl feel that he had hit upon a new style; songs with a rhythm and a feel that might mean they could achieve some significant success and maybe even rise above the poverty which was still his lot. Carl felt that music was the only possible route to a more comfortable life; he sensed that things were shaping up to make this a reality. That said, such a reality was still some way off and in the meantime he continued to do various menial jobs from which he did not earn a great deal.

Carl soon found another way to exploit his musical talent – radio. In the late forties he was a sometime member of a band called the Tennessee Ramblers and with them he appeared on a weekend show on radio station WTJS. He also made some solo appearances, for instance on *Hayloft Frolic* where in the course of a Saturday evening he played two songs. He was tempted to try out some of his own compositions but as yet lacked the confidence to give them a public airing. The radio stations he appeared on were all based in or near Jackson.

As his popularity grew, he started including Jay and Clayton in his radio appearances and this had the effect of sharpening the band's delivery. In the honky-tonks they could gradually build their sets up to a crescendo, egged on by an enthusiastic audience; beginnings and endings to songs might be quite ragged. All of this had to change for the tight requirements of radio broadcasts.

Encouraged by increasing local popularity, Carl arranged for some of his original compositions to be recorded by the band. He sent acetates to some of the majors in New York but failed to arouse the tiniest bit of interest. Carl was not deterred. The Perkins Brothers' approval ratings in and around Jackson were through the roof; and

Carl continued to be inspired and motivated by the success of artists who it seemed to him shared many aspects of the kind of high-octane music he was working hard to produce. Chief amongst these in the early fifties was Hank Williams. Apart from the fact that he wrote heartfelt, amusing and poignant songs about everyday life, his backing group, the Drifting Cowboys, were developing new sounds and creating a model which would become the template for many bands that followed. Carl was particularly impressed by electric guitarist Zeke Turner, who damped the guitar strings after hitting notes and chords; this technique added an extra rhythmic dimension to his playing and the group's sound, and bore quite a strong resemblance to some of Carl's own ideas.

The move to Madison County in 1946 had been based on a perceived economic necessity for the family but it undoubtedly had the added gain of facilitating Carl's rapidly growing musical talent. The move placed Carl less than 80 miles from Memphis – where he was soon able to experience a veritable cornucopia of musical riches not least via myriad radio stations. Blues, rhythm and blues, country and hillbilly, western swing, pop music, spiritual music, jazz – it was all readily available and he lapped it all up.

In the post-war years a considerable number of small independent studios and labels sprang up all over America, each one trying to promote a particular genre. They were working with a diverse range of small-time artists the major studios and labels up north were not interested in. In Memphis there was a particular emphasis on black music in general and rhythm and blues in particular. They were often run on a shoestring by a small businessman with a passion for music and a belief that he could find the next big thing. One such man was of course Sam Phillips. Carl's and Sam's paths would soon cross – but not just yet.

By the end of 1953 Carl had grown increasingly frustrated. The Perkins Brothers band was now well known in the area and very much in demand. However Carl was playing the same songs to the same drunken crowds – many of whom he knew personally; and he felt they only appreciated his music at a superficial level. The level of violence was undiminished and Carl himself was nearly stabbed on one occasion by a man who mistook him for someone he had clashed with earlier in the evening. The thought that this was as good as it was ever going to get filled him with dread. He was desperate to take his music beyond the limited horizons of the honky-tonk scene and "out of Jackson". He was also under financial pressure. Having recently lost his latest day job he made the decision to go full time in the honky-tonks. His new bride, Valda, supported his decision though the fact that she was expecting a baby – due in November 1953 but born prematurely in September – did not ease his situation.

Carl always preferred uptempo songs with a lot of emphasis on the beat. Towards the end of 1953 he was introduced to one of Clayton's friends called WS Holland, universally known by the nickname Fluke. At this time Fluke did not actually play drums but just from hearing him messing around and hitting rhythms on the body of Clayton's bass it was clear to Carl that his sense of timing was good. He felt that if Fluke could learn to play drums he would add another vital ingredient to the band's sound – and this is what happened, although initially a lack of money meant that Fluke had to play on borrowed kits.

A new form of popular music was gradually evolving in the fifties which reflected the desires of many younger people who were reaching out for a kind of music they could call their own. Carl's music fitted in with the new sounds. Although the term "rock 'n' roll" had been around in various forms since the twenties – often as a metaphor for sex in black music – it was only in the fifties that it started to be used widely to describe the kind of upbeat, dance-oriented music that was to set the heather alight across the western world. It owed its origins to a mysterious blending of styles: blues, rhythm and blues, country, jazz and many more.

There have been arguments, claims and counter-claims over what was the very first rock 'n' roll record and who first coined the phrase but by the mid fifties the use of the term was fairly widespread. Carl Perkins, even if he did not fully realise it at the time, was one of the musicians who was playing one form of it. Indeed when he first heard the wild abandon of Elvis Presley's high-octane version of 'Blue Moon Of Kentucky' on the radio, he was immediately struck by how similar it was to his own version – and there it was on the radio, right where he wanted to be.

Carl quickly decided that he wanted to make contact with the people behind 'Blue Moon Of Kentucky'. He caught one of Elvis' shows (still quite poorly attended in the very early days) in a gymnasium not far from Jackson. He was immediately struck by Elvis' appearance – flash, colourful clothes, thick head of hair seductively slicked back – completely different from the country and popular music stars of the day. He also clocked the dramatic effect he had on the audience – particularly the girls – who spontaneously started screaming as soon as they saw him. And the music – Carl's impression on first hearing 'Blue Moon Of Kentucky' on the radio was confirmed: everything about Elvis and his band bore a strong resemblance to the sound and the approach of the Perkins Brothers Band – in particular the presence of a guitar-playing lead singer who danced around ecstatically in response to the feeling generated by the music. Behind him was a rock-steady rhythm with a touch of country swing, some deft lead guitar lines and the driving slapping sound of the bass. It drove audiences wild with delight – but these were not the drunken country people of all ages Carl saw in the honky-tonks; these were young people who were getting high on the music. Carl experienced a surge of pleasure and relief because he now felt sure that he had been going in the right direction all along.

Moreover he reasoned that if Elvis was managing to excite young audiences and get on the radio he could too. He later reflected that the scene that met him when he saw Elvis live was like "an idling engine waitin' for someone to put the gas to it".

It was October 1954 when Carl and his brothers loaded up the car with their gear and made the trip to Memphis in the hope of getting Sam Phillips to listen to them. When they entered the premises of the Memphis Recording Service in Union Avenue, the first thing that greeted them was a life-size cardboard-backed photograph of Elvis Presley – clearly the man of the moment. Initially turned away, Carl doorstepped Sam as he arrived back at the studio in his two-tone blue Cadillac and persuaded him to listen to the band.

At first they played country songs with Jay taking some of the lead vocals. Sam was not impressed. It was only when Carl broke into 'Movie Magg' that he suddenly perked up. He liked the song, he liked the tempo and he liked Carl. He encouraged them to work up some more of their own songs and get back to him. However he made it clear that it was Carl he was interested in; he saw real potential in him – his singing, playing and his songwriting constituted an impressive package. Jay and Clayton were happy to play the honky-tonks but they lacked the driven ambition and musical vision of their brother.

Over the weeks that followed Carl and his brothers had several sessions with Sam with a view to finalising the recording of Carl's first release which would be on Sam's short-lived Flip label. 'Movie Magg' was a definite but there was debate about what would be on the other side. Sam finally decided he liked 'Turn Around', a country ballad which Carl sang with aplomb. Carl had originally called it 'I'll Be Following You' (other lyrics from the same line of the song) but had been happy to defer to Sam's choice, recognising the greater appeal of a snappier title. Sam brought in some other more experienced musicians to fill out the sound and enhance the basic skills of Jay and Clayton. Sam was still not sure how to categorise Carl. He did not want a straight competitor for Elvis in the rock 'n' roll stakes – that might just split his vote amongst the young fans. He recognised a great ability in Carl to sing country songs but there were lots of good country singers around and anyway, Carl was always going to want to sing uptempo songs. Perhaps there was some way he could get him to come up with a blend that would "revolutionise the country end of the business". Sam was always looking for new ways to sell records.

Despite his excitement at getting into the recording business with Sam, in some ways Carl was no further forward. There was no release date for his debut single but there was no let-up in the financial demands placed on him, not least because Valda had recently given birth to a second child. Despite this he was spending a lot of money on whisky, for which he had acquired a keen taste. One of his favourite brands was Early Times, which had been exempted from the prohibition-era alcohol ban on the basis that the whisky was "medicinal". He used it to calm his nerves – during shows and in the studio.

He had also bought himself a Gibson Les Paul guitar which was sold to him on favourable terms by a supportive music shop owner. He loved the fact that he was able to play around with the sounds the guitar produced and create tones that were all his own. This user-friendly classic guitar made it easier for Carl to develop his compulsively catchy sound, flitting between chords, runs, fills and any other embellishment that occurred to him on the spur of the moment – often at breakneck speed. He had plenty of opportunities to put the guitar through its paces as he continued to play the honky-tonks most nights. He also did his best to encourage the audiences to be generous when it came to putting money in the band's tip jar – though he might still only make $10 a night.

It was only by chance that Carl first heard his debut Sun single on his car radio. Sam chose 'Turn Around' as the A side. It unleashed powerful emotions as he realised that he had arrived at an important landmark on his quest to achieve stardom. The song took off locally ensuring that Carl's career moved to a new level – better venues, sell-out crowds. More importantly he was teamed up with Elvis Presley for a series of live concerts albeit that he was very much the supporting act whose reception, initially at least, was little more than polite. The audience was impatient to see Elvis, barely able to contain their mounting excitement. Carl realised Elvis' strikingly good looks enhanced by his eye-catching outfits gave him an advantage over an ordinary-looking guy like himself. Whatever, he was awestruck by the tumult when Elvis took the stage. "It was like TNT man, it just exploded. All of a sudden the world was wrapped up in rock." Reflecting on these heady times years later, Keith Richards said, "It was like the world went from black and white to Technicolor."

Elvis took Carl to his favourite clothes shop, Lansky Brothers, on Beale Street, Memphis, to help him smarten up his image. This very much fitted in with Sam's way of looking at things; he believed that artists should look special by wearing dazzling stage clothes that set them apart from the fans who came to see them – who did not want to see people who looked just the same as them up on the stage.

Carl now entered the world of life on the road and found himself touring for a time in 1955 with Elvis and also another new Sun artist, Johnny Cash, whose career was just starting to take off. The pair had a lot in common in terms of their upbringings, not least the fact that both bore the physical scars of working in the cotton fields. Gigs were generally confined to towns – Corinth and Tupelo for instance – from which they could return to Memphis after the show. This was a necessity for many who still had day jobs – unavoidable when they might only make $10–15 from a gig, less a petrol contribution and some food.

In August 1955, Sam put out Carl's first single on Sun – 'Let The Jukebox Keep On Playing'/'Gone! Gone! Gone!'. The sounds emanating from Sun were generating a lot of column inches in the local press reflecting the public appetite for this exciting new form of youth-oriented music and they appeared keen to come up with an agreed name for it. The music had elements of blues, country, the kind of uptempo high vocal sound of Bill Monroe and others. Eventually the name rockabilly was coined – and stuck, although there was a lot of crossover with rock 'n' roll. Elvis and Carl Perkins were seen as the leading exponents of this fledgling genre; others included Bill Mack and Roy Hall whose song 'See You Later Alligator' was covered by Bill Haley.

It was Johnny Cash who provided Carl with the seed of the idea that would produce his most famous hit song and with which he will forever be associated. They often talked about music and song ideas in the dressing room. One night Johnny recalled an incident in Germany when he was in the Air Force. Another soldier, who always took a keen interest in his appearance, explained to Johnny before they were heading off for a night out that he was wearing a special pair of shoes. He then issued a general warning: "and don't step on my blue suede shoes". Not long afterwards, during a gig, Carl saw a young man remonstrating with his dancing partner because she had scuffed his suedes. Carl couldn't sleep that night for thinking about how to make a song out of the scenario he had witnessed. Inspiration came when he played around with some vaguely remembered lines from children's poems and came up with, "One for the money, two for the show, three to make ready, four to go", lines which might have been used to start a running race. In no time, with some tweaking and a lot of free-flowing inspiration, the remaining lines fell into place along with a set of stop-start musical structures and Carl knew he had hit on something special.

Sam liked the song but immediately decreed that Carl's title, 'Don't Step On My Blue Suede Shoes' be shortened to 'Blue Suede Shoes'. (Valda had previously had to correct Carl's phonetic spelling "swade".) Sam was in no great hurry to record the song because Carl's previous release was still doing quite well. This gave Carl an opportunity to refine the song during gigs. Audience reaction was wildly enthusiastic. Carl continued to appear on the same bill as Elvis Presley and on occasion even stole some of his thunder. Elvis was particularly upset one night when some fans called for Carl during his set. Apart from his rockabilly sound they also liked his countrified versions of soulful pop hits of the day such as the Platters' 'Only You'.

Towards the end of 1955 Sam decided the time was right to record 'Blue Suede Shoes'. Although it proved difficult to reproduce the energy and sparkle of the live version in the studio, they nailed it in three takes. A few minor changes – "Go, boy, go" became a lot cooler as "Go, cat, go" – were needed but eventually a highly excited Sam was satisfied and felt sure he had a major hit on his hands, even though Carl was keen to work on the song some more. Subsequent events showed that Sam was not wrong.

However Christmas 1955 was still an austere affair in the Perkins household. Carl was still not making a great deal from live performances and royalties from his two recordings to date were very small. It was a source of frustration and humiliation to him that he could not afford to buy his children anything other than the most basic Christmas presents. He could not even afford a record player for himself. The man who had just written and recorded what would turn out to be one of the most famous pieces of popular music of the twentieth century had even been reduced recently to doing some shifts in the cotton fields to supplement his meagre income.

However after the release of 'Blue Suede Shoes' at the end of 1955, things started moving rapidly. Radio stations went overboard on the song (though some favoured the B-side, 'Honey Don't') and listener reaction was overwhelming. Carl became the first artist to write and perform a song that made number one in the pop, country and rhythm and blues charts. Carl was in greater demand than ever for live performances – around Memphis of course but also now much further afield. In Texas, where audiences approached 2,000 at the bigger venues, the fees he could charge nearly tripled overnight. 'Blue Suede Shoes' had struck a chord with countless ordinary people. Many of them knew all about drinking liquor from a fruit jar and only having enough money to be able to afford and cherish one item of value. Above all else though, the music touched a deep part of the human psyche – it was energising, it was fun, it made you feel good and it inspired you to cast aside the cares of the day and get up off your chair and dance. The single raced up the local charts and Carl no longer needed to appear at the bottom of bills topped by Elvis. He was also soon able to buy a top of the range Gibson guitar for $800 and a new kind of amplifier that helped to enrich the sounds he could achieve.

'Blue Suede Shoes' was not alone in taking the music world by storm; Elvis' first single for RCA, 'Heartbreak Hotel', was also enjoying huge success and for a time the pair were like a couple of boxers slugging it out for top spot on music charts all across America.

Carl and his band were soon sought after for personal appearances not just in concert halls but also on television programmes such as Red Foley's *Ozark Jubilee* in Springfield Missouri. This was a particularly emotional experience for Carl; Red Foley was a longstanding hero, not least for his tear-jerker song 'Old Shep', about the demise of a well loved dog. By the time of Carl's appearance, 'Blue Suede Shoes' had shifted around half a million units.

The following week he was lined up for even greater things with a New York appearance on *The Perry Como Show*, a hugely popular national television programme; this really was an opportunity to establish him as a national figure, set him apart from Elvis and send his career into the stratosphere.

It wasn't to be. In the early hours of the morning of March 22, 1956, the limousine Sam had hired to get them to their big date in style rammed straight into the back of a truck. It then turned over and ended up in a ditch. Fluke and Clayton suffered mainly superficial injuries. Carl and Jay were less fortunate. Jay's injuries were the more serious; he suffered broken vertebrae in his neck as well as internal injuries. Carl, who ended up unconscious under water, was rescued by Fluke. He had a broken collar bone as well as multiple lacerations. When he came to, he was in hospital. *The Perry Como Show* had gone ahead without him and a golden opportunity had been missed.

During his recuperation Carl was heartened to see 'Blue Suede Shoes' continue to perform well in regional charts as well as the *Billboard* Hot 100 – though there he had to play second fiddle to 'Heartbreak Hotel'. Sales reached a million by the end of April. His feelings were however mixed when he saw Elvis perform his version of 'Blue Suede Shoes' on Milton Berle's television show. It would become one of Elvis' trademark songs; most people nowadays associate the song with him. As Carl recovered he resumed recording and performing but there was no doubt that vital momentum had been lost. What's more, he never came up with another song nearly as memorable as 'Blue Suede Shoes' and subsequent singles in 1956, 'Boppin' The Blues' and 'Dixie Fried', failed to make a major commercial impression. It seems Carl's fairly narrow rockabilly style could not sustain mass public excitement. That said, Carl did continue to draw large, sometimes very large, crowds. In July he was top of the bill at a show near Annapolis, Maryland which attracted a sell-out 8,000 audience.

Carl did get another opportunity to appear on *The Perry Como Show* but by then Elvis had been on all the major television shows and was well on the way to establishing himself as a major star in the national consciousness, leaving Carl trailing in his wake. Perhaps in reality it was always going to be that way. Carl also got to appear at the *Grand Ole Opry*; for a country boy raised on the traditional country sounds that emanated from Nashville he was overjoyed to find himself there. However his music did not go over particularly well and it was clear that there was no prospect of it becoming a regular gig.

By the time Carl went into the studio on December 4 in the hope of laying down a new big hit single, his star, which had seemed to be burning so brightly at the start of the year, was undeniably on the wane.

3.

Jerry Lee Lewis

Legend has it that the doctor charged with bringing Jerry Lee Lewis into the world, on September 29, 1935, was drunk and fell asleep on the job leaving his parents to manage the best they could without him. This was particularly unfortunate since, so it was said, the newborn came out feet first. Unaware of the possible complications such an arrival might involve, the proud father simply grabbed his son's ankles and pulled.

Jerry Lee's parents, Elmo and Mamie, lived in a basic timber farm property in Ferriday, Louisiana which lacked electricity and running water. They were poor people who, like many others, had endured the great Depression and in a few years would also suffer the hardships engendered by the Second World War – when there was more work but precious little to buy.

Each had ascendants of note. Mamie's maternal grandparents had been well-to-do people but the wealth connection was lost when her mother married – as her parents saw it – well beneath her. Further, it was said that that there was madness in the family, carried in genetic permutations that recurred unpredictably now and then.

One of Elmo's ancestors, Thomas C Lewis, lived in a town called Fort Miro, where the city of Monroe, Louisiana, now stands. A lawyer by training he amassed a fortune through land deals, was waited on by slaves and ate off plates of the highest quality. When he died in 1819 he left an estate worth nearly $9,000. In succeeding years many members of his extended family became politicians, doctors and lawyers. Another, Leroy M Lewis, became a teacher, moved to Snake Ridge, near Mangham, Louisiana, and there made a living from farming; he and his wife, Arilla, raised 11 children. She was his first cousin and was 15 years old when they married. He was passionate about religion and music and sometimes he drank much more whisky than was good for him. Memories of wealth in the family soon became just that; Leroy ended up poor. In later years he would sometimes share a bottle with his seventh child, Elmo, Jerry Lee's father. Elmo married Mary Ethel Herron, invariably known as Mamie, in 1929, when she was 16 years old. Later that year they moved to Ferriday, Louisiana where the majority of the inhabitants were black.

Their first son, Elmo Jr, was born towards the end of 1929. Elmo and some friends and relatives got involved in the manufacture of high-octane hundred-proof bootleg whisky. A lot of people resorted to this as a way of supplementing their meagre incomes from working in the cotton fields and doing other low paid manual work. It was risky but the rewards were high. Around the time that Jerry Lee was conceived, Elmo and several others were caught by federal agents. Elmo ended up serving a few months in prison in New Orleans, though he got back home in good time for the birth of his second son.

In 1938 Elmo was sent to the same prison for the same crime as before. His incarceration this time was longer. While he was doing his time, disaster struck the family. Jerry Lee's older brother, Elmo Jr, a promising singer and a boy with a notable gift for words, was killed

in a road accident involving a driver so drunk he could barely stand –
but against whom Mamie did not press charges on the basis that God
would deal with it. Elmo was allowed out of prison but only for the
funeral and burial; the grave stone was later inscribed with the words
"Budded on earth to bloom in heaven". Throughout the ceremony
Elmo was closely supervised by armed guards and was only able to
drop flowers on the little coffin from handcuffed hands. By the time
he was released later in the year, things had changed at home. Mamie
had become the *de facto* head of the household – and she and Jerry
Lee had formed a very close bond.

As Jerry Lee grew older some things quickly became clear. The
boy loved music but did not feel the same way about schooling.
His parents appreciated music and sang enthusiastically on occasion,
usually in church, but in Jerry Lee's case it was an innate passion
and a rapidly developing skill. He listened to the old 78s he heard
on his father's wind-up record player – in particular the country
blues of the Singing Brakeman, Jimmie Rodgers, sometimes referred
to as the father of country music. He also loved religious music,
invariably performed with fire and conviction in the southern states.
He regularly wandered off to listen to the mournful blues music
performed by local black musicians. He was spellbound by tall stories
of Mississippi delta blues singer Robert Johnson selling his soul to
the devil in exchange for the ability to play the blues better than
anyone else. Jerry Lee quickly took against the strictures and dictates
of school and from an early age his attendance was patchy.

Elmo had little education himself and was determined that his son
should have the kind of opportunities that he believed schooling
made possible. In 1944, a very poor report card, overflowing with Fs,
led Jerry Lee's teacher, Mrs West, to conclude that he should repeat
the year. With some powerful persuasion from Jerry Lee's cousin
Jimmy Lee Swaggart – a future hellfire preacher – she changed her
mind. She did not really believe the boys' arguments but she did not

want to be responsible for Jerry Lee being beaten by his father. In fact he was severely leathered anyway because no matter how she re-jigged the report card, it still looked bad. Jerry never grew to like school and he did not like the nickname he later acquired there – "killer" – a comment on his wild behaviour and the meaner aspects of his nature some said. Jerry Lee later claimed it was all to do with his musical ability. Whatever, it stuck.

As well as music, Jerry Lee was also a great fan of the western movies which played at the local cinema; particular favourites were anything featuring Gene Autry or Hopalong Cassidy. He was also in awe of Al Jolson, who starred in movies such as *Down Among The Sheltering Pines*. He loved his showmanship and highly individual style. He would later say that there were only four truly great stylists: Jimmie Rodgers, Al Jolson, Hank Williams and, of course, himself.

Religion and music were inextricably linked. There were a lot of churches in the vicinity of the Lewis household even though each could only muster fairly small congregations, perhaps as few as 40 souls. These were conservative believers' churches. There was no sophisticated theological debate; whether it was Pentecostal, Baptist, Methodist or some other brand, the religious thinking was straightforward, black and white, good and bad, guilty or innocent. The attitude to marriage could be neatly summed up in the phrase: the family that prays together stays together. One Pentecostal sect, the Assembly of God – to which the Lewis family became adherents – started up in a tent. There were also travelling evangelists who fierily ranted at their audiences about human weakness, sins, hell and eternal damnation – but also held out the prospect of loving redemption for those who lived according to God's rules. There was a lot of guilt in this swirling religious stew. Needless to say, most saw Darwinism and the like as anathema, as contrary to the teachings of the good book.

When the spirit moved them in church, some danced ecstatically, spoke in tongues, and even, in the further flung reaches of the country, handled dangerous snakes and drank poison. Services usually featured hymns with the tunes hammered out on pianos. This was the bit Jerry Lee liked best. He loved to watch preachers such as Brother Janway playing the piano; he played heavy bass lines with his left hand while deftly picking out the melody with his right. Jerry Lee rapidly understood the power of music – and in particular pianos – to create an atmosphere capable of arousing and moving an audience. He loved the singing too and let rip any chance he got – in church, along with Elmo's records at home or with some of the black kids in the neighbourhood. Elmo tried him out with his guitar, on which he could knock out a tune or two, but he was barking up the wrong tree.

From early on, Jerry Lee had fallen for the magic of the keyboard, later asking interviewers why on earth he would choose an instrument with six strings when he could have one with 88. He was allowed to play the piano at the Assembly of God church (the original tent had now been replaced by bricks and mortar) when it was not in use. In addition he visited the well-to-do household of his uncle Lee and aunt Stella, where he worked hard to figure out how to make songs and rhythms out of all those black and white keys. He tried to convert the guitar riffs he heard in the Jimmie Rodgers songs he loved so much into phrases and sounds he could play on the piano.

It was not long before he was able to play tunes all the way through but right from the start he did it his way. Even slow Christmas hymns got the boogie-woogie treatment. Some called it the devil's music when he did that; those eight to the bar rhythms in the left hand just seemed to make people lose control and want to jive around.

Elmo sensed that his wayward son might really have some talent and when Jerry Lee was 10 years old, stretching himself financially until the pips squeaked, he bought a second-hand upright Starck piano – whose bent acoustic rim was said to give an upright the sound of a grand piano and make it particularly suitable for concert performances. It stood out like a beacon from the other lowly furniture in the house. There was however one negative consequence of this wondrous addition to the house – Jerry Lee was even less motivated to go to school than before.

Jerry Lee never really had much in the way of proper piano lessons – he was such a fast learner and anyway teachers couldn't (and wouldn't want to) teach him the kind of stuff he was mad keen to play. One summer he spent a month or so at the house of an older cousin who could play gospel songs as well as some boogie when his preacher father wasn't looking. Jerry Lee played for hours every day and absorbed like a sponge all the things his cousin could do. Without specifically being taught, he started to develop the ability to hammer out a pumping rhythm with his left hand whilst picking out a melody with his right and playing around with it to make it interesting.

Jerry Lee worked on learning particular songs he heard on the radio whose styles he liked such as 'Down The Road A Piece', a rollicking chunk of boogie from 1940. He would play them again and again until he had ironed out all the glitches. He also learned songs by Al Jolson. Whatever song he learned he pepped it up with his own particular brand of boogie-woogie – there was no reverence shown to the style originally envisaged for a song, even a classic like Gene Autry's 'You're The Only Star (In My Blue Heaven)'.

As early childhood gave way to teen years there were some changes in Jerry Lee's life. He acquired two sisters, Frankie Jean and Linda Gail; he did not warm to them when they were young and sometimes he revealed a seriously mean streak towards them. This was reciprocated as the girls grew older and were able to fend for themselves. One time when he was playing football – as a top player in his team he got some early lessons in female adulation – he suffered a serious hip injury. He had to wear a plaster cast for two months which meant that his leg protruded at an angle from his body. He had to be virtually carried to his beloved piano. Sometimes Frankie Jean placed a pillow under his leg to help him get into the right position to play. Sometimes she deliberately arranged things so that his leg was too high and caused him pain and discomfort. Bizarrely it appears that having his right leg sticking out from under the piano struck him as a cool thing to do; with some tweaking along the way it became one element of the showmanship he would come to be renowned for.

Several years later another piece of misfortune contributed to his piano playing style. He injured his right hand when he was working on a car. At the time he was playing sessions at a local bar and rather than let them down, he played with his right hand bandaged. The result was that he put a lot of emphasis on what he was doing with the bass lines while at the same time picking out the melody gingerly and delicately with his right.

Jerry Lee started getting into petty crime along with his cousin Jimmy Lee Swaggart. They would break into shops at night. Jerry Lee got caught after one particular solo incident when he stole some jewellery. His father and uncle Lee had to spend some money to make things right with the local authorities. Throughout his adolescent years though, the major constant was music. Jerry Lee continued to develop and improve his idiosyncratic high energy style. He listened to radio broadcasts of the *Louisiana Hayride* and the *Grand Ole Opry*. All the best and latest country music was featured and Jerry Lee had a growing ability to pick up songs and then customise them according to his own taste. He acquired a brand new hero in Hank Williams, whose version of *Lovesick Blues* was one of the most inspirational things he had ever heard. Sometimes, completely against the rules, he managed to worm his way into some of the music joints in Ferriday notably Haney's Big House. There he would hear some of the most exciting music around – Muddy Waters, Ray Charles as well as dance bands and top notch piano players such as Sunnyland Slim. It was all grist to the mill of his fast flowering piano magic.

Jerry Lee was brought up in a place and at a time when racial segregation was the norm but for him contact with black people was nothing out of the ordinary. He was also aware that segregation worked both ways. Joints like Haney's were, electively, almost exclusively black and by going there Jerry Lee was breaking a powerful social convention. However he knew instinctively that black music held a lot of the musical answers he was looking for. It was at Haney's that he heard a driving piece of rhythm and blues that would become an early favourite, 'Drinkin' Wine Spo-Dee-O-Dee'.

At the age of 14 Jerry Lee performed in public as part of the razzmatazz accompanying the opening of a new car dealership. It was Elmo who noticed that the band hired to provide the music for the event had a piano, and who persuaded them to give his son a chance to perform. He took to it like a duck to water and people loved what he did. Although he was playing some kind of secular, black even, music, the audience sensed the same kind of fervour they experienced when they sang in church on a Sunday. Much as Jerry Lee loved the performing, he was tortured by the thought that he was using his ability to peddle the Devil's music; and worse still that he got money for doing it – Elmo had gone amongst the crowd with a bag, asking for tips.

In the coming months this happened more and more as Elmo grasped his son's earning potential. Doing something he really liked and then feeling guilty about it, fearing damnation and then seeking forgiveness or redemption became a conundrum which Jerry Lee struggled with for years. However nothing in the world was going to stop him hammering out a rhythm on that piano, not even the loose women he saw in the joints where he heard the music he loved. Soon, with Elmo's assistance, he secured a regular spot on a local radio show in Natchez. He played a selection of numbers by Jimmie Rodgers, country songs and hymns. He was able to keep this going because he was popular enough to attract some sponsorship money from a local business.

However the magnitude of the feelings of guilt that racked him every now and then was immense. At the age of 15 he was convinced that he should move his life in a more religious direction. He registered at the Southwestern Bible Institute at Waxahachie, Ellis County, Texas, some 400 miles east of Ferriday. He did, briefly, make an effort to fit in with and learn from the prim and moral dictates of the institution but it couldn't last. Soon he was creeping out at night and hitching to downtown Dallas to experience the more earthy delights on offer there. He was soon expelled for playing a boogie-woogie version of 'My God Is Real' one evening in chapel; this was regarded as a deadly sin and could not be tolerated. After a mere three months he was on the bus back home.

Jerry Lee did try to take heed of the church's strictures on such compelling subjects as sex before marriage and this might help to explain why he got married at the age of 16, or possibly even younger, to a girl called Dorothy Barton who was 18. She was the daughter of a minister and unsurprisingly her parents were opposed to the marriage, not least because by the time Jerry Lee proposed the couple had only known each other for about two months. He was highly persuasive though and got his way. He actually lied about his age on the forms, claiming that he had been born in 1930 instead of 1935. He put his occupation down as farmer. Then again, it has been reported that his sister Frankie Lee's first marriage took place when she was a mere 12 years old (with falsified documents) – so perhaps he wasn't so very young in the circumstances. In the rural areas of the southern states at this time it was not uncommon for people, especially girls, to get married at a very early age. The onset of puberty was the sign that a girl should be thinking about marriage.

The fundamentalist churches were greatly exercised about the evils of fornication and many reckoned it was better for a 13 year old child to be married and having "lawful" sex than letting some country boy have his way with her outside of marriage. Girls of 15 or older without husbands or fiancées were often looked on as weird or perhaps lesbian.

A photograph of the happy couple appeared in the *Concordia Sentinel* in the section called "Ferriday Happenings". Jerry Lee displayed his trademark raised right lip, part sneer, part smile, often hard to tell which was in the ascendant at any given moment. Dorothy moved into the Lewis home and for a time, a fairly short time, Jerry Lee reverted to his church-oriented ways. He talked again about becoming a minister but it didn't last. He was a young hothead with a passion for the pleasures of the flesh and above all music. The marriage, such as it was, soon foundered. Jerry Lee, who had happily parted company from his school more than a year previously, got back into his musical pursuits with a vengeance. He resisted Dorothy's initial attempts to come and watch him playing the piano at night because in his view night clubs and bars were not fit and proper places for young married women to visit. It was a strange and contradictory view of morality.

He travelled with a friend to nearby cities where the music clubs were to be found. He talked his way into various jobs, even some solo spots in the Domino Lounge in Monroe where in a fairly short space of time he earned himself over $200. His parents might have had some feelings of unease over their son's decision to leave school early but they were certainly impressed by the realisation that he had a talent that people were prepared to pay good money for.

Even though he was still a minor, Jerry Lee started to get regular work in a variety of drinking joints where music was laid on for the customers and the owners didn't check musicians' birth certificates. If the customers liked the music any other technical difficulties could be overlooked. Jerry Lee was following his dream but along the way he was also building up a reservoir of guilt. The places he played were not at all holy; they were characterised by heavy drinking, sudden outbursts of violence and loose women. Worse still, he freely availed himself of the carnal pleasures on offer at Nellie Jackson's brothel in Natchez which, it was said, contained the first circular bed in Mississippi.

Jerry Lee was prolific when it came to sowing his wild oats, literally and figuratively. When still only 17, he met and soon impregnated a girl called Jane. Some members of her family insisted most emphatically that honour could only be maintained if there was a wedding – and in the end there was, of the shotgun variety. It was of course bigamous since Jerry Lee was still married to his first wife. This impediment was retrospectively dealt with by divorce not long after the second marriage took place in 1953. Jerry Lee was never one for paying much attention to irksome legal details.

As with his first marriage Jerry Lee did try briefly to live his life in more conventional ways. However all attempts to do proper jobs ended in failure. Jerry Lee was an uncontainable force of nature. He ended up in trouble with the law again after breaking into a shop and stealing a gun. The police caught and charged him; he only avoided a jail sentence because of his youth.

Jerry Lee poured most of his unbounded energy into music. He got a regular place in a band led by a man called Johnny Littlejohn which played at a club in Natchez called the Wagon Wheel. The band featured steel guitar and accordion in the line-up and played a mixture of country and blues and some current pop hits such as Hank Thompson's 'The Wild Side Of Life'. They played pretty much whatever the customers wanted to hear – an excellent grounding in all aspects of popular music for an 18 year old aspiring singer and piano player with notions of grandeur. They kept going as long as there were customers who wanted to hear them which often took them into the wee small hours. Jerry Lee also started to play regularly in a joint in Nashville; he was starting to get himself known in the music world although at this stage he was very much at the lower end of the food chain. That said, despite his tender years, he was able to play piano in a wide variety of styles from Cajun and country to religious and pop. It was when he was playing such places, for hours and hours on end, that he first became acquainted with the appealing qualities of drugs, which could banish feelings of tiredness for quite a while.

Jerry Lee's emergence onto the music scene coincided with the very early days of mass appeal versions of what would soon be called rock 'n' roll. Elvis Presley's first single, 'That's All Right (Mama)'/'Blue Moon Of Kentucky', was released in summer 1954 at around the same time as Bill Haley's version of 'Shake, Rattle And Roll' was grabbing a great deal of public attention. This sound added a potent new ingredient to Jerry Lee's repertoire which further set his soul on fire. That said, he was still tortured by guilt; every now and then he would tell friends that he was going to turn his back on the evil fleshpots in Natchez and Nashville and become a preacher – and he did do a bit of freelance preaching from time to time. He would tell congregations that the devil had worked his way into lots of houses and you could see his tail sticking up out of the roof – in the shape of a television antenna. It never lasted. The lure of the music always pulled him back and he continued to play with Johnny Littlejohn's band in wild places – where wine, women and song of the most unsophisticated kind were on offer most nights of the week.

Jerry Lee's second marriage proved to be a disaster. He and Jane fought like cat and dog and when things got too bad they went their separate ways for a while. A son, Jerry Lee Lewis Jr, had been born in October 1954. Later, when Jane returned after one particular period of separation (during which she took the first steps to obtaining a divorce) and said she was expecting another baby, Jerry Lee told her he did not believe the child was his. During another period apart, Jane sought and was granted an order for child support which Jerry Lee did not pay. And so it went on: lots of late night music interspersed with bouts of volatile domestic disharmony and religious guilt.

Jerry Lee knew that he would never have a proper job and that music would be his life. Equally, he was totally confident that his talent was a rare one and that playing bars and night clubs was never going to do it justice. He was aware of the growing publicity surrounding Elvis Presley and some others and he instinctively knew that he wanted a slice of that kind of action. He wanted to get caught up in the new musical tornado that was cutting a swathe through the south – but he wanted to be right out there at the front. He also heard and particularly liked a song called 'Whole Lot Of Shakin' Going On' which had been recorded by several artists without ever achieving much success; he thought he might be able to do something with it.

Jerry Lee was also influenced by Freddie Slack, a pianist and band leader whose piano driven song 'The House Of Blue Lights' was a particular favourite which Jerry Lee would later record. He also liked most of what Fats Domino did and the way he put the piano at the very heart of his compulsive style of melodic rhythm and blues. Similarly he was a great fan of Moon Mullican whose exuberant musical attack on the piano accorded closely with his own instinctive approach. He played a whole range of musical styles from country and blues to jazz and western swing. Mullican reputedly once said, "You gotta make those bottles bounce on the table". He was talking Jerry Lee's language.

He managed to secure an audition with rising star Slim Whitman who arranged for a technician to cut an acetate disc of a couple of songs. Jerry Lee seized the opportunity and did impressive versions of each – 'I Don't Hurt Anymore' by Hank Snow and 'I Need You

Now' by Eddie Fisher – big pop hits of the time. Whitman didn't reckon much to Jerry Lee but the Killer wasn't put off. He was determined to persuade some record company that what he did could make them money. The trouble was that guitars were the sexiest thing around at the time. However in response to suggestions that he should switch from piano to guitar his favoured riposte was generally along the lines of, "You can shove your guitar up your ass".

However he kept on plugging away; Jerry Lee was never short of the kind of self-confidence and self-belief which often crossed over into arrogance. If people didn't like what he did, they were wrong. All he had to do was to keep going until he found someone with sense enough to see that he was going to be a star.

It was his cousin Mickey Gilley, who would go on to become a country singer of note, who suggested he might like to head for Memphis and see if he could speak to the guy who had launched Elvis' career, a man by the name of Sam Phillips. Jerry Lee decided this was a good idea; Elmo agreed and helped to bankroll the trip from his meagre resources.

In fact they never got to see Sam Phillips, who was out of town. Instead they ended up in the studio of the Memphis Recording Service with a young engineer and former dancing instructor called Jack Clement. Jerry Lee played some country songs which Jack knew was not what Sam Phillips was looking for. He also knew that most of the many aspiring artists who came to Sun would probably never make it and did not have a lot of time to waste on no hopers. However he also knew that Sun's major successes were guys who had just walked in off the street, desperate to be heard – and he could see that this highly confident 21 year old had got something. Accordingly, he recorded him for a while – to have some material for Sam Phillips to hear – and then suggested that he go away and try to come up with a song with a rock 'n' roll groove.

Originally called the Memphis Recording Service, 706 Union Avenue is much better known as Sun Studio. Since 2003 it has been a National Historical Landmark. JOHN VAN HASSELT/CORBIS

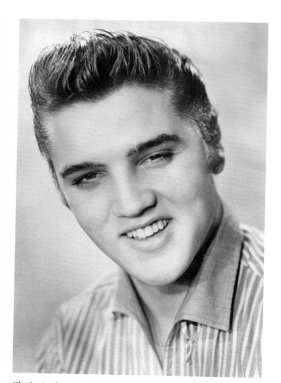

Clockwise from top left: Johnny Cash, Carl Perkins, Jerry Lee Lewis and Elvis Presley, the Million Dollar Quartet at the outset of their careers before the pressures of success had taken their toll.

The iconic shot of the Million Dollar Quartet arranged around the piano. The section with Elvis' girlfriend Marilyn Evans is usually cropped. MICHAEL OCHS ARCHIVES/GETTY IMAGES

Left: Another shot from the Million Dollar Quartet session; fifties smart casual was the order of the day. COLIN ESCOTT/MICHAEL OCHS ARCHIVES/GETTY IMAGES. Right: Shelby Singleton. Prior to his acquisition of Sun in 1969 he had produced a number of major hits including 'Harper Valley PTA' by Jeannie C. Riley. CHARLIE GILLETT COLLECTION/REDFERNS

Johnny Cash and the Tennessee Two on stage around the time of the Million Dollar Quartet session. MICHAEL OCHS ARCHIVES/GETTY IMAGES

Left: Sam Phillips with maverick DJ Dewey Phillips in Memphis c 1956. Dewey featured many of the songs Sam produced at Sun on his *Red, Hot & Blue* radio show and was the first to play Elvis' debut single 'That's All Right'. Right: Jerry Lee Lewis with wife number three Myra. When the British press revealed in 1958 that she was a minor, the public reaction was overwhelmingly hostile and his tour was cancelled. COLIN ESCOTT/MICHAEL OCHS ARCHIVES/GETTY IMAGES

Sam Phillips posing at the console. His instinctive producing style was hands on. COLIN ESCOTT/MICHAEL OCHS ARCHIVES/GETTY IMAGES

Carl Perkins receives the keys to a brand new Cadillac following the sensational success of 'Blue Suede Shoes'. He was disillusioned later when he discovered that Sam had deducted the cost from his earnings. PICTORIAL PRESS LTD/ALAMY

Sam Phillips presents Johnny Cash with a framed recording of his 1956 smash hit 'I Walk The Line'. COLIN ESCOTT/MICHAEL OCHS ARCHIVES/GETTY IMAGES

Sam Phillips with Jerry Lee Lewis in the studio. PICTORIAL PRESS LTD/ALAMY

Taken during the Million Dollar Quartet session. Sam and Elvis with Robert Johnson and Leo Soroka of the *Memphis Press-Scimitar* which ran a story on the session the following day. COLIN ESCOTT/MICHAEL OCHS ARCHIVES/GETTY IMAGES

Johnny Cash with first wife Vivian and three of the four daughters they would have together. Rosanne Cash, a highly talented singer songwriter, is on the left. AP PHOTO

Jerry Lee Lewis wowing an audience in his own inimitable way. No-one ever wanted to follow Jerry Lee. EVERETT COLLECTION/REX FEATURES

After a short but difficult period of gestation, Jerry Lee wrote 'End Of The Road'. When he returned to the studio, Jack had arranged for three session men to be there to provide a fuller band sound. Jerry Lee also had another of his cousins with him – JW Brown, 10 years his senior, who lived in Memphis and with whom Jerry Lee stayed for a while. JW was keen to form a band with Jerry Lee (although the pair barely knew each other) and he accompanied the latter to the studio. As it turned out when Jerry Lee met JW's 12-year-old daughter, Myra, his first cousin, he was immediately attracted to her, and she to him. It was the start of a pairing – they subsequently married – that would cause a great deal of upset in Jerry Lee's world a few years later.

Jack recorded Jerry Lee's new song, 'End Of The Road', and also 'Crazy Arms', a recent hit for Ray Price. When he played the recordings back to Sam Phillips soon afterwards, Sam was in no doubt that he had found another artist with that special magic necessary for success. In the case of Jerry Lee Lewis he also recognised the spirit of much of the black music he loved – the anger, the bravado, the defiance, the sorrow; despite his fair skin and blond hair, this spirit appeared to be hard-wired into his very musical being. Despite his tender years, Sam realised that there was a already a well formed talent which, with the right kind of management from him, could help to fill the large gap left when he sold Elvis' contract to RCA in 1955. That said he was slightly concerned about Jerry Lee's appearance – with a goatee beard and colourful clothes Sam found it all slightly bizarre.

Sam Phillips wasted no time in getting a record of 'Crazy Arms' to his namesake (but not his relation) the eccentric and rambunctious disc jockey Dewey Phillips, over at radio station WHBQ. He played it twice and as with Elvis in 1954, the audience reaction was wildly enthusiastic. Sam had copies pressed for public sale in less than a week. On the Sun disc, for the artist's name, it said "Jerry Lee Lewis with His Pumping Piano" – a typical commercially oriented Sam Phillips touch.

The record did not take off the way Elvis' debut single had; however it did attract favourable reviews and sold well locally. The review in *Billboard* said "[Lewis] shows a powerful feeling for country blues, and his sock warbling is accompanied by a Domino-type piano backing which brings a distinct New Orleans feel to the rendition." Sam also got Jerry Lee hooked up with promoter Bob Neal, and he soon found himself performing in lots of venues, though obviously only ones with pianos. The instruments varied greatly in quality and he quickly became an expert at identifying and avoiding damaged keys which would adversely affect his sound.

Jerry Lee Lewis knew he was on his way even if initially, for a brief period of time, Sam Phillips merely used him as a session player. Indeed that was why Jerry Lee found himself at the studio on December 4, 1956; when he arrived for work that day he had no idea that he was going to be part of a historical event of major significance.

4.

Elvis Presley

The circumstances of Elvis' Presley's birth on January 8, 1935 almost certainly had a major effect on his personality. His mother, expecting twins, delivered a stillborn baby, Jesse Garon, in the early hours of the morning in their two-roomed shotgun shack, lit by oil lamps. Approximately half an hour later Elvis Aron was born safely. The paperwork at the time had the spelling "Aron" but it appears likely that this was mistake and that the intention was to use the traditional biblical spelling "Aaron". Then again, it might be that the wish was to rhyme the name with "Garon". In any event, Elvis later expressed a clear wish that the name be spelt "Aaron" and that is the spelling that was engraved on his tombstone.

It was soon established that Elvis' mother would be unable to have any more children. As the years went by she and Elvis developed a very close, anxious relationship with each concerned about the other's wellbeing, worried that some innocent activity might result in some catastrophic harm befalling their ultimate loved one. Elvis was an only child much of whose emotional life was contained within the, at times, claustrophobic boundaries of his small family unit, affected always by the baby brother who did not survive. His mother, to whom he grew exceptionally close, held on to a kind of folksy belief, widely held at the time, that when a twin died, the other one somehow "got all the strength of both".

Vernon and Gladys Presley came from East Tupelo, Mississippi, an area where poor white working-class families lived. It bore little resemblance to the more attractive central areas of town. Eking out a living was a constant struggle and there was a thriving bootlegging industry run by people seeking to supplement their meagre incomes. The couple's historical ancestry was primarily European – Scottish or German on Vernon's side, Scottish-Irish on Gladys'. One of Gladys' great-great-grandmothers was Cherokee.

Vernon and Gladys were married in 1933. They first met at a church service and got married when Vernon was still a minor. He was 17 but stated on the application forms that he was 22. Gladys was 21 but stated that she was 19. It seems that the authorities paid little attention to checking facts back then.

People who knew Vernon often said that he was an unambitious man. Like his wife he had left school early and had taken work where he could get it; inevitably the jobs were low level and unskilled – milkman, sharecropper, any kind of manual work. That said, he accepted his responsibilities for his apparently much valued family, and when one job came to an end he doggedly pursued new opportunities in order to maintain his role as the provider.

Gladys was very different from her husband. Whereas he was taciturn, giving away little about his feelings, Gladys was outgoing and warm, voluble and feisty. It seems clear she was the dominant partner in the relationship, the driving force.

The family suffered a major blow in 1937 when Vernon was sent to the Mississippi State Penitentiary (known locally as Parchman Farm) for fraudulently altering a cheque in his favour. The sentence was three years, though he only served eight months. There were many black prisoners and Vernon would undoubtedly have heard their work chants, a West African tradition; they provided a rhythm which helped to pace the repetitive tasks they had to carry out. It might be a far fetched notion but perhaps, by some kind of osmosis, the feel of this primitive music found its way to Elvis. The folklorist Alan Lomax, who had visited Parchman Farm in the thirties, reflected on what he heard. "These people were poetic and musical and they had something terribly important to say."

Vernon's incarceration was a particularly traumatic time for the family. They lost their house and Gladys and Elvis had to spend temporary periods with relatives. This added to the generalised feelings of insecurity in the family. Though he did not talk about it much, it appears likely that the experience of being in jail did adversely affect Vernon's confidence, leaving him with a sense of failure as the main breadwinner for the family.

Elvis did not have a lot of friends; those who came into contact with him often characterised him subsequently as something of a loner. He certainly did not belong to any of the larger social groups. He was quite a gentle and sensitive boy who, for instance, did not like the idea of hunting animals – which a lot of his friends regarded as an entirely normal pursuit. He was an unremarkable student at school and was reasonably popular with his teachers one of whom described him as "sweet and average". One fellow pupil later said of him that he was a "sad, shy, not especially attractive boy".

Getting work was never easy but during the war Vernon secured steady work in a munitions factory in Memphis, coming home only at weekends. After the war things were difficult once more; life was little more than a hand to mouth existence. The family had to move around as a matter of economic necessity and at one time took rooms close to Shake Rag, a black quarter, where young Elvis was probably exposed to the rich sounds of blues music, although it was a district which white folks did not go into much.

Gladys' feelings about the preciousness of the only child she would ever have affected Elvis too. He experienced a kind of free floating anxiety concerning his parents, and fretted that they might come to harm somehow. For her part Gladys was quite possessive and protective. This made it difficult for Elvis to have anything approaching a free and easy childhood – he would sense her anxiety and work at avoiding doing things which might cause her to worry. Presciently, Elvis used to say – when his parents were going through particularly difficult financial times – that one day he would be rich and buy them a big house and a couple of nice cars. As a family, although they did most of the things other families did, they were quite insular. They spent a lot of time in each other's company. They were not prejudiced against anyone; they did not regard themselves as being above anyone, black or white.

As with most people they knew, church was a regular feature of life. From an early age, Elvis, though not especially musically gifted, demonstrated a desire and an ability to sing along with hymns; it was said he could carry a tune before he had the ability to form let alone understand the words of the songs.

When he was 10, despite his bashfulness, he sang in front of several hundred people at the annual Mississippi-Alabama Fair and Dairy Show in Tupelo. He had to stand on a chair to reach the microphone. The song he chose was 'Old Shep', the classic tear-jerker written by Red Foley. He also appeared on a radio talent show, the WELO *Jamboree*. Children and adults queued up on a Saturday morning to sing a song on air, usually gospel in Elvis' case.

He was given a guitar when he was 11 and various family members taught him the basic chords. He was an enthusiastic student and though he never became a great guitarist, he did get to be a reliable rhythm player and was able to provide a solid musical backing for his developing singing talent. He also observed people who played musical instruments with keen interest and listened to the *Grand Ole*

Opry from Nashville on the radio. Elvis got into the habit of taking his guitar into school most days; he slung it over his back. He played during breaks, sometimes putting on informal shows for the other students. When not actually playing, he was keen to talk music with anybody who would listen.

After the war, jobs were harder to come by in Tupelo once more and so in 1948, when Elvis was 13, the family moved to Memphis – where they assumed things would be easier. It was a decision of some importance for the family but of course for Elvis it put in place one of the key elements of the sensational future which lay in store for him.

The family lived in single rooms in boarding houses for a time, before eventually securing a two-bedroom apartment in a public assistance housing project, known as the Courts, for $35 a month. Elvis found the change to a new city and a new school unsettling. Always quite anxious, he was overwhelmed by his new city and did not settle easily into school; initially at least he no longer thought to take his guitar with him. Despite his obvious interest in music in the eighth grade he only attained a C, faring better in English.

Elvis heard a great deal of music on the radio. His taste was eclectic to say the least. He listened enthusiastically to country or hillbilly songs, gospel and any kind of popular music; he was also quite open to listening to and enjoying light classical songs particularly those delivered in the rich tenor tones of Mario Lanza. Unlike many of the white people he lived amongst, he also took in radio station WDIA, "The Mother Station of the Negroes", where he could experience the raw musical delights of Howlin' Wolf, a young BB King or Mahalia Jackson. The world of radio was one where a music fan could avoid issues of racial segregation completely. The airwaves were colour blind. This was harder to do in many areas of city life where restrictions based on race were commonplace. The city censor had banned the stage musical *Annie Get Your Gun* on the grounds that it featured a Negro railroad conductor.

Elvis did make friends with a small group of boys from the Courts who had some interest in music. He sometimes played guitar and sang songs for them but nobody had any sense that he had any special gift; they were struck however by the fact that he knew the words and the chords by heart – most people just remembered odd snatches of songs. At school he gradually regained the confidence to sing in front of people, at parties to mark special occasions for instance, although he always had to overcome feelings of shyness. For these informal, often impromptu performances, he tended to choose uptempo songs. One time it might be Eddie Fisher or Bing Crosby, another time down-home country or spiritual music. It gradually dawned on Elvis that as he became known as someone who could put over a song pretty well, his popularity grew – not in terms of acquiring really close friends but rather an ever increasing band of people who admired him; pretty seductive for a shy adolescent with secret ambitions to be successful. Elvis also hung out in record shops to hear the latest sounds. Some shops made this easy by setting up a loudspeaker above the door and playing a constant stream of music. He sometimes went to the local cinema where you could see a double feature for a dime.

Elvis was greatly interested in his personal appearance from his early teenage years onwards. This could be seen as a desire to be different from others, to stand out from the crowd, as if he had a sense that he was somehow destined for a life that would set him apart from other people. He grew sideboards and slicked down his hair with Vaseline and Rose Oil hair tonic. Some boys reckoned he was a sissy. He became a devotee of Lansky's, on Beale Street, the coolest clothes shop in Memphis – even though to begin with he could only drool over the colourful and stylish wares on display in the window and merely dream of owning them. Later, he became a regular customer and always appreciated the fact that when he bought clothes at first they allowed him to do so on credit. In later years he was of course their most famous customer and also an enthusiastic ambassador.

There was an impressive range of live music on offer in Memphis. Elvis regularly attended gospel shows and particularly liked the Speer Family and the Chuck Wagon Gang. He was also mesmerised and inspired by the dazzling showmanship and multi-layered vocal pyrotechnics of the Statesmen Quartet, underpinned by the brilliant bounce of the imposing bass singer Jim "Big Chief" Wetherington. These gospel groups were all white but Elvis was just as enthusiastic about the black gospel artists.

In 1953 Elvis' school, Humes High, put on its Annual Minstrel Show which featured, amongst more than twenty acts, "guitarist Elvis Prestly". He wore a red shirt and sang 'Till I Waltz Again With You'. Elvis graduated from high school in summer 1953. He was relieved to have made it all the way through; his parents were mightily proud. He got work in a machinist's shop very soon after leaving school and earned $33 a week.

Later in the summer of 1953, Elvis decided that he would like to give his mother a present of him singing. He had heard about the Memphis Recording Service, and knew that it would be a fairly straightforward matter to call by there and get an acetate recording of a couple of songs. Marion Keisker met him at reception and informed him that to record two songs would cost $3.98 plus applicable tax. He could have got a recording more cheaply in one of the department stores in the city centre. The fact that he chose to go to a professional recording studio might suggest that his ambitions went beyond simply coming up with a novelty present for his mother.

Marion had a halting conversation with Elvis during this first visit to the studio. In subsequent years she was asked about it countless times. She remembered asking him more than once who he sounded like. "I don't sound like nobody," was the response. The songs he recorded that day were 'My Happiness', a 1948 pop chart hit for Jon and Sandra Steele which Elvis had often sung before, and 'That's When Your Heartaches Begin', a ballad recorded by the Ink Spots in 1941. Marion's note indicated that Elvis might be considered a possibility when someone was required for a session or if a band was looking for a vocalist.

Elvis made a point of finding some excuse or other to visit the studio every now and then on the off chance that somebody was looking for a singer – nobody was. At the start of 1954 he cut another acetate with two songs, 'It Wouldn't Be The Same Without You' and 'I'll Never Stand In Your Way'. In his own quiet way he was pursuing his dream of making it as a singer.

Elvis started dating a girl called Dixie Locke who at 15 was three years his junior. She and some friends had let him overhear them talking about plans to go skating the following weekend and sure enough he turned up. She and her friends clearly found him an attractive proposition, a boy who was out of the ordinary, one they wanted to get to know better. Elvis and Dixie were soon an item although initially her parents, conservative church-going people, would not let him take her out; they wanted to get to know him better first and so to begin with dates were spent at her house playing board games. She was struck right away by the great interest he took in clothes and how he did not want to wear the same clothes as everybody else. On one date she recalled him wearing a short black jacket, a ruffled shirt and black trousers with a pale pink stripe down the legs. It struck her as paradoxical; although he was shy, and sensitive about comments on his appearance, he drew attention to himself with his eye-catching sartorial choices.

Dixie was quickly aware of how important music was to Elvis. They went to gospel concerts together and sometimes went to the church at East Trigg, much liked by Sam Phillips, where they listened to heartfelt gospel singing. Sometimes Elvis would simply spend an evening singing songs to her. She was struck by the fact that when he was singing it was as if he was in a zone where he was entirely comfortable; the usual shyness and hesitant conversation disappeared. He confided in her that he had failed an audition for an amateur group of singers based at a local church, although this might have been because the person he was going to replace decided against leaving the group. Not long afterwards he failed another audition for a band featuring a singer called Eddie Bond which had a regular spot at a night club. Bond loved to tell this story when Elvis became famous.

In April 1954, Elvis got a new job with the Crown Electric Company, driving a truck delivering electrical goods to building sites. He earned $40 a week. He often took his guitar in the truck and would play during breaks, much as he had done at school. The owners of the business grew very fond of their new employee; the wife of the proprietor was particularly impressed that he seemed to be so fond of his mother. There was talk of Elvis training to be an electrician at one stage though this never came to anything.

Dixie noted with surprise that Elvis routinely gave most of his pay straight to his mother; he regarded this as the natural and right thing to do. He only kept enough for a few essentials and the cost of modest outings with her. She was struck by the closeness of the bond between mother and son. Elvis had hardly ever stayed away from home overnight and his mother said that when he went out in the evening, she could never get to sleep until she knew Elvis was safely home.

Almost a year after Elvis had first visited the Memphis Recording Service and made the record for his mother, there was a major breakthrough. Sam Phillips had come across a song, 'Without You', which he felt might suit Elvis – even though he had to get Marion to remind him of the singer's name. Elvis was in the studio like a flash. They spent around three hours working on a variety of songs but nothing really clicked. However Sam was now convinced that the boy had some special X factor and now he certainly would not forget his name. Sam was also struck by Elvis' affinity to some of his black artists and later recalled, "His insecurity was so markedly like that of a black person."

Sam knew a couple of musicians, guitarist Scotty Moore and bass player Bill Black; he asked them to have an informal session with Elvis, play a variety of songs and see what they thought. He made it clear to them that in his view Elvis had something – even if he was not sure exactly what at this stage. He wanted a second opinion. Scotty and Bill were not particularly impressed beyond thinking that Elvis had quite a good voice. Sam then got them all in the studio once more and ran through a load of songs, mainly recent country and pop hits such as Eddy Arnold's 'I Really Don't Want To Know' and Leon Payne's 'I Love You Because'.

They worked late into the evening of July 5, 1954 but despite their best efforts, nothing seemed to work and Sam was beginning to have doubts about his earlier positive views on Elvis. It was Elvis himself who transformed the session. He started messing about with a song he had picked up some time before. 'That's All Right (Mama)'. It had been a minor rhythm and blues hit for Arthur "Big Boy" Crudup a few years back. Something about the way Elvis whipped it along was infectious; Scotty and Bill quickly got the vibe and joined in. Sam sprang out of the control room to see what they were doing – and then got them to do it again. It was the eureka moment he had been waiting for. He quickly got the tapes rolling and preserved for ever one of the seminal moments in the history of popular music – the sheer irrepressible exuberance of unembellished rock 'n' roll at its joyful best.

Sam took an acetate to DJ Dewey Phillips – idiosyncratic, dogmatic but with his finger on the pulse of popular opinion – whose views he respected. They listened to the song over and over again; they knew it was something special. Dewey played the song on his show the next night. Sam told Elvis in advance that this would be happening. Perhaps fearful of failure in a very public way, Elvis went to the cinema. Dewey played the song repeatedly and the public response was immediate and overwhelming with people bombarding the station with phone calls and telegrams.

Bob Dylan understood their feelings later saying that hearing Elvis for the first time was "like busting out of jail". With the assistance of Elvis' mother who, along with other family members had been glued to the radio, Dewey got Elvis out of the cinema and along to the radio station for his first interview. Dewey's only advice to Elvis was not to say anything "dirty" on air. Once the interview began he made a point of asking Elvis what school he had gone to so that the listeners would know he was not black. Nineteen-year-old Elvis, shy and deferential, found the experience excruciating. Even years later, when he was hugely successful, he rarely looked comfortable when he was interviewed; there was a nervousness, a lack of confidence, perhaps a deep-seated fear that he would be exposed as inadequate in some way.

Sam knew he had to get a single out and so he had to record another song for the B-side. In the studio they tried a range of songs but the one that worked best was a pumped-up version of the Bill Monroe bluegrass song 'Blue Moon Of Kentucky'. Sam then got demos to various key DJs in and around Memphis in order to build on the initial momentum. By the time the single was officially released on July 196,000 copies had been pre-ordered locally.

Sam set about getting as much exposure for Elvis as possible. With the help of promoter Bob Neal, Elvis, Scotty and Bill were placed on various bills with some well known stars. At the end of July they appeared at Overton Shell Park – a major local venue. This would be a real test of whether Elvis really was a rising star or just a flash in the pan. Top of the bill was Slim Whitman – a conservative country artist, a very different sort of performer from Elvis. Before the show Elvis was extremely nervous, to the extent that he stammered at the start of sentences at times. When he took the stage, he sang, played his guitar and shook uncontrollably. He was wearing baggy trousers and the effect, enhanced by Bill Black wildly slapping his bass and whooping and hollering a few feet behind, sent the crowd wild. They loved what he sang and also the way he moved; his gyrations might have been born out of nerves, but to the crowd they simply made a good thing better. It was quite remarkable. Elvis was not musically trained; he had no track record. He was a teenage truck driver with bad skin who was nervous, particularly when he was the centre of attention. And yet, he had a love of singing, a belief at some level that he had a gift and this enabled him to conquer his demons and unleash his voice and his moves on an audience which was crying out for a new musical phenomenon. After the war teenagers were looking for some kind of music to call their own, for an artist they felt represented them and their passions – and for many of them Elvis fitted the bill perfectly.

Sam and Bob Neal watched from the wings and realised they had stumbled across something bigger than anything they had ever imagined. Dixie too was watching; she too was taken aback. It started to dawn on her that their recent talk of marriage and her vision of a conventional life together, working and raising children, were fading before her eyes. She was particularly shocked by the extreme emotional reaction Elvis triggered in so many young women.

Sam was relentless when it came to promoting Elvis. He drove thousands of miles and spoke to lots of DJs, distributors and promoters in his efforts to spread the word. It was not long before Elvis was playing a lot of gigs; he also got a regular spot at a club called the Eagle's Nest. There was a sense around Memphis that something special was stirring, things were changing – and the Elvis phenomenon was at the epicentre of events. It is almost certain that his skin colour helped; a black artist with similar gifts would not have been accepted in the same way.

Sam persuaded the powers that be to give Elvis an appearance at the *Grand Ole Opry*, thus allowing him to tread the hallowed boards of the Ryman Auditorium from where the show was broadcast every weekend. The experience of rubbing shoulders with some of his musical heroes was wonderful for Elvis. He worried that Bill Monroe might be offended by his speeded up version of 'Blue Moon Of Kentucky' but in fact Monroe liked it. Despite his inexperience and the raunchy nature of his act, he received a generally warm welcome from the other artists. That said, the audience only accorded him modest applause – in stark contrast to the mob hysterics he was now regularly receiving elsewhere. There was to be none of that from the old guard of country music. It was a little livelier at the *Louisiana Hayride* where Elvis was soon offered a regular slot. This was the show, broadcast weekly on radio, which had helped to launch the careers of stars such as Hank Williams and Kitty Wells.

Finding the right venues for Elvis was a hit and miss affair in the early days. Not everybody knew who he was; not everyone liked what he did or how he looked. On one occasion he was given a gig at a venue where the highly regarded regular act could not appear for some reason. After a couple of minutes many people in the audience simply walked out. On other occasions if things were not going well or Elvis failed to develop a rapport with the audience, Scotty and Bill – very familiar with performing in front of audiences of all kinds – were well able to come up with the right line of banter to win people over. Elvis could offend some people; he sometimes cracked crude jokes, spat on the stage or belched forcefully into the microphone. He had not yet learned the art of good interaction with the paying public. Yet his instinctive way of moving on the stage was overtly sexual; he slowly worked his hips around and delivered sudden suggestive jerks in time to key moments of songs. He held and caressed the microphone in a loving trance. Elvis simply exuded sex appeal. It was all such a contrast to the shy deferential kid away from the concert performances.

Elvis didn't know what had hit him, what with late night shows and lengthy sessions in the studio. He gave up his day job which meant that his life rhythms changed completely. He ate and slept at times that accommodated his irregular working patterns. He spent long hours travelling around in an old Chevrolet with Bill's double bass strapped onto the roof. He found that he was gaining a lot of attention from girls.

As he started to earn more money he treated himself to some fancy clothes from Lansky Brothers – he seemed to have an unerring capacity to pick out the most attention-grabbing clothes – and also a Martin guitar on which his name was inscribed in black metallic letters. He bought lots of records and really did work hard to get to know a wide variety of musical styles. Music was his life's work and he was a dedicated student.

Sam was very keen to get a follow-up single into the shops as quickly as possible. The songs chosen for his second Sun single were 'I Don't Care If The Sun Don't Shine' and 'Good Rockin' Tonight'. On the face of it the former was a surprising choice. It had originally been written for the animated Disney feature *Cinderella* by Mack David, brother of Hal, of Bacharach-David fame.

By the start of 1955 word of Elvis' star quality and massive crowd-pulling powers was spreading fast; and people on the business side wanted a piece of the action. Elvis signed a management contract with Bob Neal which required the consent of Vernon and Gladys because he was still a minor. A certain "Colonel" Tom Parker, boss of promotion and management company Jamboree Attractions, had also picked up the powerful scent left by the Hillbilly Cat. Parker had run away to the circus when young and had come up the hard way. A so called "carny" he was as wily as he was tough. It is said that he painted chickens bright yellow and passed them off as canaries. He had gone from circuses and carnivals to managing singers. He had picked up the title "Colonel" in 1948 from Jimmie Davis, the governor of Louisiana, in return for work he did on Davis' election campaign. Having devoted himself for years to Eddy Arnold, whose career he took to giddy heights of chart and movie success, he was now managing Hank Snow, one of the major country stars of the day. Initially from a distance, he was keeping his commercially attuned eye firmly on events.

Elvis started to attract a lot of press attention and one journalist in particular, Bob Johnson of the *Memphis Press-Scimitar*, took a great interest in his developing career. Describing his music he wrote astutely, "'That's All Right' is in the R&B idiom of negro field jazz, 'Blue Moon of Kentucky' more in the country field, but there is a curious blending of the two different musics in both."

Eager to maintain the momentum, Sam Phillips soon released a third single, 'You're A Heartbreaker'/'Milkcow Blues Boogie'. Between the studio and the stage there was little time for rest or recuperation. Elvis was slotted into a Hank Snow tour of Canada which Tom Parker was promoting. During discussions over arrangements for the tour Parker said that for Elvis' career to take off in a big way he really needed to be with a big record label like RCA. Sam was furious about this; but even at this stage he sensed that what Parker was saying was true – though this did not stop him feeling aggrieved. As a result of his own determined efforts Elvis had become a star well beyond Memphis. However, Parker's vision was on an altogether bigger scale – he believed that for Elvis, the world was his oyster.

The reaction to Elvis on the Canadian tour and subsequent tours in America followed a familiar pattern. Large numbers of young people (mainly girls whose boyfriends were often put out by their behaviour) went crazy, like people possessed. Sometimes the audiences approached 15,000. There were near riots in some of the places they played, as there would be for the Beatles in the early sixties; and as with the Beatles it soon got to the stage where it was almost impossible to hear the music. Elvis was of course far down the bill but it became very difficult for anybody to follow him and eventually it was decided by Tom Parker that Elvis would close out the first half of the show to allow order to be resumed during the break. In this way too, no artist was placed in the invidious position of having to go onstage straight after him. Elvis soon learned to improve his onstage rapport with the audience and be a bit more at ease during interviews with journalists and DJs – although he was still awkward when it came to questions about himself. With the huge amounts of adulation coming his way on a virtually daily basis, it was hardly surprising that his confidence as a performer was increasing. Despite the surreal life he was leading, which took him so far away from the one he was used to, he continued to phone his parents and Dixie regularly; that said it was clear that he took advantage of the plentiful supply of adoring female fans on tap. By this stage it was clear that his and Dixie's relationship, with its vision of marriage and long term domestic bliss, was dead in the water. Ironically though, he was still possessive and jealous and on the increasingly rare occasions when they were able to spend time together he complained about what she had been up to when he was away.

Writing after a show in Florida a local journalist tried to sum up his appeal. "What really stole the show was this 20-year-old-sensation, Elvis Presley, a real sex box as far as the teenage girls were concerned. They squealed themselves silly over this fellow in orange coat and sideburns who 'sent' them with his unique arrangement of 'Shake Rattle And Roll'." It got to the stage where there had to be extra security to protect Elvis and those around him from the screaming hordes. Elvis did not help matters by sometimes saying at the end of his set, "OK girls, I'll see you all backstage". Tom Parker was soon convinced that with Elvis he had hit pay dirt big time, and was soon secretly planning ways to remove Bob Neal from the picture, gain exclusive control of his boy, as he already thought of him, and get him hooked up with one of the major labels up north.

For Elvis' fourth Sun single – 'Baby, Let's Play House'/'I'm Left, You're Right, She's Gone' – Sam introduced drums, which would be a feature of most subsequent recordings and live performances. He felt he wanted to emphasise more strongly the rhythm and the beat. By summer 1955 D J Fontana was the regular drummer for all studio and live work. All of the singles showed up well locally though as yet there was no national breakthrough.

It would be wrong to suggest that the rise of Elvis' career was one success after another; there was still the odd failure. At considerable expense the group flew to New York to audition for the *Arthur Godfrey Talent Scouts*, a television show featuring new acts. It was a national show which would have given them huge exposure. They failed the audition and never even got to meet the man himself. Also, at this stage of things, life on the road was sometimes far from glamorous. They would often have to grab some sleep in the back of a car as they drove through the night from one venue to the next.

However the upward momentum was unstoppable. Inquiries from major labels flooded in. If the subject of buying Elvis' contract came up, Sam did his best to fend them off by quoting astronomically high figures. He needed money but he did not really want to sell his number one asset.

In the summer of 1955 Elvis made a triumphant return to the Overton Park Shell where, as a very nervous young artist, he had made his first important professional appearance a short time previously. How much had changed in a year. There were 22 acts on the bill and Elvis was now number two, behind Webb Pierce, an established star with many hits to his name. At smaller venues he was the headliner and was supported by other but lesser rising stars such as Porter Wagoner, Johnny Cash, Carl Perkins and a young Buddy Holly. He now relished live performances and had the audience eating out of his hand. Later in the year he was touring with Bill Haley and his Comets. He was now right up there with the biggest stars in America. His rise had been meteoric. He won various awards but it seems that judging panels were not quite sure how to categorise him. In 1955 both *Cashbox* and *Billboard* chose him as the most promising new country and western artist.

The final Sun single was 'Mystery Train'/'I Forgot To Remember To Forget' and as with the previous releases the artist credit was "Elvis Presley" and in smaller letters below, "Scotty and Bill". Tom Parker came down hard on anything which took attention away from his star and once Elvis moved to RCA, all recordings were in name of Elvis Presley alone.

Jogging along below the surface of all the recording and performing activity were continuing intensive efforts on Tom Parker's behalf to wrest control of Elvis from Sam Phillips and Bob Neal. He deployed a variety of weapons in his campaign and even got Hank Snow to phone Vernon and Gladys to win them over. He was helped by Sam Phillips' continuing financial difficulties, which were still causing him sleepless nights despite a considerable degree of success with Carl Perkins and Johnny Cash.

In the end Sam bowed to the inevitable and agreed a deal totalling $40,000: $35,000 for Elvis' contract and $5,000 to Elvis for unpaid royalties due. The papers were signed in the presence of a photographer at Sun studio on November 21, 1955. The royalty rate Elvis would receive from RCA would be 5% – Sam had paid 3%. By this stage Parker was to all intents and purposes in complete control of the Elvis Presley brand although in theory Bob Neal retained an interest in his management; this last vestige of involvement came to an end early in 1956. Though happy to be moving onwards and upwards, Elvis never forgot the immense debt he owed to Sam Phillips. "If it wasn't for Mister Phillips... I'd still be drivin' a truck. He seen somethin' I never seen in myself." Sam had also given Elvis plenty of freedom in the studio which allowed him to develop production skills that he would deploy throughout much of the rest of his career.

In January 1956, just after his 21st birthday, Elvis started with work at RCA's studios in Nashville with producer Steve Sholes. The setup was very different from Sun. Sessions were timed, and rapid results were expected. Some top notch session musicians and backing singers were also brought in including Gordon Stoker of the Jordanaires who would later work extensively with Elvis. It took a while before Elvis settled into a good working groove. It seems that Steve Sholes wondered – given the success of 'Blue Suede Shoes' for Carl Perkins – if he had chosen the right Sun artist. There was even a suggestion later on that Sam Phillips might be hired as a freelance consultant to work some Memphis magic on the RCA sessions. However the first session at RCA did produce 'Heartbreak Hotel'. The song was inspired by a man in Miami who killed himself having left a suicide note which read: "I walk a lonely street".

Tom Parker and RCA did their best to publicise Elvis right from the start. RCA took out a full page ad in *Billboard* which referred to Elvis as "the most talked-about new personality in the last ten years of recorded music". Parker devoted himself full time to Elvis and established a powerful team of booking agents, publishers, promoters and television and radio contacts to get him across to the widest possible audience.

Elvis was booked to make a series of appearances on CBS' *Stage Show* hosted by Jimmy and Tommy Dorsey which went out just before the hugely popular *Jackie Gleason Show* on Saturday night. The initial appearance went reasonably well but the audience figures were not as good as hoped for. This however changed with subsequent appearances and it was soon clear that Parker's belief in the near universal appeal of Elvis was justified. He was an idea whose time had come.

One difficulty Elvis did experience was a result of his sudden transplantation from the mores of a country boy in Memphis to the far more refined manners to be found in the heightened world of rich and successful music executives and their families. On one occasion at a sophisticated dinner party, Elvis, who had a penchant for hamburgers and fries, was served rare lamb which was pink in the middle. He nearly gagged on it.

The pressure of life did start to tell on Elvis. He was often a bundle of nerves, restless, distracted, fidgety and keen to get to the next concert, recording session or interview. He used up large amounts of nervous energy. Every now and then he would simply crash out and sleep for half a day. There was one occasion when after a show in February 1956, he passed out and had to be observed in hospital for a while.

By March of that year Elvis was earning enough money to do what he had been telling interviewers he wanted to be able to do – buy a house for his parents; it was a childhood ambition fulfilled.

Elvis was now selling records in huge quantities. 'Heartbreak Hotel' had been released as a single and was only held off the number one spot by Perry Como's 'Juke Box Baby', although the latter was already sounding dated, something the parents would not be too bothered by – a final throw of the dice for the old order. His debut album – with just "Elvis Presley" on the cover by order of Tom Parker – was selling well and there was also an EP which featured Elvis' version of 'Blue Suede Shoes'.

With hardly a pause for breath Elvis next found himself being screen tested for Hollywood. Hal Wallis, famous for producing a slew of outstanding films such as *Casablanca* and *The Maltese Falcon*, liked what he saw. He felt that Elvis had a kind of magic which could pull in audiences, particularly younger audiences with their new-found economic power, in much the way that James Dean had done. There were two parts to the screen test: miming to a song ('Blue

Suede Shoes') and running through some dialogue. Tom Parker had wanted a career in movies to be part of the equation from early on. Unlike Sam Phillips and his ilk, Parker was not really a music fan. For him it was all about show business and making money. He saw Elvis following the route carved out by people like Bing Crosby, Frank Sinatra and many others who had started out as successful singers and then moved effortlessly onto the big screen. After tough and intensive negotiations Parker and Wallis hammered out a three movie deal under which Elvis would earn $100,000 for the first, $150,000 for the second and $200,000 for the third. There was even a clause, insisted on by Parker, which would permit Elvis to make one film a year with someone else if that could be arranged.

Tom Parker and his team were constantly pushing Elvis on to greater heights. In no time at all the simple notion of three musicians delivering a raw and pure form of music to set the world alight had become subsumed into the voracious world of showbiz. Elvis did a comedy routine with Milton Berle on the latter's television show which had Berle playing the part of Elvis' hillbilly brother Melvin. Part of the routine, full of corny jokes, was predicated on the view that people like Elvis, from the land of the hillbilly down south, were unable to spell. He made a return appearance later in the year when he appeared more polished, less like the new kid on the block. Live concerts were like variety shows, almost vaudevillian, and often featured acrobats, dancers, comedians – a chimpanzee act even – but when Elvis was on the bill he invariably drew the most enthusiastic audience response.

Only a few months before Elvis had been over the moon to sign a contract to appear regularly on the *Louisiana Hayride*; now this was simply a low paid nuisance which Tom Parker got Elvis out of by paying a penalty of $10,000. A regular spot in Las Vegas was more to Parker's taste and this was soon achieved. Elvis was signed up for a four week engagement at the thousand seat Venus Room at the New

Frontier Hotel for around $8,000 a week. In the publicity posters laid on by the hotel Elvis was referred to as the "Atomic powered singer".

It was not an inspired choice of venue for Elvis. The tickets were quite expensive and the audience was older and more sophisticated – they were not about to throw themselves around screaming in the aisles. Some celebrities including Liberace – one of Gladys' favourite stars – came to see him. By the end of the engagement the audience response, fairly muted to begin with had grown a bit more enthusiastic – everybody was being seduced by the new force in music. However this comparative flop had no bearing whatever on the hysterical reaction Elvis elicited from his countless young fans during his regular concerts on the road.

By the end of 1956, Elvis accounted for approximately half of all of RCA's popular music sales; money was flowing in and by the end of the year he was the proud owner of three Cadillacs (one of them painted in his favourite colours, pink and black) and a powerful Harley motor bike.

By the time Elvis played another so called homecoming concert at the Ellis Auditorium in Memphis towards the end of 1956 – headlining the Cotton Carnival – his status had soared to new levels. His place at the top of any bill was now a given. He arrived – just before he was due to go on, no hanging around in dressing rooms with lesser stars – with an official escort made up of policemen, firemen and shore patrol officers. His routines were slicker, his instinctive and, as some described them, lascivious moves had been subtly choreographed so as to appear smoother and more under control. Without warning he would hold his arms straight out to either side at shoulder height, let his hands dangle and flutter; briefly trance-like he would then launch into a series of suggestive physical jerks in time to the music. Gone were the coarser aspects of Elvis' onstage behaviour. Some said he had already lost some of that edgy danger which had been such a great feature of his early shows. One newspaper report the next day said the reception Elvis received had a "fire and enthusiasm never in memorable history granted a native son". It was announced that the city had declared July 4, 1956, "Elvis Presley Day". In the past he had invariably stayed behind to sign autographs after concerts; now, after a shortish set comprising eight songs, he was well away from the auditorium in the back of a limousine while the audience was still cheering for an encore.

Elvis was now a comparatively rare visitor to his parents' new upmarket house – which was still his only home. Whenever he stayed there, crowds of fans milled around outside. Sometimes he rewarded them with impromptu autograph signing sessions. Elvis became a virtual prisoner in the house and if he did manage to slip out to the cinema he would soon be discovered and come out to find his car vandalised by souvenir collectors.

On occasion the family visited well-to-do neighbours who would show off by getting Elvis to phone friends and relatives out of the blue. Whether they liked it or not, the lives of Vernon and Gladys had been irrevocably changed by their son's phenomenal rise. They did like a lot of the good things that came their way but Gladys in particular feared for her beloved son's safety and hankered after a different future for him, one which involved getting out of the music industry altogether, buying some kind of business and marrying and having children. She did however understand that this would never happen now.

Even as Elvis was enjoying his new-found celebrity a backlash had begun. Conservative forces in society latched on to him as the very personification of society's ills. He was seen by some as a moral degenerate responsible for juvenile delinquency, sexual permissiveness, family breakdown, a failure to uphold religious values and also the increasing integration of different races. Backstage one night an established country artist referred to his music as "nigger trash". Elvis had loved black and white music from an early age and he certainly did mix their musical styles – so how could he see anything wrong with the different races getting along better?

A lot of the negative press coverage attacked Elvis' abilities as an entertainer. A reporter in the *New York Times* said, "Mr Presley has no discernible singing ability". Another described Elvis' performance as a "strip tease with clothes on" and journalist Ben Gross said, "Popular music has reached its lowest depths in the grunt and groin antics of one Elvis Presley". His clothes were dismissively and patronisingly referred to as "loud".

Words such as "nauseating" and "noxious" were bandied about. The resort of Asbury Park, New Jersey, issued a proclamation banning rock 'n' roll music altogether following a near riot that had followed a concert there. The local mayor talked of "this hot music that seems to stir the kids up so much". The backlash affected television and radio stations; they did not want to alienate any members of their potential audiences and were forced onto the back foot. Many stated publicly that they did not want to offend anyone and that if necessary Elvis might have to tone down his act. For television's prestigious *Steve Allen Show*, Elvis appeared in dress shirt, top hat and tails and sang a very unraunchy version of 'Hound Dog' to a real basset hound. This kind of family entertainment approach was a sop to the conservative forces that were so upset by the young star. As he came on he unthinkingly wiped his nose on the top hat which he was holding in his hand. It was one of those automatic actions which indicated that he was still very much prone to nerves. Ironically, after this performance there were demonstrations outside RCA's studios by people wanting the old Elvis back. Another lesson learned was that you cannot please all the people all the time.

Elvis displayed considerable backbone in standing up for himself against often hostile questioning. Taking the general approach that he could not understand why people should criticise him in the way they did, he said in one interview, "When I sang hymns back home with mom and pop I stood still and looked like you look when you sing a hymn. When I sing this rock 'n' roll my eyes won't stay open and my legs won't stand still. I don't care what they say, it ain't nasty." Elvis also rejected the notion that his movements somehow had their origins in the ecstatic gospel singing and jiving around he witnessed in some of the churches he went to as a child.

Songwriters soon found that getting a song recorded by Elvis Presley was not quite the bonanza they thought it would be. It sometimes meant giving up a share of the income generated by the song. Otis Blackwell wrote a number of hits including 'Don't Be Cruel' and it was made clear to him that if he wanted the hottest new star in America to record it he would have to give up half the publishing rights and half the writer's share. On the face of it this was unfair, but this sort of thing had happened for years and writers still made large amounts of money.

Elvis did not have much time to relax away from the pressures of his life in music and films. When he did he went on lavish holidays in upmarket resorts with girlfriends, friends and family. One quite serious girlfriend at this time, June Juanico, and then her mother, quite innocently gave interviews to the press which touched on the subject of marriage. Tom Parker was incandescent. He made it clear that nobody should speak to the press in this way without his say-so. He was fixated on maintaining the right kind of image for Elvis in the public eye – and this did not include him getting married and thus making himself unavailable to his countless female fans. Elvis tried to laugh it off but the reality was that he had become a commodity which was under the close supervision and control of the Colonel, as he liked to be referred to, who was bent on exploiting his popularity to the maximum.

Elvis himself let it be known that he was for the challenger, Adlai Stevenson, a Democrat, in the 1956 presidential election. Many artists have assiduously avoided taking sides politically in public, in order not to alienate a large swathe of potential record buyers. It was perhaps surprising that Tom Parker did not veto such candour.

Elvis appeared in his first Hollywood film in 1956. It was a routine western about a soldier, thought to have died in battle, who returns to find his former sweetheart has married one of his brothers – the part played by Elvis. It was originally called *The Reno Brothers*. However, from early on in the proceedings Tom Parker lobbied hard to have this changed to *Love Me Tender*, the title of Elvis' forthcoming single, a proposition that became unstoppable in view of the massive demand for the record. Parker saw the film – for which he acted as a "consultant" – as a stunningly good opportunity to promote some of Elvis' songs and three were featured in the film. It was an early variation of brand placement which produced spectacular commercial results. That said, his performances of the songs were stiff and choreographed with only sanitised little vestiges of the sexy moves and jerks that had helped to make him famous. Elvis was blessed with an excellent memory which was a great asset when he had to learn new songs. When it came to his first film script, he naively memorised all of the parts, not just his own. *Love Me Tender* was the only film in his career for which he did not receive top billing. That said, the advertising posters, which described Elvis as "Mr Rock 'n' Roll in his first motion picture", had larger pictures of Elvis than the top billed stars Richard Egan and Debra Paget.

Elvis was bowled over by the magic of the film studios and soon met an array of famous names. He got to know Natalie Wood amongst others, although it seems she found him to be too unsophisticated for her taste; she visited Elvis in Memphis and stayed briefly at his parents' house where there was a no smoking, no drinking culture.

Yet another major achievement in 1956 was Elvis' first appearance on the *Ed Sullivan Show*. Sullivan had initially said he did not want

Elvis on his show but the level of his popularity soon made him see that this was commercially unwise. Sullivan ended up paying an astronomical $50,000 to have Elvis appear on three shows. It was a good commercial decision – the viewing figures were sensational – a record 54 million for one of the shows. The nation tuned in *en masse*. Tom Parker was very keen for Elvis to get on this kind of programme – he well understood the massive power of television to advertise a product. In 1950, around three million television sets were sold in America. By 1955, that figure had risen to 32 million. TV dinners had to be invented to cater for all the people glued to their sets.

Elvis performed 'Love Me Tender' on the show and made sure that he plugged the film, name-checking 20th Century Fox, and also RCA records. The single was released three weeks later with around a million pre-orders. Ed Sullivan was still acutely conscious of the righteous backlash which had engulfed Elvis in recent months and so it was decreed that there should be no shots of Elvis below the waist although this only happened during his third and final appearance on the show. Afterwards Sullivan declared that Elvis was "a real decent, fine boy" although he also professed incomprehension: "I can't figure this thing out. He just shakes around and everybody yells."

In the course of his high profile television appearances in 1956 Elvis demonstrated that his confidence as a performer, his ability to work an audience and drive women crazy with his sexy moves (despite attempts to clean up his image) had all increased dramatically in a short period of time.

Elvis's sky high public profile meant that he was soon asked to support good causes. One in particular was the March of Dimes, a fund raising initiative created by President Franklin D Roosevelt's administration in 1938 to find a vaccination for polio. Elvis underwent inoculation in front of the cameras. He was helping two good causes – a reduction in the incidence of polio and his own career.

When it became known that Elvis' character in the film *Love Me Tender*, Clint Reno, dies at the end there was outrage amongst his fans. In response it was decided that at the end of the film a ghostly apparition of Elvis would be superimposed over the final scene singing the title song – in this way the fans were left with a living image of their idol. Just before his ghostly presence disappears, Elvis delivers a cheeky little reassuring smile. The film did very well as a result of Elvis' presence but the critics were not kind. They could tell he was there because he was a star who pulled in millions of young fans, not because he was a serious actor.

In order to milk the maximum amount of cash from the film Tom Parker set up a merchandising operation with an experienced operator from California and in no time Elvis belts, scarves, lipstick, charm bracelets, jeans and many other items were flying out the door. The whole thing was soon a multi-million dollar business, light years removed from what Sam Phillips and Bob Neal could have offered.

Despite the undoubted success of Johnny Cash and Carl Perkins in the mid fifties, there was no doubt that by the time the Million Dollar Quartet session took place in December 1956, Elvis was the major star, by a long way.

5.

Johnny Cash

Some of Johnny Cash's ancestors can be traced to an attractive rural area in central Scotland, near a picturesque town called Strathmiglo. Like countless others from all over Europe, some of them sought a better life on the other side of the Atlantic. It was a new land which promised so much, but above all some relief from the grinding poverty which was their daily lot. They did not take much with them but they did take musical instruments and over generations they contributed to the rich variety of rural music which has gradually evolved into modern country and folk music in the broadest sense.

Johnny's father, Ray Cash, was a rural jack of all trades and a hardscrabble farmer; he worked poor quality land which yielded a meagre living. He grew crops for the family table such as beans and okra and also farmed cotton. In addition he travelled around the area taking whatever labouring jobs he could find to bolster the family income.

After his discharge from the army in 1919 he met and married Carrie Rivers and the couple settled initially in Kingsland, Arkansas where they lived in a variety of lowly shotgun shacks – so called because their limited size meant that if a shotgun were fired at them, everybody inside would be hit. Cotton farming was an important element of the family income, but the quality, and hence the prices obtained, fell sharply over the years, partly because the land was overworked and partly as a result of the Great Depression; it went from "fair to middlin'" to "strict low middlin'".

Johnny Cash, initially known as JR, was born on February 26 1932, the third child of a family of seven. In 1935 the family moved to Dyess, a new community created as part of a resettlement scheme by the government of Franklin D Roosevelt. It was one element of a major drive to get people back to productive work after the hard times of the Depression era. Each family which qualified for the scheme – families without sons and black families were not eligible – was given a house with about 20 acres of land, a barn, a cow and a mule. After that they were pretty much on their own. Dyess expanded quickly for a number of years and soon there was a garage, a blacksmith, a beauty salon, a small hospital and a basic cinema. In 1937, Dyess was partly inundated as a result of the Mississippi flooding close to the family home. The vivid terror of the experience stayed with Johnny Cash and was the inspiration for one of his early songs, 'Five Feet High And Rising'. His father kept on measuring the level of the flood and told the family that if the water reached five feet they would have to abandon the house. It did and the family had to be evacuated for a time.

As with so many others who went on to embrace music as a vital part of their lives, Johnny loved the songs he heard in church; they were some of his earliest musical experiences. It was the same with Carl Perkins, growing up across the Mississippi about 20 miles away in Tiptonville, Lake County; there were plenty of churches to choose from – Methodists, Baptists, Pentecostal and many more, all offering their own particular slant on the Christian faith. Although sometimes alarmed by the sheer passion of the sermons with their threats of eternal damnation for those who did not follow God's word, he loved the way that same passion found its way into the songs the congregation sang. The songs were accompanied by various musical instruments including guitar; he quickly developed a love of the sound of the acoustic guitar. These early experiences ingrained in him the beginnings of a lifelong love of music and Christianity.

In the days before television was a fixture in every home, Johnny listened to the radio every chance he got. He loved the various styles of country music he heard coming from the *Grand Ole Opry* on WSM in Nashville. Like other members of the Million Dollar Quartet he loved the music of country oriented artists such as Jimmie Rodgers, Hank Snow, Lulu Belle and Scotty, Red Foley and later, Hank Williams. Songs such as 'Amazing Grace' and 'Will the Circle Be Unbroken' were particular favourites; the latter became a tour de force in his later stage shows in the seventies and eighties. Johnny had an eclectic taste in music and whilst he loved folk and country, he also enjoyed Bing Crosby and the Andrews Sisters. One of his strongest childhood memories was trying to listen to the radio for as long as possible in the evening with his father shouting to him to turn it off.

Johnny was also a great fan of the Carter Family, a folk group which played traditional music and which has had an enormous influence on the development of country music, bluegrass and popular music in general. By the time Johnny was listening to the group on the radio they were regularly joined by children of the original members, including June Carter.

Music provided relief from the everyday drudgery of life. Like Carl Perkins, Johnny spent a lot of time picking cotton with other members of his family in his early years; like Carl also his hands were often red sore by the end of the day. In the days before pesticides the work was made even harder by the need to cut back the fast growing cow-itch vine and fend off swarms of large flies in the warmer months.

At school Johnny was an average student; naturally quick on the uptake, he frustrated his parents and teachers by underachieving – the only subjects which really appealed to him were English and history. He was an avid reader and as he grew older he revealed a penchant, unusual amongst his peers, for heavyweight historical novels by authors such as Sir Walter Scott and James Fenimore Cooper. There were opportunities to sing at school from time to time and Johnny, despite being quite shy, had no hesitation in performing in front of his fellow students and parents. He sang in public at the age of 12 in a local church and around the same age won a talent contest, possibly with a rendition of 'That Lucky Old Sun'.

Although poor, the Cash family always had food on the table and reasonably good quality clothes on their backs. In some ways Johnny's childhood had some of the idyllic qualities associated with country upbringings of the past. After school and when he was not working in the fields, he spent hours messing about in swimming holes, fishing in the river and generally leading a free and easy existence with his friends and siblings, roaming and exploring in the surrounding countryside. Johnny always retained a love of nature and the great outdoors.

Johnny was very close to his older brother Jack although they were very different characters. By the time he was 12 Johnny had already discovered the delights of smoking whereas Jack, then 14, was more interested in losing himself in Bible readings; even by his early teens he reckoned his vocation in life was to become a preacher. They did however share a love of the countryside and happily engaged in outdoor activities together for hours on end. In addition, though they approached religion in very different ways the pair shared a strong religious faith.

It came as a shattering blow when Jack was seriously injured in an accident at a workshop at their school. It seems he had been working unsupervised at a bench with a spinning circular saw and had somehow been violently pulled towards the blade. He suffered serious abdominal injuries. Since he was on his own help did not reach him for some time. By the time it did, it was already too late. Jack was rushed to hospital and operated on. He hung on for some days but his death was inevitable. Interviewed many years later, Johnny said he never really got over Jack's death and that right into late adulthood he regularly dreamt about him. He had been closer to Jack than any of his other siblings and became noticeably quieter, more introverted, in the wake of his loss.

As he moved through his teenage years, music became an increasingly important part of Johnny's life. He sang at school assemblies and at church and he loved to watch his oldest brother Roy's amateur band knocking out some country songs. Johnny's mother noticed from early on that Johnny had an exceptional voice with a distinctively rich, deep and booming timbre; she was struck by the resemblance to her late father's voice. He was sent to a singing teacher for a time but she quickly realised that he had a rare gift which could not and should not be tamed, and she discontinued the lessons.

Johnny was also a good storyteller. He wrote poems and had a remarkable memory for songs that he had only heard once or twice. He particularly liked gospel songs especially those by Jimmie Davis (who later wrote 'You Are My Sunshine') and Sister Rosetta Tharpe. Singing songs was a great morale booster in the cotton fields, especially towards the end of the day and Johnny joined in enthusiastically.

Johnny soon acquired an interest in learning to play a modest guitar his mother had bought him some years previously. Strongly motivated, he spent hours after school trying to work his fingers around the neck of the guitar to hold down the chords – a task he found extremely difficult; indeed throughout his career he never progressed beyond a very basic ability to play rhythm accompaniment – the voice would prove to be his principal instrument.

A high point in Johnny's burgeoning love of music came when the renowned Louvin Brothers played a concert at Dyess High School. These were artists he had only ever heard on the radio, on Smilin' Eddie Hill's *High Noon Roundup* programme. They played a lot of religious music, with simple messages, 'Satan Is Real', 'If We Forget God'. Johnny could barely contain his excitement as the day of the concert approached. As it turned out he got to meet one of his heroes briefly but was virtually tongue tied as a result of the overwhelming excitement he felt in his presence. As he watched the limousine pull away after the show he knew that their kind of life was what he wanted for himself. He knew that working in the cotton fields around Dyess was never going to come anywhere close to satisfying the urgent musical ambitions that swirled around in his head.

In 1950 Johnny graduated from high school. Despite his certainty that he wanted to leave Dyess, he knew he would have better prospects if he stayed long enough to complete his education. At the graduation ceremony Johnny sang 'Drink To Me Only With Thine Eyes', by now reasonably confident in his own ability and quite comfortable performing in front of an audience.

After school he took various low-level jobs none of which he liked; he particularly loathed a spell working on a car assembly line in Pontiac, Michigan (although the experience might have planted the seed for his 1976 hit 'One Piece At A Time'). He was desperate to broaden his horizons; there were few avenues open to a country boy from Dyess but one that was, and which appealed to some young men with gumption, was the armed forces. He applied to join the American Air Force. In doing so he opened up the prospect of a stable job with reasonable pay and conditions and, more importantly, a route out of the dead end world of Dyess.

He was accepted and soon found himself undergoing basic training at Lackland Air Force Base in Texas. Thereafter he was selected for a radio operator's training course at a base near San Antonio. On nights off he sometimes went into the city. One time he went roller skating and met 17-year-old Vivian Liberto – his first words to her were a blurted out apology for knocking into her. Johnny had chased a few girls before but Vivian quickly became far more special than any of the others. Unfortunately soon after their meeting Johnny got word that he was to be posted abroad. He and Vivian spent every available moment together and by the time he headed off to Germany a mere two weeks later, he and Vivian were very much in love – but with no clear idea of when they would see each other again. Johnny was posted to the Second Mobile Radio Squadron which was based in the Bavarian town of Landsberg, about 40 miles west of Munich.

Johnny had entered a new world, far removed from the hardscrabble life of rural Arkansas. He met a lot of people from all over America and beyond, often with very different life experiences from his own. After initially trying to maintain habits such as church-going and reading, he soon discovered the preferable delights of going out and getting drunk with his friends, getting into bar-room fights and chasing women. He also experienced at first hand the tensions between black and white soldiers. The US military had only recently been integrated and – unbelievably to Johnny who felt everybody should be on the same side – the soldiers sometimes ended up fighting each other, on racial lines, when they were out on the town.

He also learned a new skill as a radio operator and found himself dealing with demanding situations involving a high degree of responsibility. He became adept at sending and receiving signals in Morse code and was one of the first to pick up news of the death of

Stalin in 1953. As a highly valued operative he was sometimes chosen for special missions to other locations in different countries.

One of the fringe benefits of his job was that he could pick up the *Grand Ole Opry* on a Saturday night on radio station WSM and listen to the music he loved. However he soon had opportunities to play some music as well. He bought a cheap guitar and before long an informal group – dubbed the Landsberg Barbarians – was formed. They played songs by Jimmie Rodgers, Hank Snow and the Carter Family. Once they could play a few songs reliably together they took their guitars into town and played some sessions in local bars. Johnny also wrote some poems one of which, 'Hey! Porter', about a southern boy returning home, would later become one side of his first Sun single.

As part of his time in Germany, Johnny got to know and like many European destinations which he visited with friends during time off from his duties. It gave him an appreciation of many aspects of European culture; he was bowled over by Oberammergau where he saw the world famous passion play which is performed only once every 10 years.

Johnny was in the Air Force for over three years and during that time he did not return to America once. Despite many positive experiences it did feel like an ordeal at times. As he said later, "I spent 20 years in the Air Force from 1950 to 1954." During this time he exchanged letters regularly, sometimes daily, with Vivian. Over the course of more than three years they exchanged approximately 10,000 pages of love letters many of which formed the basis of a book by Vivian published in 2007, two years after her death.

In the course of their often intense correspondence the love the young couple felt for each other grew and grew. Vivian was the product of a fairly conservative Catholic upbringing which Johnny liked; he praised her wildly in the course of his letters – even comparing her to Mary Magdalene at one point – but also chided her when she told him about parties she had attended. Religious aspects of his own upbringing had given him a set of principles for living life by and he wanted her to stick to them too. He moralised about American soldiers who got German girls pregnant and then failed to take responsibility for their actions That said, he was not above breaching some of his own rules during his visits to local nightspots on days off. As with so many people who grew up in the rural south there was an inescapable conflict between the prospect of religious damnation for wrongdoers and the endless attractions of the pleasures of the flesh.

By the time he returned to America in 1954 Johnny and Vivian's brief romance had developed into a full blown love affair and, after he proposed marriage during a phone call from Landsberg, they were married soon after his return.

Johnny had learned to live independently in Germany. Following his return to America and his marriage to Vivian he knew that he did not want to return to his family in Dyess nor indeed to remain in the Air Force with its restrictive rules and regulations. Music was now his first love and he had worked out that Memphis was where the action was. Accordingly, he and Vivian moved there and rented an apartment with the help of savings he had accumulated during his time in Germany.

The first priority for Johnny was to get employment. He soon got a job working for a man called George Bates who was the boss of the Home Equipment Company which supplied electrical appliances; as it happened he was looking for a door-to-door salesman. To say Johnny was unsuccessful would be an understatement. He found it hard to try to persuade people to buy things which, in many cases, they could not afford. His beat took him into some of the poorer areas of Memphis and he got to know a black musician called Gus Cannon; he sometimes sat on his back porch listening to him knocking out some basic blues songs. He also listened to Dewey

Phillips' *Red Hot And Blue* radio show which featured a lot of the best music around, although not much in the way of mainstream pop. He spent time around Beale Street – he loved the atmosphere in the music joints and heard Mississippi Delta blues, jazz and country. It was an education in the joys of the best of black music which in whites-only Dyess had not been available to him. For many years his favourite album was *Blues In The Mississippi Night*, a compilation put together by folklorist Alan Lomax.

He experienced the frustration of knowing that he wanted to get into music, whilst at the same time trying to deal with reality of the need to make money – particularly since Vivian was now expecting their first baby. Johnny knew he would not last long as a salesman. He got himself onto a course at the Keegan School of Broadcasting with a view to getting work as some kind of broadcaster – for which his distinctive voice was an obvious advantage. However he gave this up after several months and continued to work for the Home Equipment Company where George Bates proved to be an indulgent boss, even lending him money from time to time.

A key development in Johnny's musical career occurred when his oldest brother, Roy, himself an amateur musician who also lived in Memphis, introduced him to Luther Perkins (no relation to Carl) and Marshall Grant. Roy was the service manager at a garage where Luther (a specialist in installing car radios) and Marshall were mechanics. They played guitar as a hobby with several other friends; like Johnny they were not musically trained. Apart from an interest in music all three came from backgrounds where religion had played a large part in their lives. They quickly became firm friends and met regularly to play music.

Johnny could see that if they were going to progress they would have to change the format of three rhythm guitars supporting his vocals. Marshall borrowed a double bass and taught himself the basics by attaching pieces of sticky tape to the neck of the bass to identify the notes. Luther bought an amplifier and Johnny immediately felt the infectious appeal of the simple rhythms Luther instinctively picked out, mainly in his comfort zone of the top three strings.

Soon, there were opportunities to perform in front of audiences – at a church service or a fund-raising event at a local restaurant; they were just happy to have the chance to hone their performing skills. George Bates was supportive and sponsored a radio appearance for the trio – he reasoned that if Johnny wasn't able to generate much income through direct sales, he could perhaps achieve more with his plugs for the company between songs.

For performances in churches Johnny featured one of his early compositions, 'Belshazzar', which, with its heavy moral religious tone, was light years away from the kind of superficial popular music many people of his age were listening to.

Like most other people in and around Memphis, Johnny became aware of the stir being kicked up by the Elvis Presley phenomenon. He saw him live a couple of times and spoke to him afterwards once. He felt there was a kind of raw purity in the music Elvis played – stripped down, no frills, just two guitars and a bass and a sensational singer with charisma. He later referred to this as "seminal Elvis". There were obvious similarities with his own trio and Johnny, struck by the electrical effect Elvis had on audiences, particularly young people, felt sure that he was on the right track. One difference was that whereas Elvis' band were all committed to music as a career and a lifestyle, Luther and Marshall had good jobs in the real world and were married with children. At this stage, music was still just a hobby for them.

Johnny was under pressure. He was increasingly drawn to a life in music but he needed to support himself and his wife. He hated his job but felt he could not give it up. Vivian, who had no particular interest in music, much less in the struggling lifestyle that was so often associated with aspiring musicians, saw considerable appeal in returning to San Antonio to be nearer her family. This was particularly understandable since their first baby was imminent. However Johnny was nothing if not determined and, like Carl Perkins, he reckoned that if he was going to make it in the music business he needed the help of someone who knew their way around. Like Carl Perkins, he thought of Sam Phillips and the recently created Sun record label.

He soon found out that Sam Phillips was a busy man. He eventually made contact by phone, saying he would like to record some songs and that he was particularly interested in gospel music. Sam told him bluntly it had insufficient commercial appeal. Johnny visited Union Avenue several times in an attempt to persuade Sam to give him a try out but he was never there. Eventually he decided that he would wait outside the studio until Sam arrived and force him to listen. This tactic worked. Sam could tell right away that Johnny was not ordinary. He listened to him singing some hits by Hank Snow, Jimmie Rodgers and the Carter Family, but the song that appealed to him most was 'Hey! Porter', the poem that Johnny had written in Landsberg, and which he had now set to music with a compulsive railroad rhythm. Sam asked him to return with his backing group so that he could consider the potential of the group as a whole. It has also been suggested that it was Sam Phillips who advised the change of name from "John", as he was most commonly known at this time, to "Johnny" in order to appeal more to a younger audience.

When Sam listened to the group he was quickly persuaded that 'Hey! Porter' was strong enough to be released as a single – much to Johnny's incredulous delight. He told Johnny that he would have to come up with another song, preferably a "weeper", for the B-side, and he quickly wrote 'Cry! Cry! Cry!' Nerves and inexperience meant that they had to do a great many takes to get it right – Luther in particular continually messed up his leads – but eventually Sam was satisfied and the single was released in June 1955, a month after Johnny and Vivian's first (of four) daughters, Rosanne, was born.

The new group had to decide on a name. Initially there was talk of the Tennessee Three but right from the start there was a feeling that Johnny's prominence in the group should be reflected in the name; hence Johnny Cash and the Tennessee Two. The initial agreement was that any income would be split 40:30:30.

Like much of Sun's output the recorded songs were unrefined, rough around the edges. However the sound was new and original – though as Marshall Grant was keen to point out, this was not by design; it was simply the best they could do with their basic instruments and limited technical ability. Apart from the hard to ignore gravitas of Johnny's rich voice, Luther Perkins had chanced upon a style of guitar playing which added an irresistibly catchy sound – part percussive rhythm, part lead – which would come to be an important element of the Johnny Cash sound. Sam understood that regardless of its lack of conventional slickness, the music had a feel which was special and which he believed the public would go for.

Johnny now threw himself into promoting the new group. He personally drove to countless bars and small venues where live music was played, and hustled for gigs. Initially they sometimes found themselves playing fairly rough dives where audiences were either apathetic or hostile; it was a steep learning curve which helped Johnny, Luther and Marshall develop their musical tightness as a group. Later he also visited radio stations to do interviews and encourage them to play his songs. One such visit gave an interesting insight into his character. He accepted the offer of a cup of coffee. The DJ said he would get him a fresh cup to drink out of since the one that was available had already been drunk out of. Johnny said he wasn't bothered because he presumed that "whoever drank out of it was human". The DJ felt this indicated strongly that Johnny did not see himself as being above anyone else.

Johnny's debut single turned out to be an impressive local hit, and made the top 20 in the national country chart. It eventually shifted around 100,000 units and after a while the group was able to charge higher fees and play in more salubrious venues. Johnny was keen to capitalise on the group's initial success with a follow-up single. This was not straightforward since so much depended on Sam, much of whose time was then taken up negotiating the sale of Elvis' contract to RCA. Once time was found for the next single, released in December 1955, the songs chosen were 'So Doggone Lonesome'/'Folsom Prison Blues'. The latter was partly inspired by the film *Inside The Walls Of Folsom Prison* which Johnny saw in Landsberg. With its stripped down sound and compulsive chugging rhythm, 'Folsom Prison Blues' became a fixture in Johnny's live performances for years and has been covered by numerous other artists ever since. Luther came up with a catchy lead guitar break of great simplicity which showed that despite his basic ability, he had an excellent ear for what worked. Unfortunately Johnny had lifted much of the song from an earlier one by Gordon Jenkins called 'Crescent City Blues'. Years later, after the song became a major hit on the back of the *Live At Folsom Prison* album in 1968, Johnny reached a financial settlement with Jenkins said to be in the region of $75,000. Subsequent releases showed Jenkins as the co-writer of the song.

Although Sam had laid down the law on the subject of religious songs, he was in every other respect a very liberal producer. He was a believer in the notion that music should be "universal" rather than strictly packaged in one category or another. Johnny spent a lot of time in the studio and had a go at songs of widely varying styles. This meant that he did record some material that was wholly unsuitable for him such as lightweight rockabilly numbers aimed at the teenage market. However the experience he gained stood him in good stead for later years. Although generally thought of as a country singer throughout his career, in reality Johnny was never an artist who could be so easily categorised. Right from the start what he played was what he liked to call "Johnny Cash music".

The group's second single proved to be a greater commercial success than the first and things started taking off for them. Promoter Bob Neal did his best to get as much exposure as possible for Johnny Cash and the Tennessee Two. The trio found themselves on bills with many of the top artists of the day – Elvis Presley, George Jones, Porter Wagoner and Wanda Jackson. Apart from honing the group's musical skills Johnny, as the frontman, had to overcome his natural shyness, learn to read audiences and how to develop a rapport with them. In the early days this involved some comedy routines including Elvis imitations. The group was also asked to appear on the popular and prestigious radio show *The Louisiana Hayride*. It did not pay well and appearances there involved a great deal of driving (the show was based in Shreveport, about 350 miles from Memphis) but it was an excellent means of reaching a large, knowledgeable audience.

By the middle of 1956 Johnny received a royalty cheque for around $5,000. He was able to give up the day job for good, though before he did he made a point of repaying all of the money which George Bates had lent to him.

However Johnny's rapid success in music led to problems at home. Vivian had a young baby and another one on the way. She welcomed her husband's meteoric rise in some ways and wanted to be supportive and encouraging, but the music scene which meant so much to Johnny did nothing for her. If she did accompany him to shows or rehearsals there was always the question of who would look after Rosanne, and when would they get back home to let the babysitter away. She was becoming increasingly concerned that the marriage which had seemed so blessed at the outset was not following a path that she felt comfortable with. However there was never any question of Johnny altering course. Indeed as his musical career went from strength to strength the reality was that he was away from home more and more.

Johnny's third Sun single proved to be the breakthrough that moved him up to a much higher level of popularity. 'I Walk The Line' was an immediate hit and ended up remaining in the country charts for 10 months and earning a gold disc, although it just missed out on the number one spot. Johnny was one of the top-selling country artists of 1956 alongside big names like Marty Robbins and Ray Price. The song also crossed over into the pop charts for a time, demonstrating that Johnny's appeal was broad based and that his music crossed boundaries – as it always would. Having only left the Air Force in the middle of 1954 it really was a meteoric rise.

'I Walk the Line' might have had its origins in Johnny's response one night to a friend who advocated the wicked pleasures available to musicians on tour. Musically it was very original, lacking a conventional chorus and making use of regular key changes which showed off the impressive range of Johnny's voice, particularly in the lower registers. It also featured an unsophisticated but effective way of enhancing the rhythmic quality of the song. Johnny threaded a folded up piece of paper through the strings of his guitar which added a percussive quality to his rhythm playing. Sam utilised a favoured enhancement to the sound, a simple but effective tape delay to create an echo which added a rich timbre to Johnny's attention-grabbing baritone.

Sam gave Johnny a fairly free rein in the studio but there were times when he was sure he knew best how to do a song. 'I Walk The Line' was a good example. Two versions were recorded, slow and uptempo. Johnny preferred the former and was upset when he heard the final version on the radio and realised Sam had chosen the latter – against his wishes as he saw it. Despite the fact that the song was such a big hit Johnny said years later that he still would have been happier if the slower version had been released.

The success of 'I Walk The Line' meant that Bob Neal was able to book Johnny on tours much further afield than the Memphis area with major stars such as Webb Pierce. For Johnny, whose memories of trying to sell vacuum cleaners in Memphis were still very close, to be rubbing shoulders with such artists backstage was something akin to a surreal dream. In August 1956 the group went on a tour of Canada where 'I Walk The Line' had been a hit. Johnny was also invited to tread the hallowed boards of the Ryman auditorium in Nashville where the weekly *Grand Ole Opry* concerts took place. There was irony in the fact that for his debut, Johnny was introduced by singer Carl Smith, then married to June Carter, who would become Johnny's second wife in 1968. Smith said of Johnny that he was "the brightest rising star in the country music of America".

At this time Johnny was perceived by the press to be a rival for Elvis Presley, whose initial rise to fame had taken place the year before. *The Nashville Banner* said that Johnny had won the hearts of the audience at the Grand Ole Opry and that he was "probably better than Elvis Presley". *The Tennessean* opined that Johnny "has sincerity, he has bombast, he has tone that carries to the rafters... He's a true country singer and Presley isn't and never has been". That said, as with other members of the Million Dollar Quartet, Johnny's reception at the highly conservative *Grand Ole Opry* was not universally positive. Some felt that his music was too far from real country music to be acceptable. This was ironic since Johnny Cash was and would always be an artist with the greatest respect for the traditions of country music.

By the time he received a call from Sam Phillips asking him to head over to the studio early in December 1956 Johnny was a rising star, though his position in the music firmament was well below that of Elvis.

6.

December 4, 1956

What is clear above all else is that nobody will ever be able to state definitively how events unfolded that day in Memphis.

A bunch of musicians got together by chance, chatted and played some songs together for a few hours. Even allowing for the fact that one member of the group was already a star, a national sensation no less, such impromptu sessions were not particularly uncommon. It would never have occurred to anybody to make detailed notes of all that happened. If Sam Phillips had not thought to set the tapes rolling at some point and call in a reporter, the chances are that the event would now be lost in the mists of time. It is fortunate for the history of popular music that this did not happen.

The recordings which have emerged, along with a lot of jumbled memories, provide a piece of music archaeology, a fascinating snapshot of a crucial moment in the development of the diverse range of popular music styles which have moved countless people all over the world ever since.

It might be argued that tapes, like pictures, don't lie. However, whilst they undoubtedly provide a lot of hard evidence of what took place, there are still questions. When were they switched on? How many people were actually participating when the tapes were rolling? Did the participants know they were being recorded? Answers to many of these questions, often contradictory, come from the notoriously unreliable medium of human memory.

The wider significance of the day only started to come to light years later, particularly after the death of Elvis Presley in 1977, and so people interviewed on the subject were trying to remember events from one afternoon many years in the past. No doubt they were influenced by things other people had said or written. WS 'Fluke' Holland, the drummer on the day, and one of the very few people still alive who was actually there, states quite honestly that his recollections of the day are "hazy" at best and that he simply cannot recall most of the specifics. However, with the aid of experts who have restored the tapes and teased out some of their long held secrets, and many participants and others who have spoken about, analysed and researched the session, it is possible to construct a fairly detailed picture of the afternoon of December 4, 1956, when the world's first rock 'n' roll supergroup, a fifties Fab Four, jammed together for a time.

Sam Phillips was keen to conjure up another hit for Carl Perkins to match the phenomenal popularity achieved by 'Blue Suede Shoes' earlier in 1956. Carl's subsequent releases that year ('Boppin' The Blues'/'All Mama's Children' and 'I'm Sorry, I'm Not Sorry'/'Dixie Fried') had not fared particularly well. Carl had also been involved in a serious car crash and from a career point of view there had been a very significant loss of momentum.

Sam was also aware that Carl, now fully recovered from his injuries, had heavy touring commitments early in the following year which meant there would be few opportunities to spend time in the studio. Like most people in America he had observed the incredibly rapid rise of his former protégé Elvis Presley, who had recorded his own version of 'Blue Suede Shoes' for RCA earlier in the year. Carl was briefly seen as a rival to Elvis; nobody seriously thought this any more but Sam was nonetheless keen to exploit his commercial potential to the full without delay. He wanted to get some new hit songs in the can with a view to keeping Carl's profile as high as possible.

Sam booked Carl and his band – brothers Clayton and Jay on bass and rhythm guitar respectively, and Fluke on drums – for some sessions. For the one on December 4, 1956 he decided that Jerry Lee Lewis should play piano and told recently hired engineer Jack Clement to give him a call. In some ways this was a surprising choice. Sam believed Jerry Lee was a star in the making and so he was perhaps not an obvious candidate for a session which would earn him a mere $15. Sam was also well aware that Jerry Lee was self-confident to the point of arrogance and might annoy Carl; put bluntly, his personality might interfere with the success of the session. That said, although Jerry Lee's first Sun single, 'Crazy Arms', had been released on December 1, he was as yet unproven – and like the great majority of artists that made records for Sun, had not yet achieved any significant success. Sam knew that Jerry Lee was an outstanding piano player and perhaps he suspected that he might just help to bring something extra out of Carl's performances; perhaps he could sweeten his hard–edged sound, making it more attractive commercially. For his part, Jerry Lee was quite happy to earn some money for the fast approaching festive season. His cousin JW Brown and his family, with whom he was lodging, had been trying to get him some regular work – without any success.

December 4 was a Tuesday, a pleasant early winter's day with no rain and little wind. By the afternoon the temperature had got up to about 18 degrees centigrade. Carl's session would probably have started in the early afternoon. Also present in the studio were Sam, Jack Clement and Marion Keisker. Various others were already there too and some came and went in the course of the afternoon. Precise details of exactly who was there and when have been lost in the sands of time.

Sam had told Carl by phone that he had found a great new piano player who would be there on December 4, and the session marked the first meeting of Carl and Jerry Lee. Carl was undoubtedly impressed by Jerry Lee's piano pyrotechnics but he was irritated by his manner. As ever, Jerry Lee was full of beans and full of himself. He did not even take compliments well. If told that his piano playing had been really good on a particular song his likely response would be along the lines of, "You ain't seen nothin' yet", delivered with a smiling sneer.

As Carl listened to his boasts he thought to himself that as the guy who gave the world 'Blue Suede Shoes', he perhaps had more reason than Jerry Lee to blow his trumpet. He also felt pangs of irritation at Sam's unbounded enthusiasm for Jerry Lee's abilities, although he had to admit that what he was able to coax out of the upright spinet in the studio was truly remarkable. In order to give the instrument a fuller, livelier sound Jack Clement inserted thumbtacks into the string hammers and then put the microphone under the piano.

There are varying accounts of just how many songs Carl and his band laid down. No doubt plenty of ideas were thrown around and various songs tried out. According to some reports Carl's father, Buck, was present for at least some of the time. This would have been a rare occurrence; according to some reports he had apparently been embarrassed when a reporter asked him questions about his son's career which he could not answer. He felt he should get to know what Carl got up to in the studio.

According to one report it was Buck who reminded Carl of an old twenties Blind Lemon Jefferson song called 'Match Box Blues'. Carl vaguely remembered a few of the key lyrics and in no time had come up with his own version which he simply called

'Matchbox'. As soon as they worked it up they knew it was a winner. Several years later no less a band than the Beatles covered it, probably because both George Harrison and Ringo Starr were Perkins fans. Another song laid down that day was a Carl original, 'Your True Love', which, along with 'Matchbox', was released as his single in January 1957. It is possible that Carl also recorded, or at least tried out, versions of Jimmie Davis' 'Sweethearts Or Strangers' and the Fred Rose song 'Be Honest With Me' as well as one of his own songs, 'Put Your Cat Clothes On'.

At some point in the afternoon Elvis, back home in Memphis for the festive season, was cruising around town in one of his Cadillacs, perhaps the one he had customised in one of his favoured colour combinations for clothes: black and pink. He might well have been doing some Christmas shopping. He was probably wearing a flashy diamond ring. He was with a girlfriend, Marilyn Evans. Elvis had met her at the New Frontier Hotel in Las Vegas where he had played a series of concerts earlier in the year. The shows had been poorly received initially although by the end Elvis had won round the bemused audiences – at least to some extent.

Marilyn Evans, a pretty brunette with dark eyes from Fresno, California, was a 19-year-old dancer who had appeared in floor shows at the New Frontier hotel as a chorus girl. He had been dating her for a short while, almost certainly not on an exclusive basis. At the time of the session she was staying with Elvis at the family home. They spent their days riding motorcycles, watching movies and eating out; speaking years later she said the day at Sun had been "great; he was young, I was young. I loved it, it was terrifically exciting and wonderful". She had been swept off her feet by the glamorous side of his star status lifestyle and was flattered when he sent her a note suggesting a date. Ironically she had no particular interest in popular music – classical was more to her taste. It is probable that with Elvis and Marilyn in the car that day was a DJ from Jackson,

Cliff Gleaves, whom Elvis had met and got to know earlier in the year when promoting his records.

Elvis drove past 706 Union Avenue and decided to stop and check out what was happening. This might have been purely on a whim in which case it would not have been unusual. Since parting company with Sam at the end of 1955, Elvis had remained on good terms with him and had stopped in at the studio on a number of occasions when he was back in Memphis. Sometimes he came by on his motorbike wearing black leathers. Jack Clement later told an interviewer that one time they thought he was a cop and that they were going to be busted. On this particular December day there were some flashy cars parked outside and this might well have sparked his curiosity.

Elvis was now a major star so his arrival undoubtedly caused a stir. That said, it was not unusual for well known musicians to drop in on sessions and listen to each other's work; in many ways his arrival was a fairly normal part of the life of a studio. Once Elvis and his small entourage had entered the building, Carl's session came to a premature end. It was not long after they had nailed 'Matchbox'. Carl later said that in some ways it was a pity; he felt that he and the band were hitting their stride and laying down tracks of real quality. If they had been able to keep going – and of course at Sun there were no time limits – perhaps they would even have come up with another piece of musical magic to rival 'Blue Suede Shoes'.

Carl had encountered Elvis at some of the rough honky-tonks they both played for a time. He had also appeared on the same bill as him on several occasions when they were on the way up and they had got to know each other reasonably well. Like everyone else, Carl had been knocked out by what Elvis did on stage. However, he had not seen him since he had hit the big time and was immediately struck by the radical change in his appearance. Gone was the acne that had caused him to wear his collar high. Now his skin was smooth like china. Before, his hair had been a nondescript sandy colour; now it was a gleaming mass of brilliantine black. As Carl wrote later, "Everything was right... he looked sharp and great". It seems the hillbilly cat was already well on the way to rock 'n' roll royalty. This was despite the fact that he, like the others on this particular day, was not dressed to impress – all were kitted out in fifties smart casual.

There are moments during the recordings when Elvis betrays a level of excitable enthusiasm, verging on anxiety, to the extent that he sometimes stammers at the start of sentences. However he had grown in confidence since the early days when Sam had described him as "probably the most introverted person that ever came into Sun Studio". In similar vein, several others commented on his former habit of nervously biting his fingernails.

Initially there was a lot of chat, back slapping, congratulations and general bonhomie. It all had the feeling of some kind of reunion and indeed for Elvis, Carl and Johnny it was – they had toured together on a number of occasions in 1955; and of course it was a reunion of sorts for Elvis and Sam, though not the first. Elvis introduced Marilyn as his "house guest". Inevitably he was the centre of attention and from the moment he arrived, events revolved around him. It was all a bit like a former pupil who has done well and who was now returning to his place of learning to take some plaudits for his success, but also to catch up on what had been happening since his departure.

There was recognition that he was extra special but they were all fellow professionals trying to make a living, keen to avoid the dead end existences of their parents, and in that sense equals; not only that but they all knew where they had come from – scratching a living from menial work was a great leveller. Elvis talked about his stint at Las Vegas, his national television appearances and perhaps also the prospect of going into the army. At the time Elvis arrived, everybody had been listening to playbacks of the songs that had just been recorded. Elvis listened too and said he was impressed by what he heard, particularly 'Matchbox'.

Before long an informal jam session started up. As with all other events of the day nobody will ever know the exact sequence of events. Some reports indicate that Jerry Lee Lewis arrived after Elvis but this cannot be right since he was playing on Carl's session earlier in the day and no-one has ever suggested that Elvis was present for that.

It seems most likely that Elvis was the initiator of the legendary jam session that followed – although any group of musicians within arm's length of instruments will soon start making music; it is often difficult to say who fired the first shot. Carl Perkins expressed his recollection of the start of the session in down to earth language. He recalled Elvis singing 'Blueberry Hill' and then "all of us scooting around the piano" with his band "kinda knocking along".

Elvis launched into several songs, with the others quickly arranging themselves near the piano. An acoustic guitar was produced and it seems it was played by, amongst others, Charles Underwood, a writer for Sam's publishing company, who probably played rhythm on some of the early songs of the session and also Smokey Joe Baugh, a Sun artist who achieved minor success; they might well also have added a few spontaneous backing vocals. It has been suggested that Cliff Gleaves and Marilyn Evans might have contributed some backing vocals but this appears to be in the realm of speculation; and unlikely in the case of Evans in view of her conservative musical tastes.

At this stage, by all accounts, the tapes were not rolling. Elvis sang several songs including 'Will The Circle Be Unbroken', 'You Belong To My Heart' (a 1945 hit for Bing Crosby) and 'My Isle Of Golden Dreams'. According to several reports, Johnny Cash sang on the last two. Carl Perkins recalls 'That Old Time Religion' being sung and it appears likely there were at least some others.

Jerry Lee Lewis, who had never met Elvis, was keen to make his acquaintance and get close to an artist who had already achieved the kind of success he believed was sure to come his way soon. Unlike Carl, who appeared to hold back a little, he was not at all overawed. He was certainly not impressed with Elvis' piano playing which, compared to his own, was fairly basic. He saw Elvis' surprise arrival as an opportunity to show off his skills. If he could impress a major star perhaps it would help his career prospects. Some reports said he had been so anxious to impress Elvis that at some point during the day he asked Sam to play an acetate of his new song 'Crazy Arms' for him. It all smacked of the kind of arrogant self-confidence that was to create so many problems in his personal and professional lives later on. It has been suggested that Jerry Lee played some songs, including 'There Are Strange Things Happening Every Day', before anything was recorded. This would certainly have been a fitting song for Jerry Lee – a rollicking piece of gospel music that is sometimes claimed as one of the first ever rock 'n' roll songs. The spontaneous pleasure he clearly takes in making music with the others captures brilliantly the essential mood of the afternoon.

It is hard to believe that the far more reserved Elvis Presley was much taken with Jerry Lee on a personal level. Carl Perkins later said that for his own part he did not appreciate Jerry Lee's "cocky brashness". Elvis invariably kept such conduct for his stage show. He was however impressed by his piano playing; he is reported to have said to reporter Robert Johnson, "That boy can go. He has a different style, and the way he plays piano just gets inside of me."

In his 1997 autobiography Johnny Cash said that he was already in the studio when Elvis arrived mid afternoon. He said he was there because Carl had invited him to sit in on his session – and Sam Phillips also recalled Johnny listening to at least some of Carl's session. He and Carl were already good friends at this stage, "friends for life" as Johnny put it, and so there would be some logic to this, but most accounts assert that Johnny arrived after Elvis, indeed that it was the presence of Elvis which inspired Sam to call Johnny and bring the four of them together. Johnny also stated that he recalled singing on 'Blue Moon Of Kentucky', 'The Old Rugged Cross' and 'Will The Circle Be Unbroken', none of which were on any of the recordings which have been released. He also said that Elvis asked him to sing some Bill Monroe songs which Johnny said he did – because he knew "the whole repertoire". However these songs might well have been performed prior to the rolling of the tapes – or indeed, perhaps there is yet another tape Holy Grail, waiting to be discovered somewhere, though this appears to be highly unlikely.

When exactly the recording started will never be known. It seems that Sam realised something special, of historical importance even, was unfolding; famous musicians did get together from time to time but this particular cohort, featuring as it did one of the biggest new stars in America, was out of the ordinary. Perhaps he sensed that they might never get the chance to play together again; if so, he was right. For Sam it was personal and emotional. As he said later, "It was like everything I had worked to achieve was there in that one little room."

As a consequence, according to many reports, he did three things – though the precise order is unclear. He called the leading Sun artist of the time, Johnny Cash, and asked him to come over to the studio to add his weight to the proceedings. He also called local reporter Robert Johnson, the entertainment editor of the *Memphis Press-Scimitar*, a good friend, and suggested that if he could get over to the studio quickly with a photographer there would be a story for him. In addition, at some point he told engineer Jack Clement to start the tapes rolling.

The microphones were positioned as they had been set up for the Carl Perkins session. Jack Clement said that in preparation for making a recording of the session he "moved the microphones around a bit" but it is very unlikely that the artists were properly mic'd up as they would be for a normal studio session. Informality was the order of the day. It appears likely that by the time the tape machine was turned on the session had been going for a while, perhaps an hour, with a number of songs, or more likely parts of songs, having been sung.

Robert Johnson arrived soon after the call from Sam; with him were photographer George Pierce and UPI stringer Leo Soroka. It seems likely that when they got to the studio the session was already underway – although it is not clear if the tapes were rolling at this point. When he wrote his regular column *TV News And Views* the next day in the *Memphis Press-Scimitar* Johnson described the afternoon as "bedlam" and referred to the music as an "old-fashioned barrel-house session with barber shop harmonies". He made specific reference to the four principals. "Carl Perkins was in a recording session... Johnny Cash dropped in. Jerry Lee Lewis was there too; and then Elvis stopped by." He went on to say, "That quartet could sell a million." The photograph of the four singers taken at the piano which accompanied the article carried the title "million dollar quartet". Robert Johnson thus came up with the name for the world's first ever rock 'n' roll supergroup. The classic photograph of the quartet also featured Marilyn Evans sitting atop the piano, but that part of the image was cropped for the newspaper article and has been omitted from most subsequent representations of the picture.

Clearly Johnny Cash was present for at least part of the time Robert Johnson was there. It might be that the pair of them left around the same time, once the photographs had been taken. Johnson certainly never made any reference to any grouping other than a quartet. In his article the next day he said that if Sam had been smart he would have recorded the session. Perhaps he arrived when Johnny was one of the contributing singers but before the tapes were switched on. If they left at about the same time then this would all fit with the version of events that holds that Johnny did sing but was not recorded; and it would also fit with his comments about the session not being recorded – he would have been unaware that Jack started rolling the tapes after he left.

Johnson's use of the phrase "million dollar quartet" was not original journalese. The term had been used to describe quartets of talented artists by the press, certainly in America, since the twenties. A recent example, in July 1956, was a photograph of film stars Betty Grable, Jane Russell, Dorothy Lamour and Marilyn Maxwell which appeared in the *Syracuse Herald American*. The term had also been used in a fiscal sense, to describe a group of tax measures aimed at raising significant amounts of money.

The photographs confirm that Johnny Cash was there and Johnson's comments raise a strong presumption that he sang. However, despite extensive expert analysis, no trace of Johnny Cash's voice has ever been found on the tapes of the session which were subsequently released on various bootlegs and official LPs and CDs. Johnny Cash claimed in his 1997 autobiography that he was "the first to arrive and the last to leave" but there is virtually no support for this view elsewhere. Carl Perkins, interviewed in 1981, said the group should have been called the "Million Dollar Trio" because Johnny just came in for the photographs and possibly to collect some money, and then left to go shopping with his wife, Vivian. One report claimed that he left because he had to go and collect Vivian from work but this is unlikely since she had two very young children and would almost certainly not have gone out to work at that time. Yet another report claimed that Vivian had accompanied Johnny to the studio with Rosanne, the first of their four daughters. Whatever the truth, none of this precludes the possibility, indeed the likelihood, that Johnny did sing for a while before the photographs were taken and the tapes switched on. Yet it is strange that Carl, who said he recalled the day "vividly", should be so certain that Johnny did not sing at all.

In his 1997 autobiography Johnny claims to remember the point at which Jerry Lee took over on the piano. He was bowled over by his playing which he had not heard before. Johnny went on to say that Jerry Lee launched into 'Vacation In Heaven' but this song does not appear on the recordings – so if it happened this must have been before the tapes were switched on. Johnny also said that nobody ever wants to follow Jerry Lee Lewis and that Elvis headed off when he started playing and that at this point he (Johnny) went next door to Miss Taylor's restaurant for coffee. However, after Jerry Lee finished playing several songs, at the end of the recordings, he and Elvis can clearly be heard saying goodbye to each other when Elvis does finally leave. Anyway at this stage of things it is hard to believe that a success story like Elvis Presley would have been in the slightest bothered by following an unknown like Jerry Lee in this kind of casual get-together. Apart from the difference in their commercial profiles it simply was not that kind of session.

In the sleeve notes to the 1981 album *The Survivors. Live*, Johnny paints a rather flowery picture of the session which does not appear to bear much resemblance to reality. "New on the scene, Jerry Lee waited politely until the singing came to a casual halt. When Elvis stood up, Jerry Lee said 'Let me at that piano'... when Jerry Lee began, he led, and Carl, Elvis and I joined in whenever the key was right". In reality Jerry Lee can be heard to make robust contributions to most of the recorded material. In addition, the stage of the proceedings that Johnny appears to be referring to – when Jerry Lee takes over on the piano – is part of the available recordings and there is no trace of Johnny's voice. This tends to refute his assertion that everybody, including him, sang along with Jerry Lee. In fact once Jerry Lee took over it was to all intents and purposes a solo performance – again the available evidence runs counter to Johnny's version of a key aspect of events.

Aware of numerous assertions that he was not at the session at all, or at least had not been present when the session was being recorded, Johnny remained adamant that he had indeed been a key participant. Having claimed that he had been there throughout, he went on to offer an explanation as to why his voice could not be heard on the recordings. Elvis was of course the undisputed star of the proceedings and so events revolved around him. Some referred to him as the ring leader. It followed therefore, Johnny explained, that songs were played in a key to suit him. This meant that Johnny found himself singing an unaccustomed high tenor, "Bill Monroe's part" as he described it, which made him less audible. He also said that he was furthest away from the microphone, a point which it would be impossible to provide evidence on now. However Jack Clement recently indicated that there were several microphones which would make it very difficult to explain how no trace of Johnny's voice has ever been identified if he had been present throughout.

Johnny's explanation really does not stand up to much scrutiny. Whichever way he sang, Johnny had a powerful voice. Leading experts have not been able to detect even one minute trace of it despite years of work. However, the microphone was able to pick up innumerable snatches of conversation going on in the studio which presumably took place further from Johnny's position which would, it is surely safe to assume, have been close to the other artists, who were picked up loud and clear. Also, Johnny had already built up a large repertoire of his own songs – surely he would have performed at least one or two of them? There are none of his songs on the recordings that have surfaced and no reference to any of his songs having been performed at all.

Johnny Cash spent much of the sixties in a drug induced haze; he almost succeeded in joining the small club of great artists who did not live past their twenties. Interest in the tapes only took off in the seventies, especially in the wake of Elvis Presley's death. Johnny's autobiography was written in the mid nineties, around 40 years after the events in Memphis, and so it appears that his robust assertions are a case of false memory syndrome – unless of course there is another tape which says otherwise lurking in a vault somewhere. However in the unlikely event that this was true, it could not support Johnny's claim that he was present and singing throughout the whole session. One of the world's leading experts on Elvis Presley, Ernst Jorgensen, who played a major role in bringing the recordings to public attention, does not think this is at all probable. He is on record as saying that in his opinion all the tapes of the session have been recovered. Referring to the 2006 CD of the session he said, "Everything that was recorded that day is on the *Complete Million Dollar Quartet* CD... when you play the three tapes [sequentially], everything fits together perfectly. You can hear Elvis come in on tape one and leave at the end of tape three. It's a myth that there is anything else out there [from those sessions]. Cash must have remembered incorrectly." It might well be that Cash sang on some songs before the tapes started rolling but it really does seem to be clearly established that he did not contribute to what took place after the tapes started rolling.

Some further evidence on the subject comes from comments by some of the people present which were recorded. At one point a female voice with a southern drawl (quite possibly that of Marion Keisker) can clearly be heard to ask if this "Rover Boys Trio" can sing 'Farther Along'. This leads to a strong presumption that a third of the way into the recording, only three artists were present. A little earlier in the tape a gravelly voice, possibly that of Smokey Joe Baugh, is heard to say "You oughta get up a quartet." This could be taken to mean that there are four people performing who are so good that they should take their quartet on the road or turn professional. On the other hand, and on balance this appears more likely, it could also be read as meaning that there were three people singing who would sound better with a fourth member. During one song, 'On The Jericho Road', Elvis, faced with the need for some low notes, says "Take young Johnny Cash to do this one." Just to muddy the waters, in the course of the final track, 'Elvis Says Goodbye', a voice can be heard saying "Johnny, I'll see you later." Does this indicate that in fact Johnny was there right up until the end of the session? Was there somebody else called Johnny present at the studio that day?

In a later interview engineer Jack Clement gave his own version of events which throws some further light on events without necessarily clarifying them. "Sam had been running the board for the Carl Perkins session, but he left after the photos were taken, went to Mrs Taylor's restaurant next door, so I sat at the board in the control room and turned up a couple of knobs, and I could hear them all gossiping and jamming in there. I remember standing up and saying, 'I'd be remiss if I didn't record this', so I stuck a tape on, moved a few mics around that were already on stands in the studio, put them in front of people, and captured everything for the next hour-and-a-half to two hours. We had 30-minute tapes, and every time I'd get close to the end I would put another one on and just let it roll." This account varies from Sam's. He said that he gave the order to Jack to roll the tapes even though nobody was properly mic'd up. Jack's account seems to imply that he arranged the microphones quite near to the various singers – which in turn contradicts Johnny's assertion that he was quite far from a microphone.

Sam Phillips, so used to exhorting his artists to give of their best during lengthy spells in the studio, adopted a different role altogether for the Million Dollar Quartet session. He was the facilitator and host of an impromptu party whose guest of honour was a rising star like no other. Far from directing the music he said later that everything was "extemporaneous". There was no set list, no pre-planning, no attempt to tease out a particular sound or create a product which would have commercial appeal. It was a case of somebody just saying,

"Do you know that song?" Somebody else would say "What key is it in?" and off they went. The participants simply played music that came naturally to them, the stuff that was in their hearts. They played for the love of it and on the evidence of these recordings would have continued to play their music whether or not they had achieved commercial success.

Writer and Sun Records archivist Colin Escott said of Elvis, "Presley let his true musical soul come up for air." Carl Perkins said Elvis sounded as he had done in the early Sun days, uninhibited and joyful – and that it was infectious. Carl also pointed out that Elvis sounded a little "keener" and higher explaining that this might have been because Sun used fairly cheap equipment which did not allow for much "bottom end". Once Elvis went to RCA it was noticeable that he oversang a lot of the time; that is, he exaggerated a lot of his vocal mannerisms, the ones that his producers had worked out sent the girls wild. There was no need for any such over-egging of the pudding for such a relaxed and informal musical jaunt. What's more, the sound they achieved had something of the raw purity and immediacy associated with the best of the Sun sound. This was partly due to the basic equipment deployed – an economic necessity – but also the fact that the musicians were all together in a small space producing their music simultaneously, interacting with one another spontaneously. There were moments when it had the feel of a live gig in a small club. It was a million miles away from the clinical precision of multi-tracking, mastering and overdubs associated with large studios.

It was not just Elvis who relished the opportunity for the kind of carefree fun afforded by the session. All four were young men under enormous pressure to perform to the very best of their ability on a near daily basis, live and in the studio, and to produce commercial returns in the fastest possible time. On December 4, 1956 in Memphis they could turn the clock back and forget all that for a brief time;

they could do what they used to do, and what countless thousands of people have done for years – hook up with some friends to make music together; a truly timeless human pursuit.

Sam could not pass up the opportunity to propose a little advantageous business following Elvis' unexpected appearance at the studio. He reminded him of the song 'When It Rains, It Really Pours', which he had recorded at Sun just before his departure for RCA. Sam's publishing company owned the rights to the song and would naturally be delighted if Elvis recorded it. The initiative worked. Elvis cut it the following year although RCA did not actually release it until 1965.

For Elvis in particular it must surely have been a delight to play music he loved without pressure from RCA producers anxious to get commercial product into the shops as quickly as possible. He had also experienced the intense pressure of having to perform to order in front of cameras for his first Hollywood movie, *Love Me Tender*, which had been released in November. Perhaps he toyed with the idea of getting back to the more carefree days of Sun – but things had moved on too far and he was now a hugely powerful brand on an unstoppable upward trajectory. It can only be assumed that Tom Parker was unaware of the session; if he had received any kind of advance warning he would either have prevented it happening or ensured that contracts were signed, fees paid, film crews booked – in order to ensure that the maximum commercial advantage was squeezed out of the day. In the modern era such a session would be unthinkable – as soon as any arrangement is made to lay down some creative work by a group of artists, the lawyers, consultants, accountants and managers would be brought in to advise on the best way to exploit the event and protect the interests of their clients. It could be said that Tom Parker was merely a sign of things to come.

It was quite sad really; in retrospect it is painfully obvious that Elvis was an ingénue, not really in charge of his own destiny. This was true to a greater or lesser extent for all of them. Despite the easygoing atmosphere on this one afternoon, their careers and by implication their lives were very much at the mercy of managers, agents and producers. What's more, there were no contracts with sophisticated clauses designed to protect their financial interests – let alone their personal welfare – in fair and transparent ways. Indeed, all would have reason to feel cheated financially in the course of their careers – not least by the host of the day's proceedings, Sam Phillips.

In the course of the afternoon the small studio premises, about the size of a small neighbourhood grocery store, must have been quite crowded at times. It is clear from the recordings that many people came and went, the numbers doubtless enhanced by the presence of Elvis. It is likely that the door between the reception area and the studio itself was left open to enable people to move around. As part of the general ebb and flow, doors can be heard opening and closing from time to time with visitors apparently oblivious to the remarkable music that was being laid down a few feet away from them. At one point the name "Charlie" is mentioned – this could well have been Charlie Feathers, another Sun artist who achieved modest success.

Carl Perkins' band, brothers Jay and Clayton and drummer WS 'Fluke' Holland, were still there when the tapes started rolling but, like others, drifted away in the course of the afternoon. Jerry Lee's cousin, JW Brown, with whom Jerry Lee was staying, might have popped in along with his wife, Lois. Later on, amongst the tantalising cocktail-party noise, the voice of a woman is suddenly clearly audible; she requests an autograph for a young relative.

Once the tapes were rolling the group (a trio so far as the recorded evidence is concerned) continued with the spontaneous session and played a series of songs which covered a remarkably wide range of musical styles emanating from the latter part of the previous century right up to current fifties pop charts. It was all there: folk, bluegrass, country, rhythm and blues, gospel, Christmas songs, jazz and pop; a substantial portion of the genome of popular music that has continued to develop ever since.

This was the music the quartet had absorbed as they grew up. For the most part it was Elvis who was in charge of proceedings. He comes over as excited, a little bit anxious but very keen to be the centre of attention; he appeared able to overcome his natural shyness because he was so sure of his talent and so keen to sing. Latterly, as Elvis becomes less involved, Jerry Lee moves centre stage. Like the young upstart he was, he relished the chance to lay out his musical wares in the presence of established greatness. He was unburdened by any self doubt. Carl Perkins on the other hand, whilst contributing much to the session, seemed to hold back a little.

All participants sound relaxed, caught up in the moment and having fun. There was an appealing boyish excitement about the way they compared notes on songs and hit upon the next one to play. They could have been teenagers talking about cars or girls. One of the questions surrounding the session which has never been definitively answered is whether they knew they were being recorded. On one view of it logic dictates that they did know; this is a view to which expert Colin Escott, on balance, subscribes. They were in a studio which had microphones set up for Carl's session earlier in the day. Johnny Cash talked about the positioning of one microphone when explaining the faintness of his vocal contribution. Jack Clement has stated that he moved the microphones in anticipation of recording what had already started to happen.

On the other hand, in his article next day, reporter Robert Johnson said that if Sam had been "on his toes" he would have recorded the session; however it is quite possible this was because he left before the tapes rolled. The presence of microphones in a studio was hardly unusual. There was a lot of general hubbub and it might be that the singers saw them but did not realise or think that they would be activated. The process of starting the recording would have taken place in the control room, away from the participants. As professional artists aware of the value of magnetic tape, they might well have assumed that tapes would only roll when the musicians were geared up to produce a really good version of a song in the right conditions – i.e. not with a party going on all around them.

Interviewed in 1978, Carl Perkins indicated that he was only vaguely aware that the session had been recorded. He was at Sun the next day and said, "Sam played a few snatches", but it was only very recently (1978) that he became aware that extensive tapes of the session existed. Confusingly, although Johnny Cash talked about the positioning of the microphone, he is also on record saying that he was not aware the session was being taped. As far as can be established, neither Elvis nor Jerry Lee have ever commented publicly on the matter.

It might well be that there is a simple answer; the boys were so caught up in the session that regardless of whether they had been told the tapes were rolling they simply forgot. Given the unguarded way in which they talked to each other, sometimes about other artists, it is hard to believe that they thought they were being recorded as they galloped through the songs. Elvis in particular gave every impression of being totally uninhibited. This was in great contrast to his manner when interviewed on radio or television; then he was often hesitant, keen to avoid criticism or controversy, giving every impression of worrying that he might be saying the wrong thing, quite guarded. This was particularly true when he suffered a strong backlash from several conservative quarters; interviewers at this time could be quite hostile. A further possibility is that they were aware that they were being recorded but never thought for a moment that the tapes would ever get a public airing, so that there was no need for any kind of discretion on their part.

Towards the end of the recordings Elvis drops out – presumably to talk to Sam and others, possibly in the control room, and make preparations for his and Marilyn's departure. At this point Jerry Lee takes the opportunity to move centre stage. To all intents and purposes the latter part of the recordings is a solo performance by the Killer starting with a virtuoso rendition of his debut Sun single, 'Crazy Arms'. Prior to this Elvis had said, by way of complimenting Jerry Lee's playing, that the wrong person was at the piano. Without hesitation Jerry Lee said this is what he had been saying all along and told Elvis to "scoot over". He eventually stopped playing around the time Elvis was leaving and it was time for goodbyes to be exchanged all round.

Towards the end of the recordings Elvis can be heard to say, "That's why I hate to get started in these jam sessions, I'm always the last one to leave." Goodbyes are exchanged along with firm expressions of desire to do it all again soon; it was not to be.

A few days after the session Sam sent a press release to the DJs on the Sun mailing list. He quoted the feature written by Robert Johnson in the *Press-Scimitar* and also included a photograph of the quartet. At the bottom – in his own handwriting – he added:

"Our Only Regret. That each and every one of you wonderful DJs who are responsible for these boys being among the best known and liked in show business could not be there *too*!

We thought however that you might like to read first hand about our little shindig – it was a *dilly*!
Sincerely grateful, Sam Phillips."

Jack Clement said that he would arrange to send acetates of the session to the participants but he later told an interviewer that he had never got round to it.

It seems the session kicked off around the middle/late afternoon with Elvis' arrival. When did it all come to an end? Carl Perkins recalled Elvis leaving around eight in the evening; given that he was the star attraction his arrival and departure times pretty much define the parameters of the Million Dollar Quartet session. Of those five hours less than half were actually recorded and even less than that is available on publicly released recordings.

The Million Dollar Quartet recordings say more about the origins of popular music than a million words ever could. Given the backgrounds of the participants the session also provided a glimpse of some of the key artists who represented the rise of the south as an important musical force. Up until the mid–fifties most popular music that was successful in national terms came from the north, in particular from New York. The phenomenal success of the quartet in the years that followed meant that the big guns who had ruled the roost for so long were faced with the reality that new forces were massing and that a fiery wind of change was blowing up in their direction to shake up their more genteel world.

Away from the wider picture and on a more personal note, Sam sensed the significance of the session for the individuals involved. He said later, "I think this little chance meeting meant an awful lot to all those people, not because one was bigger than another, it was kinda like coming from the same womb."

7.

The Songs

So what specific songs did the Million Dollar Quartet play on December 4, 1956? Colin Escott described the session as "the cultural flashpoint that caught rock 'n' roll at the moment of creation". A striking feature of the big bang they generated was to be found in the astonishing range of music the quartet of young men unleashed that day.

It will never be known exactly how many songs they had a stab at after the Carl Perkins session had come to an end with Elvis' arrival – but before the tapes started rolling. From the various accounts of the session it is possible to state the most likely candidates, though the way they were played and the chatter in between songs can only be guessed at. These were songs which, just like the ones that were recorded, contribute to the overall snapshot of the origins of the rock and pop music the session provided.

Claims have been made – in the course of subsequent books and interviews – for a number of songs to have been sung during the afternoon prior to those on the recordings which have reached the public domain. They are all perfectly credible choices for the quartet, the kind of music to which they were all naturally drawn.

Who exactly sang them is not clear. What is clear is that the quartet had a great many songs at their musical fingertips. The number of songs that were recorded as well as those sung before the tapes rolled – more than 50 in all – is impressive but is merely a sample. It can surely not be doubted that if a similar session had taken place a few weeks later they could easily have come up with another 50 songs, and many more besides, all of them ready to burst forth at a moment's notice – triggered by a brief question, a couple of chords or a guitar lick.

It appears reasonably likely that the following songs were played, in whole or in part, before engineer Jack Clement set the tapes rolling. That said, some of the titles of some songs have been reeled off many years after the event by participants giving wide ranging interviews and who might simply have been detailing songs they half-remembered playing from that general era. The principals all played countless gigs over many years and recorded large numbers of songs in studios all over America. How could they possibly know for sure what songs they played decades previously one particular winter's afternoon in Memphis? Carl Perkins even referred in one interview to the blues classic 'Big Boss Man' – which was not in fact written until four years after the Million Dollar Quartet session took place.

However many of the following songs really were performed by the quartet on December 4, they are certainly typical of the range of songs that were recorded that day.

Blueberry Hill

This song was originally recorded by Gene Autry in 1940 for the film *The Singing Hill* but was soon picked up by other artists and producers who realised the simple little song had the makings of a classic. Countless artists have put their own stamp on the song but it is the version by Fats Domino, released in 1956, which has best stood the test of time. Domino's influential oeuvre has encompassed piano-based rhythm and blues, rock 'n' roll, zydeco, Cajun and boogie-woogie. It was almost certainly his version – lilting rock 'n' roll – which the quartet was best acquainted with. According to several reports, Elvis started the session with this song. Needless to say the piano parts would have been putty in Jerry Lee's hands.

'Blueberry Hill' has been recorded by numerous acts over the years, from the Glenn Miller Orchestra in 1940 to Led Zeppelin, who performed it live at the Los Angeles Forum in 1970 at a concert from which a bootleg album called *Live At Blueberry Hill* subsequently appeared.

Will The Circle Be Unbroken?

This Christian hymn, written in about 1907 by Ada Ruth Habershon and Charles H Gabriel, is one of the best known and best loved of all religious anthems. The lyrics aim to provide comfort for people who have recently been bereaved but over the years, singing the song in unison has come to be seen as an anthem appropriate for groups of people standing together in the face of adversity of any kind, announcing their common resolve to overcome their difficulties to the world. Countless concerts by traditional country-oriented musical groups, right up to the present day, feature the song as their finale, with the audience joining in. The quartet was probably able to sing bits of it before they could read and write.

Modern arrangements vary from medium paced and soulful to uptempo and joyous. Most are based on a rearrangement of the song in the thirties by AP Carter, of the legendary Carter Family, whose music provided the foundation upon which much of modern folk and country music has been built.

As evidence of its continuing appeal and relevance, the song was used as the title for a famous recording in 1972 by the Nitty Gritty Dirt Band which brought together musicians young and old to record traditional old time songs. Bill Monroe was a notable refusenik.

My Isle Of Golden Dreams

The Hawaiian guitar sound became hugely popular in America in the early part of the twentieth century as musicians from the archipelago brought the instrument with them on visits to the United States. This process was boosted by songs like 'My Isle Of Golden Dreams' which mixed the sound of the Hawaiian guitar with sentimental English lyrics. This particular song was written in 1919 by Walter Blaufuss and Gus Kahn. A song like this would have been very suitable for Elvis who had an outstanding gift for romantic ballads; some reports have it that Johnny Cash sang on it too.

American enthusiasm for the sound of the Hawaiian guitar faded in the late twenties but the instrument, in the form of the steel guitar, became permanently established as the signature instrument of country music whose followers have loved its sweet emotional sounds ever since.

Though mainly as novelty numbers, Hawaiian songs enjoyed regular resurgences of popularity in subsequent years, notably in the hands of Marty Robbins and Bing Crosby.

There Are Strange Things Happening Every Day

This is a traditional black American gospel song often adapted to various musical styles according to the preferences of performers and audiences. Although there have been many versions over the years, the most famous is that by Sister Rosetta Tharpe, the electric guitar-toting firebrand Christian advocate. She recorded it in 1944 and regularly featured it in her live concerts. Some have claimed it as the first ever rock 'n' roll record, others as an important precursor of rock 'n' roll. This was partly due to the rocking nature of the song but also to Tharpe's stage presence and attack; she swung her hips and moved around the stage as she picked out catchy licks on her steel-bodied guitar. The song's popularity was such that it crossed over from the gospel charts to the "race" (later rhythm and blues) charts. Its popularity continues and there have been recent versions by Tom Jones and Michelle Shocked.

It would certainly have been a suitable vehicle for Jerry Lee who would doubtless have underpinned the song with a rollicking piano foundation.

That Old Time Religion

This traditional call and response song, alternatively called '(Give Me That) Old Time Religion', might trace its origins to English folk music. It has been a southern gospel rallying call since the late nineteenth century in America, loved by both black and white spiritual singers and their audiences. A standard for well over a century, it is a song the quartet would all have known well from early in their lives. Carl Perkins said he recalled it being sung at some point during the session and Johnny Cash said he remembered singing on it.

Blue Moon Of Kentucky

Written by Bill Monroe, this song has been discussed elsewhere. As one side of Elvis' first single, it would have been an obvious choice for inclusion at an informal jam session. In his 1997 autobiography, Johnny Cash said he remembered singing it.

The Old Rugged Cross

Religious numbers featured strongly in the quartet's spontaneous selection. 'The Old Rugged Cross' is a Christian song, loved by millions of people across the world, which was written in 1912 by a Methodist evangelist called George Bennard, whose ancestors came from Scotland. The song has long been a standard, popular with black and white artists and audiences. It has been recorded by singers from Elvis Presley and Patsy Cline to Al Green and Willie Nelson. It even turned up in an episode of the popular British science fiction television series *Doctor Who* in 2007.

I Won't Have To Cross Jordan Alone

This is a gospel standard, originally copyrighted in 1934, which has been recorded by numerous artists; it has long been a fixture in American church hymn books. It would have been as obvious a choice of religious number as any of the others that definitely were performed that day. As with many other spiritual songs, it is concerned with the comfort offered to believers through religious faith. In 1962 Johnny Cash included it on his second album of religious material for Columbia, *Hymns From The Heart* (the first was *Hymns By Johnny Cash,* released by Columbia in 1959 not long after Johnny's arrival at his new label). One of the reasons he had grown dissatisfied with Sam Phillips was his resistance to Johnny's wish to be allowed to record gospel songs for Sun.

When I Take My Vacation In Heaven

In a similar vein, 'When I Take My Vacation In Heaven', sometimes simply called 'Vacation In Heaven', is a gospel song, originally published in 1925, which has enjoyed considerable popularity over the years. It was also included on Johnny Cash's 1962 album, *Hymns From The Heart*.

It was co-written by Herbert Buffum, a Christian evangelist whose output was prolific – around 1,000 published songs in his lifetime. When he died in 1939 one newspaper described him as "The King of Gospel Song Writers".

Tutti Frutti

A major hit for Little Richard in 1955, the often indecipherable 'Tutti Frutti' is among the most famous rock 'n' roll songs ever recorded, right up there with anything by Elvis, Bill Haley or Buddy Holly. The unaccompanied rhythmic onslaught that sets it off, "A-wop-bop-a-loo-bop-a-wop-bam-boom", is arguably the most memorable opening to any piece of popular music. In 2007 a panel of experts assembled by *Mojo* placed the song at number one on its list, The Top 100 Records That Changed The World. They characterised the record as no less than the "sound of the birth of rock 'n' roll". RCA clearly saw that it was perfect material for Elvis and it was included on his debut album for them – albeit with the lyrics toned way down from some of the original words which were aggressively sexual. This song would have been a lot of fun for Jerry Lee Lewis and a real opportunity for him to show off his skills.

This Train (aka This Train Is Bound for Glory)

This well known gospel song was first recorded in 1925 though it had been sung in churches for some years prior to that. In 1935 a version was recorded with the title 'Dis Train', a probable indicator that the origins of the song lay in black music. Sister Rosetta Tharpe recorded a version in the early fifties which, with her trademark electric guitar, sounded a lot closer to rock 'n' roll than anything that might normally be heard in a church. The song was also brought to wider public attention by the work of folklorists John A Lomax and Alan Lomax.

The song has been covered by a great many artists in a wide range of musical styles from blues and folk to reggae and zydeco. A shortened version of the main hook line of the song provided the title for Woody Guthrie's autobiographical book, *Bound For Glory,* which was later used as the basis for a biopic on Guthrie's life.

Bruce Springsteen borrowed the theme of 'This Train' on his song 'Land Of Hope And Dreams', which was written in 1998 or early 1999, and debuted live with the E Street Band in March 1999.

According to some reports Elvis also sang 'You Belong To My Heart', which was also sung later on, when the tapes were rolling.

★ ★ ★

Various recordings of the Million Dollar Quartet session have been released over the years. It is however the 2006 SONY BMG release, the culmination of much painstaking research and expert audio restoration, which provides the fullest account of the music that was played. The following commentary on the songs and instrumentals follows the order of this release.

1. Instrumental. (1.44)

This rhythm and bluesy opening jam probably features Carl Perkins and his band, brothers Jay and Clayton with Fluke on drums, plus Jerry Lee Lewis, whose unmistakeable pumping left hand enlivens the number and adds a powerful rhythmic undertone. There are no composer credits and it has not been identified as any particular song. It is a driving, though fairly aimless, piece of improvisation with Carl's rockabilly guitar and Jerry Lee's relentless piano to the fore most of the time before it fizzles out. Apart from Jerry Lee's contribution, the playing is unspectacular though competent, but the band sounds tight. Fluke lets rip on the drums every now and then, demonstrating a real confidence in his ability despite a total lack of training and a fairly short career. Carl later said he did not think his guitar playing was particularly good that day. It all sounds like the sort of musical backdrop you might expect to hear at any number of smoky bars and honky-tonks on a Saturday night in small town fifties America – the kind of place Carl and his brothers had headlined countless times. Perhaps this was a piece Carl and his brothers had in reserve for those occasions when they had worked their way through their repertoire and needed something else to keep the crowd happy.

Although it is only speculation, this instrumental might have been played after the initial unrecorded songs, and after the photographs had been taken and Elvis was saying goodbye to Johnny Cash and the men from the press. Alternatively, Elvis might simply have been taking a break, chatting to Sam or others, possibly in the control booth. Perhaps the sound of Carl playing about with one of his recent big hits towards the end of the number made him think it was about time he was getting back to the musical fray.

2. Love Me Tender/Mr Sandman. Instrumental. (1.02)

Carl's session was over, the quartet had probably worked their way through some songs together, posed for some photographs, and now, for a spell, Elvis was apparently absent – but in their thoughts. Carl and Jerry Lee start the song quite tentatively but soon get the hang of it. They are of course familiar with it since it has been a national hit; both were well able to play songs by ear. Jerry Lee embellishes the sound with some flowery piano phrases. Fluke hits a few beats but there is no rhythm to get hold of so he gives up. Voices can be heard in the background.

'Love Me Tender' was an updated version of a sentimental ballad of the Civil War era, written by George R Poulton and W W Fosdick and published in 1861. It was originally called 'Aura Lee' (and sometimes known as 'The Maid Of Golden Hair'). It became popular with barbershop quartets and also soldiers at West Point where it had become a graduating-class song in the nineteenth century. It was embedded in American history, popular with several generations.

Elvis' recording had been released at the end of September 1956, one of a veritable blitz of releases by RCA, keen to recoup the money they had spent on Elvis' contract and exploit his massive commercial potential. Already it was clear that they had cleaned up his image – the sleeve photograph showed a clean cut Elvis with a non-sneering smile; the only complaint a parent might have had being the length of his hair. The song too was a long way from the rougher rockabilly sounds Elvis delivered for Sun, an indication that Tom Parker was keen to maximise his appeal by moving him closer to the mainstream. Taken along with such a traditional song, the unthinkable had happened – the name Elvis could just possibly start to be associated in listeners' minds with an epithet such as all-American.

Elvis performed the song on *The Ed Sullivan Show* on September 9, 1956. The following day RCA received a million advance orders, making it a gold record before it was released – something which had never happened before.

The composers of the song are stated to be Vera Matson and Elvis Presley. In fact neither of them contributed to the composition at all. The melody was written in the mid-nineteenth century and by the fifties was public domain; the modern lyrics were written by music producer Ken Darby, the husband of Vera Matson, who was in charge of music for the film *Love Me Tender.*

It was Darby who came up with the idea of using an old melody and adding new words. It was a formula which Elvis used again successfully with 'Wooden Heart' which featured the melody of the German song 'Muss Ich Denn' and 'It's Now Or Never' which was based on 'O Sole Mio', a late nineteenth century Italian song, its literal translation 'My Sunshine'. Darby did not wish to be credited but did want to earn royalties and so stated the composer to be his wife, Vera (using her maiden name). Elvis was credited as a co-writer. This was part of a harsh commercial reality at the time, dictated by his publishing company Hill & Range – anyone wanting to have one of their songs recorded by Elvis, and thus to achieve huge guaranteed sales, had to give up a large chunk of the writing credit. When asked later why he put his wife as co-writer along with Presley, Darby responded acidly, "Because she didn't write it either." Aware of the massive commercial pulling power of his boy, Tom Parker enforced such practices with enthusiasm. That said, Elvis invariably contributed greatly to the production of his songs – changing arrangements and lyrics to achieve the best result and so perhaps, to some extent at least, the writing credit could be justified in his case.

The song reached number one on the main *Billboard* chart at the start of November 1956 and stayed there for five weeks, a period which included the day of the Million Dollar Quartet session. The song had followed 'Hound Dog'/'Don't Be Cruel' onto the top spot. It was the first time an artist had succeeded himself on the top spot; in addition it was part of a record run of 16 consecutive weeks at number one by the same artist – a record which was only surpassed in 2004. 'Love Me Tender' became a standard for a while and was recorded by many other artists including Paul Anka and Engelbert Humperdinck.

The song is also closely associated with Elvis' entrance into the world of movies. His debut film was originally going to be called *The Reno Brothers*, with established actors Richard Egan and Debra Paget in the starring roles. In the course of production however, the RCA single 'Love Me Tender' created so much interest that it became the title of the film after much pressure from Tom Parker; three other Elvis songs were quickly included on the soundtrack and although Richard Egan retained top billing, it was Elvis' image which dominated the publicity posters.

After playing 'Love Me Tender' for approximately 50 seconds, Jerry Lee cuts into 'Mr Sandman' with some support from Carl. Fluke tries to add some drums momentarily but gives up after a while, apparently unable to get a handle on the song. This was traditional clean-cut pop, with completely innocent lyrics – the sort of thing that happened before rock 'n' roll came along and shook everything up. It had been a number one hit for the Chordettes in 1954.

Now a standard, the song has been covered and adapted by a wide variety of artists. It was a Top 20 UK hit for Max Bygraves at the beginning of 1955. In 1978 the trio of Dolly Parton, Emmylou Harris and Linda Ronstadt recorded a version. The song is a gift for a piano player with its chord progression in the chorus which follows the circle of fourths for six chords in a row.

3. Jingle Bells. Instrumental. (1.57)

No doubt the festive season was already well underway by early December, with Santa Claus much in evidence in the shops, and thoughts of Christmas would naturally have come to mind. This family favourite is familiar to all, young and old, and Jerry Lee and Carl deliver a fairly straight, jaunty rendition, respectful of the traditional nature of the song – though naturally with Jerry Lee at the piano it bounces along at a fair lick.

Though they had only met for the first time that day, Carl and Jerry Lee play together as if they were used to each other's musical company. One of the best-known and commonly sung winter songs in the world, it was written by James Lord Pierpont (1822–1893) and originally published under the title 'One Horse Open Sleigh' in the autumn of 1857. It was first recorded in 1898 by the Edison Male Quartette on an Edison cylinder as part of a medley of Christmas songs.

Even though it is commonly thought of as a Christmas song, it was originally written and sung for Thanksgiving. It is one of the best known and best loved of all secular songs, albeit one associated with Christmas in the minds of many. It duly earned its writer a place in the American Songwriters Hall of Fame.

As with other songs sung by the quartet, 'Jingle Bells' represents traditional values and customs; this is quite ironic when the four young performers were often associated with behaviour which was deemed by many to be a threat to good morals and the American way of life.

4. White Christmas. Instrumental. (2.05)

As 'Jingle Bells' peters out, Carl neatly morphs the chords into those of 'White Christmas' after momentarily revisiting 'Don't Be Cruel'. Themes of family and tradition are once more to the fore. Written by Irving Berlin in 1940, 'White Christmas' is a secular song which looks back nostalgically, with all the trimmings, to a bygone image of Christmas, with references to such festive delights as glistening treetops and sleigh bells in the snow. Given the song's strong association with Christmas, some commentators have referred to it as a secular hymn. Bing Crosby's version, which was featured in the film *Holiday Inn*, is the biggest selling single of all time according to *Guinness World Records*. It was recorded in 1942 with backing vocals provided by the

Ken Darby singers. The huge success of the song might, as with 'Aura Lee', be related to its warmly sentimental nature and the connection to a time of war. Elvis went on to record the song in 1957 for *Elvis' Christmas Album*.

Jerry Lee delivers a colourful and showy version of the song with Carl adding occasional guitar flourishes and Fluke messing about on the hi-hat, trying to find a beat amongst Jerry Lee's Liberace-like twists and turns. Once more their instinctive choice of song shows a respect for tradition, indeed a real taste for tradition – in contrast to the public perception of them which was based on the new cutting edge sounds with which they were exciting their younger fans – and upsetting many in the establishment.

5. Reconsider Baby. (2.45)

This is the point at which Elvis is first heard singing on the recordings; the point at which he returns to the music and takes over the show. Although others provide backing vocals, it is Elvis who now leads the singing – until he hands over to Jerry Lee Lewis towards the end of the session. He is the undisputed main man; that said Carl Perkins had probably been singing without much of a break for several hours by this stage and might well have been content to have Elvis sit in the driving seat.

'Reconsider Baby' was written by blues guitarist and singer Lowell Fulson, one of the founding fathers of West Coast blues, a sub-genre which features elements of jazz, rhythm and blues with piano and guitar solos to the fore. It developed when blues players moved from Texas (or in Fulson's case Oklahoma) to California in the thirties and forties and then blended the music they brought with the music they found in their new home. West Coast blues favours smooth vocals and is generally more accessible than some of the purer, harder edged types of blues.

Fulson enjoyed a lengthy career but 'Reconsider Baby', released on Checker Records, a subsidiary of Chess Records, remained his biggest hit. A blues classic. Once more the instinctive draw for the quartet was towards outstanding songs, iconic examples of particular key styles. At times Elvis' singing is barely audible whereas the piano and drums remain constant; perhaps he was moving around as he was singing, putting himself out of range of the fixed microphone emplacements. Fluke provides a rock solid shuffle beat.

Elvis covered this song in 1960 for his album *Elvis Is Back!* It has since been done by many artists, including Eric Clapton who has often featured it in his live concerts. Fulson's original version was inducted into the Blues Foundation Hall of Fame in the "Classics of Blues Recordings" category. It is also included in the Rock and Roll Hall of Fame's list of the 500 Songs That Shaped Rock And Roll.

6 7 & 9 Don't Be Cruel. (2.20; 2.20; 0.36)

Elvis recorded 'Don't Be Cruel' in June 1956 and it was released with 'Hound Dog' on the other side in July. The bosses at RCA were on a mission to release the largest possible amount of Elvis material in the shortest possible time but it was certainly not a case of quantity over quality. In 2004, the song was listed at number 197 in *Rolling Stone's* list of the 500 Greatest Songs of All Time. The fact that Elvis performed it during all three of his appearances on *The Ed Sullivan Show* contributed to its massive commercial success. The record quickly reached number one on the *Billboard* chart, to be followed onto the top spot by 'Love Me Tender'. It was all part of an *annus mirabilis* for Elvis when virtually everything he touched turned to gold. Everybody round the piano seemed to love the song since they had three shots at it.

It was written by Otis Blackwell who penned a number of Elvis' early smash hits including 'All Shook Up'. It has been suggested that Elvis might have copied some of Blackwell's vocal mannerisms which he would have heard regularly as he listened to acetates of him (Blackwell) singing the songs he sent in for consideration.

Blackwell also wrote 'Fever', a big hit for Peggy Lee that Elvis would record in 1960. As was the case with other writers, he was told that he would have to give up half of the publishing royalties (a third according to some reports) and also concede a co-writing credit to Elvis on the basis that anything Elvis recorded would sell in big numbers. The financial loss to him was enormous but as someone who had known real poverty not long before, he was prepared to accept the situation; the reality was that he would still make an enormous amount of money from the songs he wrote for Elvis – half of a lot was better than all of a little. In any event, this sort of thing was nothing new; other stars, including Al Jolson, claimed credits for songs they didn't write – and Elvis did contribute his own shape to the production of the songs in the studio.

Bones Howe, one of the recording engineers who worked with Elvis, said that he changed arrangements of songs during sessions and contributed ideas about phrasing and instrumentation. He took some of the key decisions. In this way, he actually contributed to how songs turned out and, it can reasonably be argued, their commercial appeal. This approach was very uncommon for artists in the fifties. Elvis was very hands on, he listened to songs over and over again, and tweaked them until he drew out the magic. He had a big say in what happened in the studio and if he didn't like something, it usually didn't get done. This approach became commonplace in subsequent years but back in the fifties Elvis was, as with much of the music he brought to the world, an influential innovator.

For all his shyness, Elvis was never happier than when he was entertaining people. In the relaxed atmosphere at Sun Studio that December afternoon he was in his element; he liked to be the centre of attention and much of what was captured on tape finds him at the heart of things – anxious to tell his stories, stammering slightly in his enthusiasm to get out what he had to say, always giving the slight impression that he was having to overcome a certain reserve.

Elvis became particularly animated when telling the assembled group about Billy Ward and his Dominoes, a black rhythm and blues vocal group with a well choreographed stage show. Earlier that year he took time out from his schedule at Las Vegas, where they too were performing, to watch them – "four times straight". He loved their charismatic lead singer, Jackie Wilson – although he does not appear to have been aware of his identity at the time. Elvis described the way Wilson imitated him when he sang 'Don't Be Cruel' and proceeded to return the compliment.

"I heard this guy in Las Vegas, Billy Ward and his Dominoes, there was a guy out there that was doing a takeoff on me – 'Don't Be Cruel'. He tried so hard until he got much better, boy, much better than that record of mine." Elvis sweeps aside expressions of dissent at this point. "No, wait now, I mean, he was real slender, he was a coloured guy... he had it a little slower than me..." At this point Elvis asks someone what key he had done it in – already he was accustomed to the idea that in the studio he could fire off questions which somebody somewhere should be able to answer.

Somebody suggests "D". He then starts singing the song – Elvis pretending to be Jackie pretending to be Elvis. Jerry Lee quickly picks up the vibe with a plonking bass line which complements Elvis' rhythm perfectly. Again Elvis' voice fades in and out as, presumably, he moves away from the microphone.

He then continues his narrative, interspersed with snatches of singing to illustrate points he was making, in enthusiastic bursts – with his audience apparently spellbound. "He got the backing, the whole quartet... he was hitting it, boy." (At this point Elvis apparently imitates some of the stage moves he liked so much which in turn triggers peals of laughter from the people in the studio.) He continues, "Grabbed that microphone, and on the last note he went all the way down to the floor, man, looking straight up at the ceiling. Man, he was cutting out. I was under the table when he got through singing ... and all the time he was singing, them feet was going in and out, both ways, sliding like this." Elvis was greatly amused by Wilson's pronunciation of telephone as "tellyphone". The others were all amused too, one describing Elvis' story as "classic". Elvis jokes good-naturedly that he was so good – "sang the hell out of that song" – that he wanted to shout out, "Get him off, get him off".

The remarks are self-evidently spontaneous and unguarded; it is surely clear that he was unaware, or at the very least had forgotten, that he was being recorded. They also reveal great generosity to a fellow performer, an honest appreciation of his skills which he does not see as any kind of threat. He did though say that Jackie's version of 'Hound Dog' earlier in the evening had not been so good because he was "trying too hard".

As he sings the song the others can be heard whooping and laughing especially at his imitations of Wilson's accent and stage moves. Elvis reprises the song immediately after 'Paralyzed' and once more jokes about Jackie Wilson's accent explaining, "He was a Yankee you know." Somebody says, "All he needed was a building or something to jump off." Elvis agrees that would have made a "big ending".

Elvis remained an admirer of Jackie Wilson until his career was prematurely ended in 1975 when he suffered a major heart attack during a concert. He died in 1984. Elvis admitted openly that he borrowed some stage moves from Wilson. For his part Wilson was quick to counter criticisms of Elvis. "A lot of people have accused Elvis of stealing the black man's music, when in fact, almost every black solo entertainer copied from Elvis."

8. Paralyzed. (3.00)

During 'Don't Be Cruel', when Elvis takes a break from singing to talk about Jackie Wilson, someone, probably Carl, asks about him doing 'Paralyzed' in the same way but Elvis declines, at which point a woman's voice can be heard pleading with him to do it. The moment passed but once the first two takes of 'Don't Be Cruel' come to an end it seems Elvis has a change of heart and the ensemble drifts into the song. Once more Elvis imitates Jackie Wilson's delivery – slower than his own version – and once more he asks what key it is in before he starts singing. For this song Jerry Lee is more restrained – more like the lowly session musician he was supposed to be.

With Elvis now in full flow, the session takes on the feel of an informal concert and there is enthusiastic applause from those fortunate enough to be in the studio – little did they know what historic events were unfolding before their eyes. Despite the best efforts of the engineers who restored the tapes, there are moments when some damage to the originals cannot be disguised – although it is to their immense credit that this barely affects the overall listening experience.

'Paralyzed' was another song written by Otis Blackwell but once more the writing credit is shared with Elvis who had recorded it in the Hollywood studio Radio Recorders for RCA earlier in the year. It appeared on his 1956 album *Elvis* and was also released on an EP. As a sign of Elvis' star status the studio was locked when he recorded it and a guard vetted people who came and went – only those approved by Tom Parker gained admittance.

Even for a private recording engagement such as this Elvis felt he was on show and made sure that his clothes would make him stand out from the crowd. He wore black slacks, yellow socks, a red checked shirt, and black oxfords with red inserts. By contrast, for the Million Dollar Quartet session he wore genuinely casual clothes, confident that he was among friends for whom he did not need to make a special sartorial effort.

The song was not released as a single, possibly as a result of some uneasiness amongst DJs and others about the title, with its connotations of disability. This might have been an early example of a kind of political correctness; there is some irony if so. In a mixture of altruism and favourable publicity, Elvis had agreed to become a supporter of the March of Dimes. This was a high profile national campaign aimed at raising funds for research into a new vaccine for polio, responsible amongst other things for childhood paralysis. Perhaps Elvis' own people were also uneasy about the associations which might be created in listeners' minds. Despite such considerations, Elvis did feature it when he appeared on *The Ed Sullivan Show*. Apart from being photographed receiving a vaccination, he also recorded a public service announcement in support of the campaign.

10. There's No Place Like Home. (3.36)

Carl Perkins kicks off this song which is often simply referred to as 'Home Sweet Home'. He starts tentatively picking the notes of the melody which Elvis quickly picks up on after humming it mellifluously for a few moments. "Is that 'No Place Like Home', Carl?" he asks. Things develop from there. The group choose a mid-tempo upbeat delivery, eschewing the more common slow ballad interpretation. Carl plays some tasty country-rockabilly guitar while Jerry Lee lays down some honky-tonk piano in the background. At this stage it appears that Carl's backing band, certainly Fluke on drums and Clayton on bass, are still playing in support.

There is a lot of to and fro chatter in the background – some of which relates to the song. Elvis is asked if he has recorded the song for a new album – he had not but then he asks if there is a copy "here". Presumably he means a Sun recording. The response is

"Yeah, somewhere, I'll have to find it." At other times the subject is football. It all goes on as the music continues.

This is a song with a history stretching back to 1822. It was originally an operatic aria from Sir Henry Bishop's opera *Clari* also known as *The Maid Of Milan*. The lyrics were written by John Payne. The melody was used by Rossini in *The Barber Of Seville*.

It has been adapted, and indeed had liberties taken with it, countless times over the years. However the powerful emotional message of the song, about the vital human desire to have somewhere to call home – a house, a region, a country – has never varied and has struck a chord with people all over the world. In Japan, a version which is akin to a secular hymn is regularly played at weddings. Not surprisingly it was very popular during the American Civil War; so popular that, according to some reports, senior officers tried to ban it because it might make soldiers more likely to desert. The song has been part of the rich embroidery of popular American music for nearly 200 years. In the early days it was a song that was marketed to families as something they could, and perhaps should, sing at home.

Elvis' rich and honeyed tenor voice does full justice to the song, suggesting that even at this early stage in his career he was able to work his vocal magic on any musical style.

11. When The Saints Go Marchin' In. (2.18)

'The Saints', as it is often referred to, is a traditional gospel hymn which could be said to fall under the general umbrella of folk music in the broadest sense. It marks the start of a run of eight religious-oriented songs which the ensemble performs with effortless confidence. Given their experiences during childhood, it was really inevitable that gospel would be one of the styles they would turn to early on in the session.

The song is often featured as a standard by jazz bands. There is however no definitive way of performing it and extra verses are sometimes added. In New Orleans it is often part of the musical accompaniment to funerals; a dirge on the way to the cemetery, uptempo Dixieland on the way back – which is how Elvis & Co do it. Jerry Lee can be heard singing backing response vocals with real fervour, reflecting his heavy personal involvement with so many aspects of evangelical religion throughout his 21 years. The listener can imagine the dilemma he regularly faced. Talking about his live performances he once said, "I'm out here doing what God don't want me to do, I'm leading people to hell." He was a sinner who would not stop sinning, but who always felt able to ask God for forgiveness. At the end he says with feeling, "I sure do love that spiritual music."

Earlier versions of the song emphasised its apocalyptic nature – "When the sun, refuse to shine" – taking much of its imagery from the Book of Revelation, but excluding its more horrific depictions of the Last Judgment. Such aspects of religion would have been very familiar to the quartet as they were growing up and experienced the onslaughts of hellfire preachers for whom joy and damnation were inextricably linked. As time has gone by the lyrics have generally been softened. Louis Armstrong popularised the song in the thirties to the disapproval of his sister who felt that his version wrongly took the focus off the religious nature of the song.

Elvis later recorded his own version for one of his gospel albums.

12. Softly And Tenderly. (2.42)

"Do you know 'Softly And Tenderly?'" somebody asks. "Gimme a key," snaps Elvis, eager to get into another song. Carl starts playing some notes. "That's a little bit high Carl." He brings it down – songs are invariably geared up to Elvis' vocal range; in consequence Carl and Jerry Lee's vocals sound a little strained at times as they try to fit Elvis' preferred keys. It is a given that Elvis knows the words.

The full title of this song, which dates back to the late 1870s, is in fact, 'Softly And Tenderly Jesus Is Calling'. It was written by Will L Thompson and is a Christian hymn, a meditation on impending death, which was sung at the memorial service for Martin Luther King in 1968. Although Elvis is inevitably the lead singer, Jerry Lee does his best to keep up with him, oblivious to any notion that it might be appropriate for him to defer to a major star. That said Jerry Lee never sounds like a lesser star in the firmament; completely familiar with the song he sings lead and harmonises with ease, imbuing it with real gospel energy. A listener who did not know otherwise might well think he was black.

There is constant background chatter which appears to be very convivial. People were clearly not yet in awe of Elvis as they would be soon, when the idea of a lot of people making noise when he was in a studio, some of them unconnected to the music, would be out of the question.

13. When God Dips His Love In My Heart. (0.23)

As with the other religious songs, 'When God Dips His Love In My Heart' is one which will have been familiar to most of the people Elvis and the others grew up with; it would have been a favourite at church and in gospel concerts. Perhaps the first version they heard was the 1946 recording by the Blackwood Brothers, the white gospel quartet of whom Elvis in particular was a great fan.

It was not just that they all knew so many religious songs – they clearly loved listening to them and singing them. It is hard to avoid the feeling that modern country singers include a few religious songs in their repertoires because some expert in the publicity department has said they will go over well with some sections of their potential demographic target. No such thinking applied with the quartet in the fifties.

Although sometimes attributed as "traditional", the song 'When God Dips His Love In My Heart' was written by Cleavant Derricks, whose whole life was devoted to religious matters. He was a pastor, a church builder, a choir director, a poet and the composer of around 300 religious songs. His initial motivation for embarking on his writing career was to inspire and give hope to people, especially poor black people, whose lives had been made even worse by the ravages of the Great War and the Great Depression. That said, Derricks understood that his concerns applied just as much to poor whites as they did to poor blacks and as the years went by many of his gospel songs were sung by black and white people, though not often together initially; as with many areas of life, churches were divided along racial lines. They were sung by innumerable mass choirs, quartets and Sunday night gatherings around the piano in little country churches. It can be argued that they succeeded in helping people to rise above many instances of racial segregation and an atmosphere of prejudice, both commonplace during this era. Ironically Derricks, a black man, did not receive anything like the financial rewards he should have done while his publishers raked in large profits from the songs he wrote.

The ensemble just has a very brief stab at the song. In what might be a fragment of a longer version, Jerry Lee is singing lead and the uptempo rhythm is emphasised by hand–clapping and some vocal sounds from Elvis which might have been an indication that on this occasion he did not in fact know the words.

14. Just A Little Talk With Jesus. (4.09)

Towards the end of 'When God Dips His Love In My Heart', with Jerry Lee in full flow on lead vocals, Elvis cuts in and brings the song to an abrupt end. "I know one Carl… 'Just A Little Talk With Jesus'… remember that?" Carl does and they quickly start it up. Jerry

Lee is once more relegated to piano player and backing singer albeit one who is doing his level best to be at the forefront of the action, providing the calls for Elvis to respond to – something he had clearly done many times before.

This is another inspirational gospel song from the pen of Cleavant Derricks which was originally copyrighted in 1937 as 'Have A Little Talk With Jesus'. An instant classic, black and white audiences quickly took it their hearts; they loved the simple and direct message of the comfort provided by religious belief and devotion. It was framed in language that resonated with ordinary people leading lives that were often hidebound by poverty and where physical pleasures were few.

After doing the song for a while, Elvis gets Carl to slow down from uptempo gospel swing to a more soulful tempo. Once more he is in charge, making things happen in the way he believes brings out the best in the song. This was his *modus operandi* regardless of whether he was in an RCA studio or enjoying an informal jam with friends in Memphis. Carl delivers some tastefully picked country style leads.

15. Jesus Walked That Lonesome Valley. (3.28)

"Remember some of those real old ones Carl?" Elvis inquires. The impression is given that the session is all about Elvis with Carl as a kind of first mate. Elvis' remarks are rarely addressed to Jerry Lee. Apparently not even waiting for a reply, he launches into the song; Jerry Lee positively explodes with delight when he realises which song is kicking off and again does his best to hijack it. He is in his element with music like this and makes no attempt to restrain his exuberance; on this one he outshines Elvis. He comes alive in the joy of the moment, breaking into a kind of delirious falsetto at times. As for Elvis, his singing is natural and relaxed, free from the exaggerated mannerisms which were often in evidence on his later official RCA releases such as 'Jailhouse Rock' and 'Are You Lonesome Tonight?'.

The song is sometimes described as "traditional" which is partly right; it can also be attributed to William L Dawson, born 1899, who, as well as being a famous composer, was a teacher and arranger of music. For this and other songs he drew on the lyrics of traditional American folk songs. He also used melodies of old spiritual songs whose origins were lost in the mists of time.

His *Negro Folk Symphony* of 1934 garnered a great deal of attention at its world premiere; it was later revised and revamped with greater emphasis on African rhythms. The composition attempted to convey elements of native music that were lost when Africans came into bondage outside their homeland. The music the quartet chose to play really did connect to deep roots which spread far beyond the comparatively limited geographical boundaries of where they had been brought up.

At this stage it appears there are fewer people in the studio since there is hardly any applause at the end of the song – and what handclapping there is appears to come mainly from the musical participants themselves. Throughout the session there is an ebb and flow of people.

16. I Shall Not Be Moved. (3.49)

"Here's an old one," says Elvis by way of introduction. The group launch into the song with real gusto, all contributing to the lead vocals.

'I Shall Not Be Moved' is a traditional African American spiritual whose origins might well date back to the slave era. It has also gained worldwide popularity as a protest song in the form, 'We Shall Not Be Moved'. The song's format meant that it was easy to remember and it lent itself to group singing where all participants could feel included and express straightforward ideas. It consists of a series of verses, each of four lines. The title is repeated three times with one new line being introduced each time; this new line can easily be adapted to suit particular new situations. It came to be strongly associated with the Civil Rights Movement.

This version stresses the song's religious origins, which is how it would have been experienced by all participants as they were growing up. If unaware of the true situation, a listener to the recording might reasonably think it was made in church on a Sunday afternoon not least because of the "Glory Hallelujahs". The image of "the tree that's planted by the water" is one that seeks to express a message of hope, security and faith – to equip people for the trials of life. It imagines a better world ahead.

At the end Jerry cannot contain his glee. "Boy this is fun... I like this." You can hear the irrepressible grin all over his face. Someone, possibly Smokey Joe Baugh, as a comment on the lack of a bass for this gospel song, says in a deep voice, "You oughta get up a quartet," a remark that is usually taken as evidence of the absence of Johnny Cash. Elvis jokily ripostes, "A who-et?"

17. Peace In The Valley. (1.33)

Before this song starts, there is talk of doing 'Softly And Tenderly' again but after doodling for a while, and after Elvis apologises for burping, he leads the way into 'Peace In The Valley' against a background of doors closing and opening, people coming and going. There are no drums and on this song Jerry Lee takes a break from the piano, just providing backing vocals. Occasional snatches of a woman singing in the background are also detectable.

'Peace In The Valley' was written in 1937 by Thomas A Dorsey and was originally performed by Mahalia Jackson who, apart from being an outstanding gospel singer, was also a prominent civil rights campaigner. Dorsey originally played jazz and rhythm and blues but switched to writing religious music in the thirties. According to some sources it was he who coined the term "gospel music". It was one of Elvis' favourite styles of music throughout his life and he would often listen to it for pleasure in his spare time, away from the pressures of the studio.

'Peace In the Valley' has been covered by countless artists and is one of the first gospel songs to sell a million copies. It is not hard to see the link between traditional gospel music and the soul music which developed from the late fifties onwards. The version freshest in Elvis' mind could have been Red Foley's 1951 country hit.

In order to please his mother, Gladys, Elvis sang this song – against the wishes of the producers – during his 1957 appearance on *The Ed Sullivan Show*. It was probably the moment when most people started to see him not as a satanic figure who was a threat to women and the morals of the nation but actually a nice boy who believed in God and American values. Later in the year he recorded a version for RCA.

As the song draws to a close, Jerry Lee says to Elvis with great sincerity, "Yeah that's brilliant. It is, it's beautiful."

18. Down By The Riverside. (2.26)

As they mess about between songs, Jerry Lee appears to suggest, tentatively, doing 'My God Is Real', but is quickly outgunned as the others get going with 'Down By The Riverside'. Elvis sparks it off once he has checked what key Carl was playing in before – A. This is the last in this continuous run of religious/spiritual songs but the singers have lost none of the fervour shown in the previous songs. Somebody, possibly Fluke, adds percussion from about halfway through by hitting something metallic rhythmically, but it is not a conventional drum-kit sound.

Carl Perkins recalled people working in the cotton fields singing this song in unison in order to raise their spirits and get through the day. A traditional gospel song, it was known during the American Civil War and also has associations with slavery in the Deep South. The words have been adapted to many situations over the years.

It falls into a category of folk music which is beyond mere entertainment; rather it is a traditional part of the fabric of particular communities, especially the rural working class, a unifying activity in which everybody can join. Such songs can be readily understood by anyone and the themes they cover include war, civil rights, work, satire and love. Such music is timeless; in the years following the Million Dollar Quartet sessions, many other artists deployed folk music in their opposition to the Vietnam War and the government's unpopular economic policies. 'Down By The Riverside' is still sung regularly all over the world, little changed, as an anthem of hope and triumph over adversity.

19. I'm With A Crowd But So Alone. (1.16)

The indefatigable Jerry Lee suggests another religious song – 'Jesus Hold My Hand' – even as Elvis launches into an imitation of Ernest Tubb doing 'I'm With A Crowd But So Alone', and managing to sound like Hank Snow along the way. This is clearly a spoof with Elvis trying to force his voice lower than its usual comfort zone. Such imitations were not unusual and were more affectionate than mocking – Johnny Cash regularly imitated Elvis during his live concerts around this time.

Country singer Ernest Tubb, "The Texas Troubadour", was someone Johnny Cash in particular looked up to; Tubb gave Johnny a lot of useful advice early on in his career and acted as an informal mentor. Country through and through, he was at the height of his career in the mid fifties. It was a career which lasted more than half a century during which time he scored numerous hits and helped to popularise country music beyond the strict confines of Nashville and environs. In 1955 he had enjoyed an enormous hit with 'The Yellow Rose Of Texas'.

'I'm With A Crowd But So Alone' was co-written by Tubb and Carl Story, an influential bluegrass musician sometimes referred to as "The Father of Bluegrass Gospel Music".

20. Farther Along. (2.08)

The group returns to religious music at this point following a request from a woman in the studio, probably Marion Keisker. "Would this rover boy's trio play 'Farther Along'?" There have been suggestions in the past that the request came from Elvis' companion on the day, Marilyn Evans, but in a recent interview in 2008 (probably her first on the subject) during which she listened to a recording of the session, she denied this. "I wouldn't pick up a Southern accent that fast." The request does provide a particularly strong piece of evidence in support of the proposition that Johnny Cash was not present when the recordings were made – quite apart of course from the fact that his voice is nowhere to be heard and none of the recorded conversations make direct reference to him.

The rover boy's trio can indeed play 'Farther Along'. The fact that so often they all knew all the words of the religious songs provided a strong flavour of a bygone era when a certain level of social cohesion was achieved, and cultural values shared, through the practice of all children in particular areas learning the same songs. Apart from knowing the words, the trio of vocalists give an excellent close harmony rendition of the song; clear evidence that even at this early stage, their credentials as top notch vocalists were established beyond question.

The lyrics of 'Farther Along' were written in 1911 by an itinerant preacher called Reverend W A Fletcher. A gospel music promoter, JR Baxter, then arranged for the words to be put to music. The theme of the song is that in heaven all truths will be revealed and all questions – in particular those relating to the many injustices in the world – will be answered. To this day the song is included in the repertoires of many of the top traditional country artists.

Just after the song finishes a female voice can be heard to say, "There go the strings," which might refer to the departure of Carl's brothers.

21. Blessed Jesus (Hold My Hand). (1.26)

Jerry Lee was not to be denied. The ensemble now turns its attention to the song he had mentioned just before Elvis launched into 'I'm With A Crowd But So Alone'. His appetite for religious songs was huge. This fairly brief rendering is a vocal duet by Elvis and Jerry Lee with acoustic guitar courtesy, presumably, of Carl. Elvis and Jerry Lee sound as if they have been regular singing partners for years despite a brief breakdown halfway through.

'Blessed Jesus (Hold My Hand)' is essentially a prayer put to music. It is a heartfelt plea for God's protection through life's journey and even more importantly for the believer, the reward of a place in heaven at the end.

22. On The Jericho Road. (0.52)

This song flows almost seamlessly from its predecessor. When after a few bars of the song Elvis says, "Take young Johnny Cash to do this," he surely provides yet more evidence of Johnny's absence.

The Jericho road runs from Jerusalem to Jericho; it is a difficult road, very steep, a place where in the past robberies routinely occurred. In the song it serves as a metaphor for the difficult and perilous journey of life that everybody has to go through on the way to eternal happiness – a journey that can only be successfully negotiated with the help of Jesus in the view of Christian believers. The underlying message of many of the songs is the same, it is just framed in different ways; a bit like country love songs.

Once more the song is an Elvis – Jerry Lee duet with acoustic guitar backing.

23. I Just Can't Make It By Myself (1.04)

This soulful gospel song, initiated once more by Elvis, was written by Herbert Brewster. A trained minister, he experienced a great deal of racial prejudice at the outset of his career when he tried to get work; as a result, he set up the Brewster Theological Clinic. He also worked as a pastor at other churches most notably East Trigg Avenue Baptist Church in Memphis. The congregation was black but quite a lot of white people, including Sam Phillips and Johnny Cash, regularly tuned in to the radio broadcasts of the services. Elvis Presley attended services there from time to time. Yet again the song contains the same message of obedience and reassurance which is found in so many religious songs.

Though afflictions fill my soul
I'm determined to make the goal
I've gotta have Jesus
Cause I just can't make it by myself

Elvis stammers slightly in his enthusiasm to propose the song; in the end he gives up and just starts singing it. It is striking that once he starts singing, in other words once he is in his natural element, his vocals are almost invariably smooth and consistent.

24. Little Cabin Home On The Hill. (0.46)

Just as the previous song is starting to fizzle out, a voice is heard. "Jack said sing some of Bill Monroe." No further encouragement was required following this command, which was presumably passed on from Jack Clement in the control room. The ensemble fire straight into a medley of brief extracts from four Bill Monroe songs; along the way Elvis amuses the others with an imitation of Monroe's high tenor voice.

Kentucky-born Bill Monroe (1911-1996), whose ancestry can be traced back to Scotland, was a towering figure in the history of country music. He was the founder of bluegrass (the name came from his backing group the Blue Grass Boys) and everyone making music that day in the studio had the utmost respect and admiration for him. Bluegrass, in particular the uptempo songs, had a significant influence on the development of rockabilly and in turn, with some adaptation, rock 'n' roll. Carl Perkins described the thrill of playing a John Lee Hooker blues tune to a bluegrass beat.

Bill Monroe was brought up in a musical family and apart from playing mandolin and fiddle, he had a very distinctive high tenor voice ("high lonesome") which soon became an essential element of all traditional bluegrass bands. He added Earl Scruggs to the Blue Grass Boys in 1945; his brilliantly innovative banjo playing proved to be hugely popular with fans. Also included in the line-up at this time was Lester Flatt (with whom Bill Monroe wrote 'Little Cabin Home On The Hill') and this particular grouping, which also featured fiddle and bass, came to be seen as the "Original Bluegrass Band". It included the key elements which came to define the bluegrass genre – breakneck tempos, tight vocal harmonies and technically advanced instrumental breaks. This line-up did not last for very long – Monroe continually changed the personnel in order to give a chance to promising young players – but the songs they recorded in

1946 and 1947 are now regarded as classics and include the four laid down during the Million Dollar Quartet session.

The B-side of Elvis' first single was an uptempo version of Monroe's 'Blue Moon Of Kentucky'. When Elvis met Bill Monroe for the first time he was worried that the great man might be offended by what he had done to his song but on the contrary, he was complimentary, and indeed suggested that his band might lift a few ideas from the Elvis version.

Although Bill Monroe is most closely associated with bluegrass, he also played country and gospel music. He won countless awards in his lifetime and it is noteworthy that he was inducted into the Rock and Roll Hall of Fame as an "early influence". Once more, Elvis and the others were instinctively drawn to musical styles which constituted an important element of the DNA of popular music. In the years that followed, their musical genes found their way into much of the material the quartet produced and passed on to the world.

Elvis recorded a version of this song (though it was entitled 'Little Cabin On The Hill') in 1970.

25. Summertime Is Past And Gone. (0.14)

"Y-y-y-you know what I like?" Without further ado Elvis has a go at the first line of the song but doesn't remember where to go after that. Carl tries to help but it quickly fizzles out. The spirit was keen but the memory weak.

The lyrics of the song are typical of many classic Bill Monroe songs of this era – poignant folksy classics about love and loss.

Summertime is past and gone
And I'm on my way back home
To see the only one I ever loved

Now the moon is shining bright
It lights my pathway tonight
Back to the only one I ever loved

26. I Hear A Sweet Voice Calling. (0.36)

Having failed to ignite the previous song there is some chat about other possibilities – Elvis suggests 'Christmas Time's A Comin'' – but that comes to nothing. Then someone suggests 'I Hear A Sweet Voice Calling' which someone describes as a "pretty thing". They have a go but beyond providing a hilarious opportunity to mimic Bill Monroe's high voice, this one also fails to take off. Clearly the boys did not know their Bill Monroe songs as well as they knew the religious material – but then again they had not learned them all through their childhoods.

Bill Monroe recorded this song in 1946 and then again in 1956; presumably it was the latter version that was fresh in the minds of the ensemble. Following a long established country tradition of tragic tear–jerking songs, often with religious overtones, it is about a dying girl who is sure there will be a place for her in heaven. Popular music has always found room for songs like this. In the seventies Terry Jacks had a major international hit with 'Seasons In The Sun' about a boy dying of cancer.

27. Sweetheart You Done Me Wrong. (0.28)

Elvis initiates this song which seems to take off well with an uptempo bluegrass beat emphasised by someone working a bass drum pedal (or something similar) in time to the music. Reflecting the feel of the song somebody says, "Yeah, sounds like a party." Like the other Bill Monroe songs however, this one soon falls away. Once more the maudlin lyrics are typical of Bill Monroe's music.

171

You told me that your love was true
Sweetheart, I thought the world of you
But now you've left me all alone
I have no one to call my own
Now sweetheart, you've done me wrong

28. Keeper Of The Key. (2.08)

Carl now wonders aloud if anybody knows Wynn Stewart's 'Keeper Of The Key'. He leads the singing with Jerry Lee providing harmonies and positive comments about the song. After a pause Elvis yet again asks about the key – A – and it seems that he might have a go at it himself but this does not happen; Carl sings this one.

The song brings the ensemble into the orbit of one of the most prolific and successful writers of everyday country songs of all time – Harlan Howard, one of four writers of this particular song. Howard's career lasted for more than half a century and his songs have been recorded by countless artists including Patsy Cline, Ray Charles and the Judds. Asked for his definition of a good country song Howard is reported to have said, "Three chords and the truth."

The song had been a minor hit for Wynn Stewart earlier that year. Along with Buck Owens and Merle Haggard, Stewart was associated with West Coast country music and the Bakersfield sound – stripped down honky-tonk, a driving beat, with the instrumental emphasis on electric guitars ahead of steel guitars.

As the song finishes Jerry Lee says, "Yeah, that's the way I done it... on the piano... a while ago." Does he mean the ensemble played the song earlier in the day or does he mean he did a few weeks ago in another context? This is not clear.

29/42. Crazy Arms. (0.17; 3.36)

Initially Elvis just has a brief pass at this song which comes to nothing – he is just doodling.

'Crazy Arms' was Jerry Lee's first Sun single and had been released a few days before the Million Dollar Quartet session took place. In some ways it was a surprising choice of song for the launch of Jerry Lee's recording career since it had been a major hit for Ray Price and his Cherokee Cowboys just a few months before. It spent 20 weeks at the top of the country charts – proof that despite the arrival of the young rockabilly devils on the scene there was still room for a good traditional country song. It was co-written by Ralph Mooney, a highly accomplished exponent of the steel guitar, country music's signature instrument, which features prominently on the Ray Price version.

Jerry Lee and Sam clearly believed that with its swinging 4/4 shuffle rhythm and soaring melody, it was a song Jerry Lee could put his own mark on.

For his part Jerry Lee was doubtless keen to show it off to the assembled group. However he had to wait until later in the session, when Elvis was otherwise engaged, to play something approaching the full version, in his own unmistakeable swaggering stomping style – a star performance by a star in waiting.

30/35. Don't Forbid Me. (1.19; 0.50)

"Have you heard Pat Boone's new record?" asks Elvis by way of introduction to 'Don't Forbid Me'. Elvis tells everyone the song had been written for him and that a copy of it had been "over my house for ages, man. I never did see it, so much junk lyin' around". Elvis kicks it off with Carl providing rhythm guitar. "That's Pat Boone?"

says Jerry Lee during a vocal pause. Someone else says, "He's got a hit, man."

'Crazy Arms' was a piece of straightforward country music from which the guys moved effortlessly to the clean-cut mainstream pop of 'Don't Forbid Me' which Elvis returned to a few minutes later. They were easily able to turn their hands to a wide variety of musical styles; for them what mattered most was the quality of the song.

'Don't Forbid Me' was written by Charles Singleton (who later co-wrote the Frank Sinatra hit 'Strangers In The Night') and recorded by Pat Boone in November 1956; though his reading of the song sounds straight and fairly unexciting, it provided him with his second number one hit in 1957.

31. Too Much Monkey Business (0.05)

32/34/39. Brown Eyed Handsome Man (1.14; 1.53; 0.17)

Jerry Lee tries to generate interest in 'Too Much Monkey Business' but Carl, who says shortly afterwards that he has just "come off a five-week tour with Chuck Berry", quickly moves them onto another Chuck Berry song, 'Brown Eyed Handsome Man'. Not long afterwards Elvis responds to a question about 'Too Much Monkey Business' making it clear he prefers 'Brown Eyed Handsome Man'. He says, "It's all right but I like this one better."

They have real fun with the song, stumbling over the words, stopping and starting, and getting some help with the lyrics from one of the women present in the studio. One or possibly more children can be heard in the background adding to the party atmosphere.

Whilst there is no one person who can legitimately claim to have invented rock 'n' roll, Chuck Berry surely has as strong a claim as any artist alive or dead. It was inevitable that the ensemble would come across one of his songs sooner or later. Their sheer delight in the irresistible fun qualities of the song is palpable, although they break down several times as they try to get the words right.

Despite their apparent preferences, when released in 1956 on the Chess label (in both 7″ 45 rpm and 10″ 78 rpm), 'Too Much Monkey Business' was in fact the A-side and 'Brown Eyed Handsome Man' the B-side. It was Chuck Berry's fifth single and reached number four on *Billboard's* R&B chart.

Despite the light-hearted feel of the song it was inspired by the kind of racial tensions which were all too prevalent in parts of fifties America. It was written by Berry after a visit to California when he had witnessed a Hispanic man being arrested by a policeman in questionable circumstances, an incident which prompted a bystander to intervene on his behalf. One commentator has surmised that the song is subtly challenging racial attitudes in suggesting for instance that the very white and very beautiful Venus de Milo would "lose both her arms in a wrestling match to win a brown eyed handsome man" (ie a black man). Elvis later said that Chuck Berry told him the song was originally called 'Brown Skinned Handsome Man' but that, "They made me change it."

One point that emerges from the sessions is a clear lack of racial prejudice on the part of members of the quartet – no mean feat at a time when it was so prevalent. Then again, their eclectic taste in and respect for all types of music by black and white artists would surely have made it illogical for them to have held any such views.

These songs, along with many others, are now standards which have been covered by innumerable artists. For all the new sounds that came out of Britain during the Swinging Sixties, it is striking to note how many of Chuck Berry's songs were relied upon to populate albums, even those by some who would go on to record fine material of their own. 'Too Much Monkey Business' was covered by the Hollies, the Yardbirds and the Kinks. The Beatles recorded it for a live appearance on the BBC Light Programme; and that was just one song. The Rolling Stones modelled much of their early work on Chuck Berry's pioneering style and the Beatles covered a number of his songs including 'Roll Over Beethoven' and 'Rock And Roll Music' on their albums. The worldwide influence of Chuck Berry on popular music for well over half a century cannot be overstated.

To the musical base of rhythm and blues he added simple catchy melodies, hooky country-style guitar riffs and witty tongue-in-cheek lyrics all about the things that mattered most to a younger audience such as cars, dancing and the opposite sex.

Carl Perkins had got to know Chuck when the pair found themselves on the same bills in the mid fifties. He immediately recognised Berry's importance and was struck by his wide musical knowledge. As well as modern stars such as Bill Monroe, he was well acquainted with the music of hugely influential figures such as Jimmie Rodgers, "The Singing Brakeman", one of the founders of modern country music who melded blues and white rural music with New Orleans-style jazz. Carl also identified with his childhood. "He told me about how he was raised very poor, very tough. He had a hard life. He was a good guy. I really liked him."

Chuck Berry's influence is by no means limited to his music; that was only part of the story. He was also one of those early pioneers who injected a high degree of showmanship into their performances – who can hear the words "duck walk" without thinking of Chuck Berry? Ever since the late fifties, no matter how much talent artists might possess, they have also needed something special about their appearance and stage presence to make them stand out from a very crowded field. In every respect Chuck Berry was right up there with the most important and original artists of the fifties.

As with Elvis, Chuck Berry had a massive appeal to the rapidly growing teenage market. He gave them a style of music they could identify with because of its uptempo rough-edged sound and lyrics about their everyday concerns; music that gave them a way to be defiantly different from the older generation. Elvis recognised this and had regularly featured 'Maybellene', Berry's debut single, in his live shows.

Another similarity between Elvis and Chuck Berry was the fact that each produced what many critics have agreed was their best music, their genius in its purest form, during comparatively short spells with their first labels: Sun in the case of Elvis, Chess in the case of Chuck Berry. It was during this period that he produced such enduring classics as 'Roll Over Beethoven' and 'Johnny B Goode'.

Chuck Berry set standards that countless others aspired to. One of the first musicians to be inducted into the Rock and Roll Hall of Fame when it opened its doors in 1986, it was said of him that he "laid the groundwork for not only a rock 'n' roll sound but a rock 'n' roll stance". Keith Richards said, "Chuck was my man. He was the one who made me say 'I want to play guitar'. Suddenly I knew what I wanted to do." John Lennon said that "if you tried to give rock 'n' roll another name, you might call it Chuck Berry".

All members of the Million Dollar Quartet recognised him as a towering figure in their musical world and all absorbed aspects of his music and showmanship into their own highly distinctive styles – though it was Elvis and Jerry Lee who focused most on developing the showmanship aspect.

Eavesdropping on Elvis and the others talking excitedly about Chuck Berry and which of his songs they prefer, what strikes the listener is that these young guys were not a bunch of aloof stars but rather wildly enthusiastic music fans, just like the hordes who came to see them and bought their records week in week out.

All members of the quartet had grown up loving nothing better than making music with their friends in their homes, and Elvis in particular continued to do so for a while after he was famous. Although the setting for the Million Dollar Quartet session is a recording studio, the listener is also hearing what one of these informal get-togethers would have sounded like, even to the extent of having non-musician friends chattering away in the background. Although each is associated in the public mind with particular types of music it is clear above all else that essentially they just loved music period.

33. Out Of Sight, Out Of Mind. (0.37)

"Hey I'll tell you one I like." Elvis' knowledge of songs was seemingly inexhaustible. This pop song, with its doo wop crooning, was an ideal vehicle for Elvis' smooth soaring tenor; and his simple acoustic guitar backing fitted the feel to a tee. It was first recorded earlier in 1956 by the Five Keys and was written by Ivory Joe Hunter and Clyde Otis, two black men who had considerable success in a white dominated world.

Otis was one of the very first black executives of a major record company – Mercury. He produced records by Brook Benton, Dinah Washington and Sarah Vaughan, amongst many others. He also wrote or co-wrote hundreds of songs which were recorded by artists from Bobby Darin to Aretha Franklin. Ivory Joe Hunter started out as a rhythm and blues singer and pianist but latterly he also achieved recognition in the fields of blues and country. Each man enjoyed a substantial degree of success and 'Out Of Sight, Out Of Mind' was merely one passable piece of pop they conjured up together; a small part of a huge body of work. Hunter alone is estimated to have written or co-written more than 7,000 songs.

The year after the Million Dollar Quartet session, Elvis invited Hunter to visit him at Graceland. They spent a day together, talking and singing songs. Hunter said later that he was struck by Elvis' courtesy and spirituality. Even at this early stage he felt moved to say, "I think he's one of the greatest."

36. You Belong To My Heart. (1.10)

"You know a song that'll come back some day?" says Elvis. "It'll make a splash… it's an old popular song." This one could be said to have an interesting and unusual provenance for a song plucked out of the air in a jam session in Memphis. It is an English language version of the Mexican Bolero song 'Solamente Una Vez' meaning 'Only One Time', which was popular both in Mexico and Cuba. It was written by Agustín Lara (1897-1970), a Mexican singer who was also a prolific composer. He often wrote songs with Spanish themes some of which, such as 'Granada', have become standards.

The English language version (whose lyrics bear no relation to the original Spanish language lyrics) was featured in the Walt Disney film *The Three Caballeros*. Bing Crosby also recorded a version in 1945. Subsequent cover versions have included such diverse artists as Gene Autry, Cliff Richard and the Three Tenors. The lyrics were written by Ray Gilbert whose many writing credits included 'Zip-A-Dee-Doo-Dah' in 1947.

Elvis sings the song, with effortless and convincing passion, adding colour by mixing the English and Spanish lyrics, and humour by camping up his vocal delivery.

37. Is It So Strange. (1.21)

Country singer Faron Young, aka "The Singing Sheriff", wrote 'Is It So Strange'. One of the most popular purveyors of smooth honky-tonk of his day, his career lasted around 30 years and included major hits such as 'Hello Walls', 'Live Fast, Love Hard, Die Young' and 'It's Four In The Morning' (the last-named being his only UK hit).

Before he starts singing Elvis jokes that Faron had sent the song to him but that he, "Didn't want to give me none of it. He wanted it all". This is presumably a (slightly sheepish-sounding) reference to the practice of compelling writers to give up a large part of the writing credit if they wanted Elvis to record their songs. In fact Elvis recorded it for RCA in 1957.

During this number, which Elvis sings solo and accompanies himself on acoustic guitar, a child's voice can be heard in the background, giggling at times. When Elvis stops singing he is addressed by a woman: "My little granddaughter (Susan) is a big fan of yours, would you put your name here." Elvis, by now very used to dealing with such situations, displays characteristic courtesy, completing the transaction with a very polite, "Thank you ma'am," as if he was the one being done the favour.

38. That's When Your Heartaches Begin. (4.58)

Elvis starts talking about this song, which he had clearly mentioned before at some point. "I lost the dub on it." This is the longest individual song by nearly a minute. It has a particularly treasured place in the history of Elvis Presley since it was one of the two songs that started it all; one of the songs he recorded at the Memphis Recording Service for his mother in July 1953. He says he had lost the disc but according to other reports he gave it to a friend of his who had provided the money for him to make the recording in the first place. By 1956 his voice is transformed – it is now smooth and assured, delivering his own interpretation of the melody with confident aplomb.

He next recorded it in rather different circumstances for RCA in 1957, when it appeared as the B-side of 'All Shook Up'. The song's three composers Fred Fisher, William Raskin and Billy Hill were all born in the late nineteenth century and were mainly associated with music from a different, bygone world. Fred Fisher, for instance, wrote music to accompany silent films and also co-wrote 'Whispering Grass'. Billy Hill, one of the most successful songsmiths on Tin Pan

Alley in the thirties, co-wrote 'Have You Ever Been Lonely' and 'The Old Man Of The Mountain'.

'That's When Your Heartaches Begin' was first recorded in 1937 and in 1941 the Ink Spots also recorded a version which might well have been the one Elvis heard when he started to take an interest in the sounds coming out of his father's radio set. The Ink Spots were a popular black vocal group whose heartfelt songs were characterised by sweet melodies with soaring vocals and gentle arpeggiated acoustic guitar backing. The conservative, unthreatening nature of their songs and their clean-cut image made them acceptable to white audiences. They were major contributors to the development of the doo wop style of popular music. Their influence on Elvis is crystal clear on some of his later songs, in particular 'Are You Lonesome Tonight'. A particular feature of such songs, which Elvis here demonstrates, is the practice of speaking one or more of the verses in an emotionally charged voice – something he did with considerable skill in various songs over the years.

Elvis expresses the view that if someone could sing it right, "a guy with a really deep voice", it would sell. Could this be yet another reference to the self-evident absence of Johnny Cash?

40. Rip It Up. (0.23)

Elvis has fun with this one which he does in response to a request from a spectator; but he only really does the opening line. He deliberately gets the opening words wrong: "It's Saturday night and I just got paid… laid." This caught the mood of much of the session. It is delightful to listen to these artists simply being themselves and not putting on a show manipulated to fit in with the demands of promoters or television producers.

Writers Robert Blackwell (no relation to Otis Blackwell) and John Marascalco were certainly an appropriate presence at the Million

Dollar Quartet session – even if their contribution can be measured in seconds. Like the quartet they were in the early stages of their stellar careers. They contributed to the composition of some of the most memorable rhythm and blues and rock 'n' roll hits of the golden era of the fifties and early sixties. Together they wrote 'Good Golly Miss Molly' and 'Ready, Teddy' for Little Richard. 'Rip It Up' was recorded by Bill Haley and his Comets and also by Little Richard in 1956. Marascalco also wrote songs with Fats Domino and a young Harry Nilsson amongst many others. Blackwell went on to work extensively as a producer and was involved with the early careers of stars such as Ray Charles, Sam Cooke and Sly and the Family Stone. Later in his career he produced some songs for Bob Dylan's album *Shot Of Love*.

41. I'm Gonna Bid My Blues Goodbye. (0.55)

"Did you ever hear ole Hank Snow do a song called 'I'm Gonna Bid My Blues Goodbye'?" With that Elvis launches into a brief take on the song, once more, it appears, accompanying himself on acoustic guitar – unlike Carl, his ability level was merely competent.

Close to the height of his career in the mid fifties, Hank Snow was one of the leading country artists of the immediate post-war era, whose inclusion in the session was highly fitting. All four members of the quartet grew up listening to his music on the radio and for all of them he was something of a hero as well as a strong influence.

A natural showman, Snow, whose main early influence was Jimmie Rodgers, wrote, recorded and regularly performed a clutch of classic hits including 'I'm Moving On' and 'The Golden Rocket' in the fifties. Born in Canada he eventually became an American citizen in 1958 and settled near Nashville – the logical place for him to live. His career spanned over 60 years and when he was 61, he became the oldest country performer to achieve a number one hit, with a song called 'Hello Love'.

Elvis brings the song to an end and moves away from the microphone. There is chatter, a door opening and closing and he is gone. His involvement in the music is now at an end. The last thing he can be heard saying is, "That's why I hate to get started in these jam sessions, I'm always the last one to leave, always."

There is a brief pause and then Jerry Lee can be heard seizing his opportunity and starting up on the piano which he now plays solo until the end.

43. That's My Desire (preceded by Crazy Arms). (2.02)

Before he starts 'That's My Desire', Jerry Lee grabs his turn in the limelight with a swaggering version of his first Sun single, 'Crazy Arms', released at the beginning of December. This time he was able to play it all the way through – earlier he could only deliver a brief snatch of the song because Elvis was still in charge of things at that point. This was the start of a run of five solo songs by Jerry Lee.

He does full justice to 'Crazy Arms'. His virtuoso display provides a detailed picture of the Jerry Lee Lewis piano technique, a veritable master class; the pounding left hand, the flowery embellishments with the right, the syncopation, it was all there. Johnny Cash later described him as "the master of the keyboard". The piano playing is remarkably clear unlike Jerry Lee's vocals which sound as if they were laid down in a different room from the microphone.

Jerry Lee plus piano really could cover all angles – a backing band was merely an optional extra. The song is now a country/honky-tonk standard which has been covered by everyone from Bing Crosby to Linda Ronstadt. Perhaps the quartet's spontaneous attraction to such material was a sign of the kind of musical instinct that led them to be so successful themselves.

After 'Crazy Arms' Jerry Lee moves onto classic, old school pop territory with the kind of song that his and his friends' parents might have listened to. 'That's My Desire' was co-written by Helmy Kresa who was the principal arranger and orchestrator for Irving Berlin. Since Berlin could not read or write music, he got Kresa to fulfil this role for the songs he wrote at the piano. Amongst many others, Kresa worked on 'White Christmas'.

Over the years the song has been covered in various styles by artists including Louis Armstrong, Dion and the Belmonts and Frankie Laine.

44. End Of The Road. (1.44)

"Sing 'End Of The Road'," is the request from a female present, possibly Marilyn Evans. Jerry Lee says, "I might as well do another one" with an audible smile. 'End Of The Road' is one of the few songs recorded by Jerry Lee which he wrote himself. Again he gives a star performance which brings out the very best in a routine but highly catchy little song. Unaccompanied, his playing once more takes the breath away; his legendary skills are already well established and clearly in evidence.

45. Black Bottom Stomp. (1.11)

This rollicking jazz instrumental, imbued with hints of ragtime and Dixieland, provides Jerry Lee with an opportunity to show off another side of his effortlessly dazzling piano skills. On some early Million Dollar Quartet releases it is referred to as "Jerry's Boogie." It was written by Ferdinand Joseph LaMothe (other spellings of this last name are often quoted), better known as Jelly Roll Morton, in 1925, and was originally called 'Queen Of Spades'. He recorded it in 1926. His version was a multilayered musical affair. In one fairly brief number he maintained listener interest with a range of techniques – stomps, breaks, backbeat, two–beat, four-beat, melody played all over the keyboard, increasing volume, reducing volume – and Jerry Lee does much the same in his interpretation. It might have been impromptu but it revealed the studious nature of his exploration and understanding of the music of key figures in the development of popular music from an early age.

Jelly Roll and Jerry Lee had other things in common apart from a gift for playing the piano, in particular a confident belief in their own abilities which regularly crossed over into arrogance. Jelly Roll often claimed that he had single-handedly invented modern jazz. Whilst his contribution was undoubtedly considerable, such a claim has been challenged by many commentators, although it is true that his number 'Jelly Roll Blues' was in 1915 the first published jazz composition. He is even said to have falsified details of his birth date in order to make the claim more credible. Jerry Lee got up to similar tricks when it came to his early marriages. The pair also had colourful private lives with an impressive array of relationships with women to their credit.

46. You're The Only Star In My Blue Heaven. (1.12)

The inclusion of a Gene Autry song creates a connection between the Million Dollar Quartet and cowboy music, which has been an important strand of country music for as long as there has been country music. He was one of the most successful of a small number of singing cowboys which also included Roy Rogers. He is probably best known for the western song 'Back In The Saddle Again' although he was also responsible for some favourite Christmas songs including 'Rudolph The Red-Nosed Reindeer' and 'Here Comes Santa Claus'. Jerry Lee brings the song to an abrupt end as Elvis plus some others leave the building; he gets up to join in the farewells.

47. Elvis Says Goodbye. (0.40)

During the goodbyes the irrepressible Jerry Lee can be heard to sing the line, "You're the only star in my blue heaven," a couple of times. Elvis says, "Good night boys, I'll see you again," suggesting that the session has gone on well into the evening. Jerry Lee says, "Yeah, mighty glad to have met y'all." Elvis is heard saying "Thank you sir" to someone.

It is poignant to think that these casual events, which the participants probably intended to repeat some time, never in fact happened again. It had been a once in a lifetime event. Johnny Cash, Carl Perkins and Jerry Lee Lewis did subsequently get together a few times, but never all four. Elvis' fame took him away from the possibility of such carefree spontaneous encounters for the rest of his life.

The recordings, a remarkable piece of audio archaeology, provide an extremely rare glimpse into a crucial stage in the development of western popular music. In the course of an unguarded and uninhibited jam session – without pre-planning or pre-agreed set lists worked out by managers and producers, four giants revealed the musical DNA which they would transmit to the world. As Colin Escott said, "This is what the founding fathers of rock 'n' roll music heard and played solely for the love of playing it."

8.

Reunions

The Survivors Live

It could have been one of the major musical happenings of the seventies, and a shot in the arm for all four careers, every one of which was in historical decline. "The Million Dollar Quartet Rides Again" would have been the hottest ticket in town. A national tour, endless analytical documentaries on television, merchandising mania, talk show appearances and advertisements for the new album all culminating in a sell-out gig at a massive auditorium in New York – the video of the show would then have been a best seller. However, as with the magic of the original session, it could only work with Elvis on board and Tom Parker would never have agreed to it; his boy didn't share the limelight with anybody, not if he had anything to do with it. Then Elvis' death in 1977 put an end to any such lingering thoughts forever, just as John Lennon's murder in 1980 snuffed out any chance of the Beatles coming together again. A formal reunion was not even a theoretical possibility.

After 1977 there were, of course, times when the remaining members of the quartet found themselves on the same television show or present at the same awards ceremony. However there were also a few specific occasions when the trio did get together and make music together, and some commentators did loosely describe such occurrences as reunions of the Million Dollar Quartet – though in reality this is not what they were.

In 1981, Johnny Cash was touring Europe with a new version of his troupe known as the Great Eighties Eight. Along with Jerry Lee Lewis and Carl Perkins he was one of the stars slated to appear at a rockabilly music festival in Rotterdam – the Rockabilly Reunion. In the course of the evening of April 19 the trio got together for an encore to Johnny's section of the show, and sang some old songs, much to the delight of the audience. The audience particularly loved it when Jerry Lee followed Carl onto the stage and said, "God bless you – you got a piano over there?"

Johnny was due to play a solo show at the Sporthalle in Böblingen, near Stuttgart, on April 21 and, as it happened, neither Jerry Lee nor Carl was performing that night. After some deliberation by the artists and their respective management teams, the idea emerged for the three stars to appear together during the second half of Johnny's show on April 21 – and for the event to be recorded for subsequent release. It was not thought of as a Million Dollar Quartet reunion but memories of that day in December 1956 doubtless crossed the minds of some. Almost all of the songs selected for the occasion would have fitted easily into the selection the quartet hit upon that day.

In some ways it was as if the intervening quarter of a century had evaporated and they were continuing where they left off after a short break, minus one quarter of the group. As in 1956, it all sounded fairly rough around the edges although this time they did play complete songs for a paying audience. The emphasis was on informality and a lot of high-spirited fun for all concerned. The trio took the opportunity to play some of their favourite songs in an unreconstituted display of classic country, rockabilly, gospel and rock 'n' roll.

They took turns at leading on some of the old favourites including 'Peace In The Valley' which was featured in the 1956 session and which, poignantly, they dedicated to Elvis; he was there in spirit.

Other than that they went for some of the songs that made them famous. Carl was first to join Johnny on stage and it wasn't long before he gave the fans the one they really wanted to hear – 'Blue Suede Shoes' – although it sounded more like a bit of fun pop music than the revolutionary, game-changing explosion that was released in 1955.

Jerry Lee joined everybody on stage after Carl had performed a few songs. He raised the roof with 'Whole Lot Of Shakin' Going On'. In marked contrast to 1957, when Sam Phillips had been concerned about the sexual nature of Jerry Lee's delivery of the song, everyone knew that in the liberated age they now lived in no-one would be bothered in the slightest by his current take on the lyrics: "My name is Jerry Lee Lewis, love to do it all night long." Also featured was the underrated Cash classic 'Get Rhythm'. Most of the other choices were old songs. A robust version of 'Will The Circle Be Unbroken', which might have been sung at the original session before the tapes started rolling, was a particular crowd pleaser.

An album was released in 1982 with the title *The Survivors Live*. The other tracks were: 'I Forgot To Remember To Forget', the old Elvis song; 'Goin' Down The Road Feelin' Bad', an old traditional song also known sometimes as 'Lonesome Road Blues' and recorded by many artists including Woody Guthrie and Bill Monroe; 'That Silver Haired Daddy Of Mine', another old song co-written by Gene Autry; 'Matchbox', the blues song re-worked by Carl Perkins, which he had recorded back in 1956 prior to the start of the Million Dollar Quartet session, indeed the principal reason he had gone into the studio that day; 'I'll Fly Away', written in 1929 and one of the most frequently recorded gospel songs ever; 'Rockin' My Life Away', a Jerry Lee Lewis classic that combines rock 'n' roll and boogie woogie and is a perfect vehicle for his compulsive piano riffs; and 'I Saw The Light', written and originally performed by Hank Williams and now a country/gospel standard.

There were other songs which failed to make it onto the final list: 'Rockabilly Fever' featuring Carl Perkins, a medley of boogie-woogie numbers played by Jerry Lee Lewis, and 'When The Saints Go Marching In', featuring the entire Great Eighties Eight plus the two special guests. For the earlier show in Rotterdam, the trio also sang 'Daddy Sang Bass', a fixture in Johnny Cash's live repertoire which was written by Carl Perkins.

Johnny Cash wrote the sleeve notes with the kind of comments, about Carl in particular, relating to his alcoholism, only a very close friend would get away with. Talking about the days when they toured together regularly he said, "Sundays were unusually bad days for Carl. The stores were closed and if he had forgotten to get a double supply on Saturday, he would tremble and sweat backstage. Once on the stage, the audience never knew how he was suffering." Of Jerry Lee and his exceptional musical gift allied to his religious anguish he said, "His personal relationship with the Giver of that talent is his personal affair."

The critical response to the album in 1982 was not particularly enthusiastic. It is never easy to produce live albums which attract a lot of praise from commentators; it was particularly difficult when the project had been thrown together at such short notice and when the artists were turning out material they had performed thousands of times before.

Detractors might say that in contrast to 1956, when the tapes rolled and a kind of magic was preserved forever, the tapes that rolled in 1981 did not record anything very special. The music the trio produced sounded rather dated and safe. The singles they produced in the fifties at Sun, and the kind of musical magic captured at the session on December 4, 1956 were a different story altogether. Then they were young, new, different and edgy. Most parents and authorities felt threatened and unsettled by them. Ironically, they had helped to create a permanent demand among young people for ever more groundbreaking artists with the power to shock – so that each new wave of young fans could have their own heroes who upset their parents just as the members of the Million Dollar Quartet had done years before. That said, the album did serve to emphasise the point that the music they had created in their heyday had genuine enduring quality, and was still capable of generating visceral excitement for people, many of whom were not born in 1956.

Class of '55

Amidst a massive publicity effort, a well organised get-together took place in 1985, roughly marking the 30th anniversary of the musical careers of the three survivors of the Million Dollar Quartet plus Roy Orbison, standing in for Elvis. These four had performed as a unit before, in 1977, when they appeared on Johnny Cash's glitzy Christmas special. By way of tribute to Elvis they sang 'This Train Is Bound For Glory' after fulsome introductory praise by Johnny Cash. This traditional American gospel song, first recorded in 1925, was chosen in recognition of Elvis' love of religious music.

The meat of the 1985 project was a four-day recording session which produced the album *Class of '55: Memphis Rock & Roll Homecoming*. The very fact that the year quoted is 1955 not 1956 confirmed that the project was not specifically related to the Million Dollar Quartet session. Rather it was a general tribute to the emergence of rock 'n' roll in Memphis in the heady Sun years of the early fifties and in particular the music produced by Sam Phillips on the Sun label. That said, bringing together the surviving members and adding a fourth with a highly distinctive singing voice suggests that thoughts of the Million Dollar Quartet were part of the creative process that led to the project taking shape. All of the principals showed inevitable signs of age. All wore glasses to read the lyrics – in Roy's case they were shaded to protect his chronically weak eyes. Carl was sporting his latest rug-like wig. Johnny and Roy had put on a fair bit of weight. Jerry Lee had a few wrinkles.

The producer chosen for the project was Chips Moman who had been in charge of Elvis' 1969 album *From Elvis In Memphis* which marked a return to form following years of lightweight movie soundtrack albums. Recording took place in Memphis over four days, two at the reconstituted Sun Studio – a project Sam had advised on – and two at Moman's American Sound Studio.

The sessions were turned into major media events which included a high profile press conference with the principals in attendance. Everything was filmed and later became the subject of a television special. Elvis' presence was evoked in traded memories and the lyrics of some of the songs. Jerry Lee was a little less deferential than some when he said Elvis would have been there too, "If he hadn't of overshot the runway".

Recalling the event, Jack Clement, the engineer for the original Million Dollar Quartet session, described it as "one big party... everybody had a big time". There was a lot of reminiscing, a lot of hugs, a lot of laughs and some tears prompting Johnny Cash to call it a "lovefest". Johnny, Carl and Roy were particularly close friends but the demands of constant touring meant they rarely saw each other. This was even true of Johnny and Roy who were next door neighbours in Hendersonville, near Nashville. Four days in each other's company was a real bonus.

Sam Phillips presents Carl Perkins with a plaque marking one million sales of 'Blue Suede Shoes'. COLIN ESCOTT/MICHAEL OCHS ARCHIVES/
GETTY IMAGES

Elvis preparing for one of his ground-breaking appearances on the *Ed Sullivan Show*. Guitarist Scotty Moore is in the background.
CBS PHOTO ARCHIVE/GETTY IMAGES

Left: Sun Studio, Memphis. At the time of the Million Dollar Quartet session in 1956 the unit on the corner was home to Mrs Taylor's restaurant. DAVID O. BAILEY/ALAMY Right: Roy Orbison in the late fifties. Sam Phillips failed to see his potential as a soulful ballad singer.
MICHAEL OCHS ARCHIVES/CORBIS

Downtown Memphis in the fifties including a sign for Elvis' favourite clothes shop, Lansky Brothers.

Elvis at Lansky's. From an early age he wore clothes that made him stand out from the crowd.

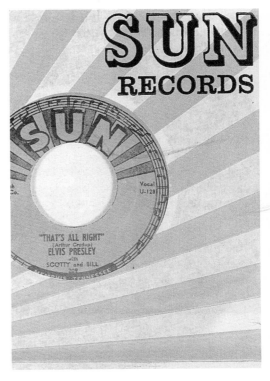

The single that launched Elvis' career in 1954. He was already a major star by the time of the Million Dollar Quartet session in 1956. GAB ARCHIVE/REDFERNS

Sam Phillips sells Sun Records to Shelby Singleton in 1969. SUN ENT CORP

One of Sam Phillip's pioneering ideas – an all-girl radio station. Marion Keisker is second left; Sam's then wife Becky is front right with necklace. MISSISSIPPI VALLEY COLLECTION

Johnny Cash and the Tennessee Three in 1968, by now featuring W S 'Fluke' Holland on drums. THE BILL MILLER COLLECTION

Johnny Cash with special guest Carl Perkins on his television show in 1971. Johnny said they were 'friends for life'. BETTMANN/CORBIS

Left: Johnny Cash with Jerry Lee Lewis during a sound check before a concert in Nashville in 1982. THOMAS S. ENGLAND/TIME & LIFE PICTURES/GETTY IMAGES

Right: Class of '55. Memphis rock & roll homecoming. Roy Orbison stood in for the late Elvis Presley on the album which commemorated the hugely influential music which emerged from Memphis in the fifties.

Once more Roy Orbison makes up a quartet, on this occasion for the 1977 Johnny Cash Christmas Special. The quartet sang 'This Train Is Bound For Glory' which they dedicated to Elvis. ALAN MESSER (WWW.ALANMESSER.COM)

The surviving members of the Million Dollar Quartet backstage. In 1981 after coming together by chance in Germany they recorded a live album together. KIRK WEST (WWW.KIRKWESTPHOTOGRAPHY.COM)

Million Dollar Quartet – the musical stage show. Apart from the Sam Phillips role, candidates for the leading parts were mainly chosen on musical ability. MINNEAPOLIS STAR TRIBUNE/ZUMA PRESS/CORBIS

Last man standing. Jerry Lee Lewis performing during the finale of the stage show on Broadway in September 2010.

Despite much bonhomie, there were considerable logistical and technical problems, not to mention the challenges of managing four powerful personalities and their respective drug and alcohol preferences. Carl Perkins said of Jerry Lee Lewis that he was "wilder than a guinea hen" throughout the sessions. Johnny Cash later related one incident when Jerry Lee tried to walk on his hands causing lots of pills to pour out of his pockets onto the floor right in front of a photographer. Some things hadn't changed.

Unlike *The Survivors Live,* the songs chosen for the project did not include any that were featured in the Million Dollar Quartet session in 1956. This was meant to be a new musical statement though of course one that paid tribute to the past. Some new songs were written for the album which reflected the story of rock 'n' roll and which looked back nostalgically to the early fifties.

The standout song was the album's opener, 'Birth Of Rock And Roll', written by Carl Perkins and his son Greg. The lyrics neatly summed up the way it all started.

The other songs were:

'Sixteen Candles'
This doo wop classic is the only song that actually dates from the Million Dollar Quartet era. Jerry Lee's delivery is characteristically over the top. Some might say a song about a man's passionate romantic feelings for a young girl was not the most inspired choice for Jerry Lee. Perhaps it was ironic.

'Class Of 55'
A sentimental rear-mirror take on the old days sparked by a chance meeting between old friends. Co-written by producer Chips Moman, the song, a slice of soulful pop sung by Carl, was unashamedly nostalgic.

'Waymore's Blues'
A chugalong piece of countrified blues written by Waylon Jennings. The quartet share lead vocals and adapt the lyrics to make them more relevant to the project in hand, part of which was the powerful memory of Elvis. Jerry Lee adds vocal embellishments in the manner of a hellfire preacher.

'We Remember The King'
This song, written by all four participants, is a sentimental tribute to Elvis; the message is enhanced by the rich gravitas of Johnny Cash's baritone voice. As with other songs on the album the song is heavily produced with the addition of a chorus, brass and strings – the complete antithesis of Sam Phillips' approach at Sun.

'Coming Home'
An emotional rendering by Roy Orbison of the story of a person's journey to some kind of religious revelation. Roy's emotionally penetrative voice shows him to be a worthy stand-in even for a singer as great as Elvis. There were times during the sessions when Roy, who was suffering from a heavy cold, chose to record some of his contributions away from the camera and any unnecessary personnel. He was still struggling with unimaginable personal tragedy. His wife had been killed in a motorbike accident and two of his three sons had died in a house fire.

'Rock And Roll (Fais Do Do)'
This is a fairly bland piece of sanitised rock 'n' roll pop, once more over-produced and with outdated, cringe-worthy lyrics.

'Keep My Motor Running'
This straightforward piece of bluesy rock owes a great deal to Chuck Berry for the music as well as the lyrics. Jerry Lee leads and Carl provides some tasty old style rockabilly guitar. Once more the addition of embellishments such as a prominent horn section fills out the sound without adding much. A case of more is less. It is like an anodyne variety show version of the rough and edgy sounds of the fifties.

'I Will Rock And Roll With You'
This song, written and sung by Johnny Cash, was originally released on his 1978 album *Gone Girl* (his 58th). Johnny personalised the lyrics to suit the theme of the album.

'Big Train (From Memphis)'
The grand finale. Sun originals Sam Phillips and Jack Clement were in attendance for the recording and joined everyone else to sing on the chorus. There were other notables in attendance too: Dave Edmunds, Rick Nelson, June Carter Cash, and the Judds. The song was written by John Fogerty who said his inspiration came from the old Sun records of the early fifties. Some also interpreted the song as a metaphorical tribute to Elvis.

At nearly eight minutes the song was very much on the long side with an ending that stretched for miles and which included vocal snippets of some of the most famous Sun songs, including 'That's All Right (Mama)' and 'Blue Suede Shoes'.

In contrast to the singles the quartet had released earlier in their career, the songs on the album sounded tame and complacent. It was probably an inevitable consequence of the passage of so many years. Neither critics nor fans went for the album in a big way – it briefly reached number 15 in the *Billboard* country charts and then dropped back. Its commercial prospects were not helped by legal wrangles which resulted in the album not being well promoted.

The album purported to be a return visit of sorts to the glory days of Sun *et al* in the fifties but with the possible exception of Carl Perkins' opener, it lacked the spirit of those heady times. The fact that Chips Moman applied so many production embellishments didn't help. He did not appear to understand that for the Million Dollar Quartet and their ilk, the best music was the most stripped down. There was irony in the fact that much was made in the songs of the magic of the early Sun sound which Moman singularly failed to recapture.

The sessions were later turned into a television special by Dick Clark Productions, *Coming Home: A Rockin' Reunion*, which was broadcast in 1989. They were also covered extensively in the press, in particular *The Commercial Appeal*, the mid south's biggest selling newspaper.

A series of interviews were recorded as part of the sessions and released as *Interviews From The Class of '55 Recording Sessions* which in 1987 won Grammy Award for Best Spoken Word Album for the four performers plus producer Chips Moman, Sam Phillips and Rick Nelson.

Tapes/Bootlegs/Releases

When the final goodbyes had been said and everybody had left the studio on December 4, 1956, it was, for Jack Clement, the end of another day's work, albeit quite a special one. He put the tapes of the session in metal containers and then put them away in a cupboard. He told the participants that he would send them acetates of the session but has said in subsequent interviews that he never got round to it. However it seems likely that somebody, perhaps Sam, made arrangements for this to happen. Copies were later found in Elvis' vault at Graceland – after his death – and Carl Perkins is thought to have possessed a copy as well.

There was a frisson of excitement in the press the day following the session as a result of Bob Johnson's article in the *Memphis Press-Scimitar* but after that it was business as usual; there were always more artists to record and aspiring hopefuls to consider. In the months that followed, Jack did listen to parts of the tapes occasionally, but says that Sam Phillips never showed any particular interest in them.

Sam grew less interested in the studio business as the years went by. Jack Clement said he became bored by it. In part at least this was because he no longer discovered artists who created that magical buzz that made him believe he could once more take the music world by storm.

From time to time he received offers for the business and the back catalogue but these initiatives came to nothing until 1969 when Sam agreed a sale to Shelby Singleton, a successful and shrewd music producer and record label executive. He had started up and run a number of labels and had a knack for identifying hit material from unlikely sources. He produced the 'Boll Weevil Song' for Brook Benton in 1961 and 'Harper Valley PTA', a massive worldwide hit for the then unknown Jeannie C Riley, in 1968.

As part of the deal to purchase Sun, Singleton took delivery of a large quantity of boxes full of badly catalogued tapes running to around 10,000 hours. Singleton began trawling through this material; in the mid to late seventies he embarked on a major programme of re-releasing material by Sun artists including the big names, Johnny Cash, Jerry Lee Lewis and Carl Perkins, in order to capitalise on their success in the seventies. He agreed a licensing deal with the British Charly label which released material in Europe where the music from the Sun archives went over particularly well.

It was during his searches of the tapes that Singleton came across the Million Dollar Quartet session. If he had chosen not to go through all the countless Ampex tapes from Sun in this way, it is possible that these priceless tapes might simply have festered at the back of a cupboard, eventually becoming unusable, and thus lost to the world forever. It seems the tapes – or at least about 35 minutes' worth of them – came to light in about 1978. Interest in items of this sort became intense after Elvis' death; there was a huge worldwide desire for recordings, information and artefacts relating to all aspects of his life and career.

When it became known that Singleton was planning to release extracts from the Million Dollar Quartet session – there were suggestions in some quarters that thousands of copies had already been pressed but this has never been substantiated – lawyers acting on behalf of Elvis' estate, Johnny Cash and Carl Perkins quickly swung into action in an attempt to prevent this happening. A protracted court battle followed. Elvis' label took the view that when the session was recorded in 1956, albeit in the most casual way, Elvis was under contract to them and nobody other than them had the right to releases the resultant material. Nobody was in any doubt that the main value of the tapes lay in the presence of Elvis. Apart from preventing release of the recordings, RCA was seeking an order that they were the rightful owners of all recordings which featured Elvis and that they and they alone were entitled to market them. Further, they sought an order that they had the exclusive right to use Elvis' name, image or biographical material in connection with the promotion and marketing of records and tapes which featured him.

Johnny and Carl's representatives stated in the course of the proceedings that the recordings were private and that there had never been any intention that they be issued publicly. Carl Perkins put forward the argument that since the "practice" session that day was his session then he had at least some claim on the material that was recorded – even though on a commonsense view it was clear that as soon as the Million Dollar Quartet session started the Carl Perkins session was over.

Johnny Cash's position was complicated by the fact that his voice was not audible on the tapes; however his name was associated with the session and photographs proved he was there at some point and so he joined the legal attempts to prevent release of the material. The point of all actions was not that the recordings should never be released, simply that they should not be released by and for the exclusive benefit of Shelby Singleton. Carl said that once they were released he would like at least some of the income to be used to help underprivileged children, a particular passion of his and a cause he felt sure Elvis would have approved of.

At some point – when exactly is not clear – some of the tapes were bootlegged and released in Europe. Accordingly some aficionados and collectors were extremely excited to be afforded the opportunity to listen to parts of the 1956 session for the first time in more than 20 years; to eavesdrop on a vital moment in history that up until then had been for most of them a matter of speculative conjecture rather than absolute fact.

Following a legal settlement of the court case and an appropriate licensing deal, an LP, *The Million Dollar Quartet*, was released in Europe on Charly/Sun in 1981. It featured a section of the recordings with 17 tracks, mainly religious material, lasting about 35 minutes.

Additional material came to light in the following years and double albums (in LP and CD formats) entitled *The Complete Million Dollar Session* were released on Charly/Sun in 1987. The lack of any evidence of Johnny Cash's voice on the recordings resulted in the word "quartet" being dropped for this particular release which contained 40 tracks, close to the entire amount of commercially usable material that has ever some to light. In 1990 RCA released the same recordings for distribution in America as *Elvis Presley – The Million Dollar Quartet*.

In 2006, the fiftieth anniversary year of the session, Sony BMG released what is almost certainly the definitive version of the Million Dollar Quartet session. It included a further 12 minutes of previously unreleased recordings which were apparently found on a recording of the session in an archive in Graceland. Strenuous efforts were made to ensure that the tracks appeared in the order they were originally recorded so that the album is as true to the actual events of the day as humanly possible. That said, not everything that was found was used – the tapes included items like Carl's band tuning up for instance, of interest to real anoraks but not commercially justifiable.

The 2006 double album runs to 79 minutes and includes certain items omitted from previous releases, for instance nearly a minute of the song 'Jesus Walked That Lonesome Valley'. This is a real boon since it adds in a section of the song when Elvis and Jerry Lee work themselves into a religious lather when trading some of the lines. There have been other releases of the Million Dollar Quartet session including a two-disc picture vinyl edition on the Universe label in 2007.

Ernst Jorgensen, one of the world's leading experts on Elvis Presley, had worked on Elvis' material for RCA from 1991; he was responsible for a number of acclaimed box sets bringing together songs from various elements of Elvis' career and was closely involved with the Million Dollar Quartet project. He also believes that so far as humanly possible the songs are now in the correct order. Thanks to the expert work of audio-restorer Kevan Budd the sound quality is probably as good as it ever will be. All aspects of the sound were an improvement on previous releases.

However there still remain the tantalising sounds of conversations amongst other people present in the studio; for the most part it is not possible to make out what they are saying. Perhaps these exchanges contain some historical gems; perhaps they are just light and banal.

After more than half a century, thanks to the assiduous efforts of several technical experts, a record of the Million Dollar Quartet session now exists, which provides a fascinating and eminently listenable glimpse into the very origins of rock 'n' roll.

9.

Subsequent Careers

SAM PHILLIPS

In the wake of the Million Dollar Quartet session, Sam continued to do what he had been doing for years – find, nurture and promote new talent. Jerry Lee Lewis became the focus of much of his attention after the sensational success of 'Whole Lot Of Shakin' Going On' in 1957 launched him into the stratosphere. For a time it seemed that he might have found a star with enough extra-special talent and charisma to rival Elvis. In November 1957 his follow-up single, 'Great Balls Of Fire', was another massive hit and his position was strengthened when Elvis headed off to the army. However defeat was snatched from the jaws of victory in 1958 when Jerry Lee took his show to Great Britain. A journalist revealed the fact that Jerry Lee's wife, Myra, was underage; as more facts about his marriages came out, the public reaction was overwhelmingly hostile and the tour was cancelled.

After Jerry Lee's return to America, there was a feeling that the British experience need not affect Jerry Lee's career elsewhere. This was very short lived. However, it soon became apparent that the wider American public too would be unforgiving. Sam arranged for Jerry Lee to issue an apology in the trade press in an attempt to recover ground but it was all to no avail. Jerry Lee's standing would be restored only after several years of penance; ironically it was in the same Britain that had shunned him that he found acceptance in the more tolerant sixties era.

Although Sam had sold Elvis' contract to RCA in 1955, the pair remained on good terms. When Elvis' mother, Gladys, died at a young age in 1958, Elvis was deeply shocked and upset. Sam was one of the few people able to provide comfort to the grief-stricken singer.

In 1957, Sam launched a new label, Phillips International, in an attempt to break into new musical territory. Success was immediate but short lived. The instrumental 'Raunchy' by Bill Justis sold around three million copies and 'Mona Lisa' by Carl Mann was a modest hit but there were no significant follow-ups; Sam soon closed the label down.

In some ways Jerry Lee's spectacular fall from grace signalled the beginning of Sun's decline. In 1958 Johnny Cash and Carl Perkins moved to Columbia. Each had become disenchanted with Sam. Each felt their royalty earnings were too low. Johnny was still determined to record religious music – something Sam was equally determined to resist on the basis that he continued to believe the music was not commercial. Sam continued to release singles by Jerry Lee Lewis but they made little impact. Jerry Lee eventually moved to Mercury in 1963.

Although chart success was rare and fleeting, Sam did work with other artists of note. Roy Orbison's debut Sun single, 'Ooby Dooby', was a minor hit but Sam failed to see where Roy's strengths lay. He tried to turn him into a rockabilly artist, apparently failing to see his potential as a romantic balladeer.

Charlie Rich had a hit with 'Lonely Weekends' in 1960. A decade later, long after he had parted company with Sun, he found success with a series of smooth country-oriented ballads including 'Behind Closed Doors'. A young singer called Harold Jenkins worked with Sam at Sun but it was only later, after changing his name to Conway Twitty, that he made the big time.

The premises at 706 Union Avenue became too small and crowded and Sam acquired a new studio in Memphis at 639 Madison Avenue which became known as the Sam C Phillips Recording Studio; its facilities were far superior though most people found the atmosphere sterile when compared to Union Avenue. The new studio was home to some regular session musicians of outstanding quality such as Steve Cropper and Booker T Jones.

Sam also had studios in Nashville and Tupelo for a short time. One of the people who worked in the Nashville studio, Billy Sherrill, went on to become famous but ironically he was strongly associated with the Nashville Sound – all sweet orchestrations and angelic choruses – a million miles away from the raw, rough around the edges music that Sam was renowned for.

As time went by Sam became less involved in hands–on music–making. He concerned himself more with strategic executive decisions about which people to record and what songs to put out. However it seems he had lost his knack of picking winners. Memphis in the early fifties had been a real hotbed of exciting musical talent which he exploited to the full for a brief magical spell. However the bigger labels quickly woke up to what was happening and moved in to hoover up much of the best talent. In addition they realised the potential of the many talented black artists making music; back in the day, recognition of black talent had been a kind of unique selling point for Sam and Sun. On top of everything else the sixties produced myriad new musical styles which were unfamiliar to Sam. The album format became increasingly popular while Sam resolutely clung to his preference for the immediacy of singles. Speaking later Roy Orbison summed it all up: "The industry just outgrew him overnight and he didn't know it."

The power of the Sun name was such that Sam did get offers from various parties to buy him out during the sixties. He finally did a deal with music polymath Shelby Singleton in 1969. The price tag for the Sun name and catalogue was never made public but is reported to have been around $1m. The studio in Madison Avenue has continued to produce music by a wide variety of artists.

The money Sam received added to his wealth, which was already considerable. He had been one of the early investors in the Holiday Inn hotel business which expanded rapidly in subsequent years. Amongst other projects Sam also invested in the Sun Studio Café with various locations around Memphis.

In association with his family – his two sons also went on to be successful music producers – he founded the Big River Broadcasting Corporation which owns and operates several radio stations. They also invested in new record labels.

Sam was in demand for interviews and television appearances as popular music increasingly became a subject of interest to commentators and academics. He was the subject of television specials which invariably cast him as one of those responsible for the Big Bang that led to rock 'n' roll.

On occasion his behaviour in public was erratic. He was incoherent during an appearance on the *The David Letterman Show*; clearly under the influence of some kind of mind–altering substance he simply failed to engage with his host who, in despair, resorted to producing photographs of some of the stars he had worked with in a futile attempt to focus him.

Much of the significance of the enormous contribution Sam Phillips made to the development of popular music only became apparent in retrospect, as it rapidly grew into a massive industry which reflected social, cultural and economic developments in the world. In 1986,

Sam was part of the first group inducted into the Rock and Roll Hall of Fame along with Elvis Presley and Jerry Lee Lewis. Speaking after receiving the award he said that to be involved in "the broad expanse of rock 'n' roll takes an element of mind expansion that people less creative would term insanity".

Remarkably he was also inducted into the Blues Hall of Fame and, in 2001, the Country Music Hall of Fame – rare for any artist, truly remarkable for a non–performer. Eight of the songs recorded at Sun, including inevitably 'Blue Suede Shoes', won Grammy Hall of Fame awards – which honour recordings of lasting qualitative or historical significance. There were many other awards which reflected the influence he had on the development of popular music in all its forms.

As the years went by, he took on the mantle of elder statesman and was regularly dubbed, "The Man Who Invented Rock 'n' Roll". He was involved in the restoration of the premises at 706 Union Avenue and their transformation into a tourist venue and working studio.

Talking about his own attributes he said, "I have one real gift and that is to look another person in the eye and be able to tell if he has anything to contribute, and if he does, I have the additional gift to free him from whatever is restraining him."

A heavy smoker most of his life, Sam Phillips died of respiratory failure on July 30, 2003 just before the original Sun Studio was designated a National Historic Landmark.

CARL PERKINS

After the Million Dollar Quartet session, Carl continued to cut records at Sun with minimal success. It appears that Sam came to feel that Carl's own compositions lacked commercial appeal since he got him to record a number of cover versions such as 'Roll Over Beethoven'. However, to the frustration of all concerned, nothing came remotely close to repeating the spectacular success of 'Blue Suede Shoes' which Elvis recorded and released on an EP around the time of Carl's accident. The song was a hit for Elvis and is nowadays associated in most peoples' minds with Elvis rather than Carl.

Carl continued to tour regularly but he only headlined smaller venues and the fees he could charge dropped considerably. He also toured with other stars of the day and in the sixties found himself on bills with Patsy Cline and George Jones amongst many others.

Along with Johnny Cash, Carl helped to transform Jerry Lee's stage show; they advised him to loosen up on stage, kick his leg out, get up on the piano, in short to follow his natural instincts and get rowdy. Jerry Lee only needed to be told once and his electric stage act was soon born. Carl and Jerry Lee were invited to appear in a low grade rock 'n' roll exploitation movie called *Jamboree*. Carl had a choice of songs. He chose an unexceptional number called 'Glad All Over' which meant that Jerry Lee got the other one, 'Great Balls Of Fire', which turned out to be one of the greatest rock 'n' roll anthems of them all.

There were tensions between Carl and Sam. Carl felt that Sam paid too much attention to Jerry Lee's career at the expense of his own. He was also starting to wonder if he was receiving all the royalties he was entitled to. When, along with Johnny Cash, Carl was approached by Don Law about switching from Sun to Columbia, he did not need much persuading, making the change when his contract with Sun terminated early in 1958. Sam did try to dissuade him, deploying the argument that a big label like Columbia would not understand Carl or his music in the way Sam did. Given Carl's almost total lack of commercial success with Sun, the argument did not carry much weight.

However Carl's time with Columbia was no more successful than his latter days at Sun. He did not warm to the studio culture of the big label – strict time limits with an expectation that results would be achieved quickly. He cut quite a few records but once more producers got him to record too many cover versions. Carl soon got the feeling that they did not want to invest heavily in him. When his contract with Columbia expired in 1963, it was not renewed. Entering contracts with labels large and small which were not subsequently renewed, and a lack of commercial success, became the pattern for the rest of Carl's career.

One of his main problems was the stunning array of competition that emerged in the fifties, acts like Chuck Berry, Little Richard and Buddy Holly, not to mention the other members of the Million Dollar Quartet. He was undoubtedly a figure of importance but he was not in their league. It seemed that Carl's fairly narrow style of rockabilly – aspects of which had been lifted and sanitised by some of the new clean-cut stars on the block – simply lacked significant commercial appeal. The undoubted fact that he lacked movie star looks did not help either. He also struggled with alcohol addiction for years.

At one stage in the early sixties Carl seriously contemplated giving up music altogether and buying a farm. However an offer to tour Britain with Chuck Berry caught his attention; he accepted and found himself caught up in the Swinging Sixties. He was surprised to discover that many musicians and fans in the UK were familiar with his music and held him in very high regard indeed. He found himself appearing with groups like the Animals, the Swinging Blue Jeans and the Nashville Teens. Top of the list of admirers however were the Beatles. Carl spent a day with them at Abbey Road, playing and talking music until the early hours. Before the Beatles wrote almost all of the material that appeared on their albums, Carl's songs were amongst their favourites. Three of his compositions, 'Matchbox', 'Honey Don't' and 'Everybody's Trying To Be My Baby', made it onto Beatles records.

Carl became a regular visitor to Britain although he never sold large numbers of records. He was recognised as a key player in the creation of rock 'n' roll and was also venerated as the "King of Rockabilly". It was galling for him though to see the people he had known as equals in the fifties enjoy stellar careers. Even Jerry Lee was eventually rehabilitated, initially as a country singer, allowing him to move forwards and upwards.

Carl was fortunate in his marriage – his wife, Valda, stood by him through good times and bad. However, he did experience personal tragedy. His brother Jay never fully recovered from the injuries he suffered in the car crash in 1956 when Carl too was badly injured. He died of a brain tumour in 1958 – which led to Carl drinking more. Clayton Perkins shot himself in 1973. He and Carl had had an increasingly difficult relationship as a result of Clayton's heavy drinking and violent behaviour.

At the end of a concert in the late sixties Carl raised his hand to wave to the audience. His hand came into contact with the moving blades of an unprotected rotary fan. He suffered serious tendon injuries and it was months before he was able to play a guitar. Not long afterwards he was shot in the ankle in a hunting accident.

In 1965 Johnny Cash asked Carl to play guitar as part of his large travelling show. A few concerts turned into a 10-year engagement with Carl an established part of the troupe. It was an arrangement which provided Carl with a considerable degree of financial security when he was making very little money from record sales and concerts. With Johnny he toured widely in America and abroad – on one occasion they visited Vietnam – and played guitar on a number of his albums. Carl appeared at Richard Nixon's White House with Johnny. The disadvantage of this professional relationship was that Johnny and Carl's friendship suffered. They had been the best of friends in the fifties but things were freer and easier then. Now Johnny was the boss and Carl the employee; each felt uncomfortable at times and were both relieved when Carl decided to quit in 1975. Carl formed a band, CP Express, with his sons Greg and Stan. Carl and Johnny remained close friends thereafter. Each struggled with substance abuse although it was reported that Carl finally managed to become sober some time in the seventies.

For years Carl had made half-hearted attempts to recover money he felt he was due from Sam Phillips all to no avail. He instigated legal proceedings in the late seventies. His action was defended vigorously by Sam and the nature of the exchanges was acrimonious at times. It was revealed that Carl had not read the contracts he had signed. He had simply put his trust in Sam and for years found it extremely difficult to question or doubt him – or any other authority figure for that matter. This was not at all uncommon; in the fifties the interests and wellbeing of the artist were usually secondary concerns to the people who made money out of them.

In the end Carl won a partial victory and was awarded just over $36,000. Carl was left with a strong feeling of resentment that Sam had failed to pay him money he was entitled to at a time when he was raising a young family – although at the time he had been grateful for the income he did make from Sun. That said, his feelings did ease a little over time and he always acknowledged the debt he owed Sam for seeing his potential and giving him his major break.

Carl never stopped writing songs. He collaborated with other artists including Bob Dylan and Dolly Parton. He wrote 'Daddy Sang Bass' which incorporated snatches of 'Will The Circle Be Unbroken' for Johnny Cash. In 1981 he was delighted to be asked to renew his acquaintance with Paul McCartney who invited him to Montserrat to play on his *Tug Of War* album; Carl spent eight days there and wrote a song for the album, 'My Old Friend'. His presence on the album resulted in him immediately being able to charge more for his live appearances – a stark reminder of the continuing power of the Beatle's magic.

During the eighties Carl received numerous awards as the powers that be started giving official recognition to the role he had played in the birth of rock 'n' roll. In 1987 his home town of Tiptonville opened the Carl Perkins Museum. In the same year he was inducted into the Rock and Roll Hall of Fame. The committee was evidently unaware of the bad blood between Carl and Sam since they chose Sam to present the award. He made a long and rambling speech after which Carl joked, "He got a standing ovation just for quittin'." He was also inducted into the Nashville Songwriter's Hall of Fame and the Rockabilly Hall of Fame.

In the early eighties Carl became increasingly concerned about the damage caused to society by child abuse and proudly lent his name to a charity – The Exchange Club Carl Perkins Center for the Prevention of Child Abuse – which continues to help thousands of children annually to the present day. Each year he was involved in fundraising concerts and telethons.

It was gratifying to Carl that new generations of musicians such as the Judds, Steve Earle and Rosanne Cash respected and acknowledged his contribution to the development of popular music. Carl continued to play concerts – he always received a particularly warm welcome from his many fans in Europe – and to write music. He also made some cameo appearances in a few films.

One particular highlight of his later years was a filmed concert, *A Rockabilly Session: Carl Perkins And Friends*, which featured some high quality playing by George Harrison, Dave Edmunds, Ringo Starr and Eric Clapton amongst others.

He headlined a concert in Memphis in 1992 to mark the 15th anniversary of the death of Elvis Presley. The concert also featured early Presley band members Scotty Moore and D J Fontana as well as Elvis' backing vocal group the Jordanaires.

Many of Carl's recordings for various labels, which achieved little or no commercial success when originally released, were later re-

released in lovingly put together compilations by the specialist re-issue label Bear Family. Carl continued releasing albums up until 1996, his final offering being, appropriately enough, 'Go Cat Go', which included contributions from Paul Simon, Bono and George Harrison. His last major public appearance came in 1997 when he agreed to perform at the Music for Montserrat all star charity concert at the Albert Hall in London.

Carl's final years were blighted by ill health. In 1992 he was diagnosed with throat cancer. After intensive treatment he did recover but was greatly weakened. Following a series of strokes, he died on January 19, 1998. He was 65.

JERRY LEE LEWIS

As with other members of the Million Dollar Quartet, when fame and success came, they came quickly. After the session on December 4 Jerry Lee's first Sun release, 'Crazy Arms', was a moderately successful local hit though not on a scale which would permit him to stop doing session work for other artists to earn a living. One oddball record he played on was 'Flyin' Saucers Rock 'n' Roll' by Billy Lee Riley and the Little Green Men.

However, Sam was convinced he was onto a winner with Jerry Lee and that success on a grand scale could not be far away. Thanks to the sale of Elvis' contract he had sufficient funds to promote and invest in Jerry Lee's career. Indeed one source of tension with other Sun artists at the time, in particular Carl Perkins and Johnny Cash, was the perception that Sam was devoting too much time and energy to Jerry Lee. He would later say that he had devoted a lot of time to launching their careers too and that now it was someone else's turn.

Sam and Jerry Lee had a close working relationship; Sam acted as a restraining and organising influence on Jerry Lee's wild and reckless instincts whilst still encouraging his protégé to express himself musically to the full. Jerry Lee toured extensively and found himself on bills with now legendary names – Fats Domino, Buddy Holly and Paul Anka for instance. He even headed over to Australia for several dates. It was during a tour of Canada early in 1957 that Carl Perkins and Johnny Cash encouraged him to loosen up dramatically on stage, get rowdy, use his feet instead of his hands sometimes – it was advice which Jerry Lee took much as a firework reacts when somebody lights the blue touch paper. This created problems during a tour with Chuck Berry. Chuck was top of the bill but Jerry Lee, believing that this was his rightful place, worked the audience up into a state of frenzy, making it hard even for Chuck Berry to follow him. He is even reputed to have set fire to a piano with lighter fuel on one occasion in an attempt to steal the show

Having found his natural stage persona, the shattering breakthrough came soon afterwards with Jerry Lee's second Sun single, 'Whole Lot Of Shakin' Going On'. It was a song Jerry Lee had played live, sometimes improvising the words when his memory let him down. When it was tried out in the studio in February 1957, Sam immediately realised its potential. However he was concerned that the obviously sexual – aggressively so in Jerry Lee's hands – lyrics would offend the many conservative elements in fifties America. He released it as the B-side to 'It'll Be Me' but it was soon clear from public reaction, as reported by DJs and verified by sales requests, that 'Whole Lot Of Shakin' Going On' was the hit. An appearance on the nationally broadcast *Steve Allen Show* had the same kind of effect on the nation as Elvis' initial America-wide unveiling on *The Ed Sullivan Show*. This was rock 'n' roll of the rawest, purest kind and people loved it – even if there were still those who saw Jerry as proof positive that rock 'n' roll was taking the country on a one way road to moral collapse.

Jerry Lee let rip as never before, battering the piano, standing up, sitting down, shaking around, all the time leering suggestively at the camera. His blond wavy hair, which initially appeared quite well coiffed, was soon flying around all over the place. The record, which had initially been a sleeper, took off and ended up reaching the top spot in the country and rhythm and blues charts and number two in the pop charts.

Not long afterwards came the opportunity to appear, along with Carl Perkins, in the rock 'n' roll B movie *Jamboree* and the fateful decision to let Jerry Lee sing 'Great Balls Of Fire'. The song gave Jerry Lee the other half of a brace of songs that ensured legendary status for the tormented kid from Ferriday.

Once more it seemed that Sam's Midas touch had weaved its magic and that a worthy successor to Elvis had been found – the fact that Elvis was about to head off to do his military service only served to help Jerry Lee's prospects. Working in the studio with Jerry Lee was not always easy though. The recording of 'Great Balls Of Fire' was held up for a time because he argued religion with Sam while the session men waited helplessly. He asserted robustly that he was doing the devil's work recording this kind of music and that people would go to hell as a result. He had been drinking. Sam used his powers of empathy and diplomacy to get Jerry to concentrate on the music.

By the end of the year 'Great Balls Of Fire' sat astride most national music charts. It was the best selling record Sun ever produced. Jerry Lee, now one of the most sought after artists in the country, had achieved what he felt was his due; he appeared unstoppable and a new single, 'Breathless', was soon released. Around this time there were allegations that Sam had been involved in a payola scheme – financial inducements to influential DJs to play the song – which were never proved.

However problems of an altogether greater magnitude were just round the corner for Jerry Lee. He was booked for an extensive tour of Britain in the middle of 1958. On arrival in London a sharp-eyed reporter noticed a young girl in the entourage. He soon established that this was Jerry Lee's third wife, Myra. Jerry Lee said she was 15; in fact she was 13. She was also his first cousin. Jerry Lee simply could not understand the fuss but the story spread around Britain in a wildfire blaze of negative publicity. There were calls for the Home Secretary to deport him immediately. Twenty-seven dates had been booked but after three poorly attended performances (with people calling out "cradle-robber" and the like) the tour was cancelled and Jerry Lee and Myra headed back home. Fans were not appeased by the fact that the set list included religious material such as 'My God Is Real'.

Unfortunately for Jerry Lee and much to his surprise, the scandal also brought his career in America to a shuddering halt. Eventually Sam arranged for an apology, in the form of a long exculpatory letter from Jerry Lee, to be issued in the trade press but it was already too late. Jerry Lee was shunned by television and radio. He went from fees of $10,000 a night at prestigious venues to nearer $200 at the kind of places he was hoping he had left behind for good. It was one of the most spectacular falls from grace ever. Perhaps if he had been established as a star for longer than just a year or so he could have ridden out the storm; as it was, his apparently unstoppable ascent fell back to the runway in a ball of flames.

Sam did stand by Jerry Lee, always believing in his great qualities as an artist. However the singles he released made little or no impact without airplay and television and press coverage. They even resorted to the use of a pseudonym, 'The Hawk', for one release but DJs saw through this – it was impossible to disguise his highly distinctive piano playing. One exception to Jerry Lee's generally dismal showing was a cover of the Ray Charles song 'What'd I Say', which stayed in the charts for around two months.

Sam and Jerry Lee parted company in 1963 when Jerry Lee moved to Mercury's Nashville-based subsidiary label Smash.

Ironically Jerry Lee did find a degree of success in Britain, and other European countries, with covers of rock 'n' roll hits. When he toured there again in the mid sixties he received a generally favourable response, in stark contrast to the situation back home. Times had changed and the album *Live At The Star Club, Hamburg* was generally well received.

However it was only in the late sixties that Jerry Lee's career took off again in America, after he switched from rock 'n' roll to country music. In many ways it was a logical move since country music has long majored in sinning, inappropriate relationships, backsliding, indulgent women, guilt and religion. Jerry Lee was even able to work his dazzling piano playing into the country mix, albeit in a slightly watered down form. His many difficult life experiences also qualified him to put across a country song with heartfelt credibility. Jerry Lee was accepted with open arms by many but not all in the country music firmament. There were those who suspected his motives in switching to country – was it a purely opportunist move? – and who found it hard to forgive and forget what they saw as his immoral lifestyle.

To the surprise of some Jerry Lee accepted a very different kind of role in the late sixties when he played Iago in *Catch My Soul*, the rock musical based on *Othello*. The critics were not kind to the musical but Jerry Lee received many favourable comments on the energy and excitement he brought to his role.

Although a regular critic of many aspects of the rock music ushered in by the Beatles and the Stones – not least for the long hair he regarded as unmanly and against Christian teaching – he appeared on a bill with the Doors in 1969. He also appeared on a Monkees television special.

Jerry Lee enjoyed a string of top quality country hits starting in 1968 with 'Another Place, Another Time' and continuing with gems such as 'What's Made Milwaukee Famous (Has Made A Loser Out

Of Me)' and 'Once More With Feeling'. He was once again able to command large fees for his concert appearances. As the seventies wore on he revisited his rock 'n' roll past and had a hit in 1972 with a new take on the old Big Bopper hit 'Chantilly Lace'. The hits kept coming until the start of the eighties by which time a middle-aged Jerry Lee was totally rehabilitated and once more able to pull in audiences all around the world.

The events that led to Jerry Lee's professional demise almost came to look like a good career move. As the years have gone by people have been far more inclined to be indulgent, indeed impressed, on hearing of Jerry Lee's colourful past life. However the reality is that his personal life has been marred by tragedy of the worst kind. Jerry Lee has been married seven times and had four children (other people have claimed to be his children but paternity has not been established). One of his children with his third wife, Myra, Steve Allen Lewis, drowned in a swimming pool mishap when he was three years old; this led to a dramatic increase in his father's ingestion of pills and liquor. His son Jerry Lee Lewis Jr, one of the children from his second marriage, to Jane Mitchum, was killed in a car accident at the age of 19. Lewis' fourth and fifth marriages both ended with the deaths of his wives; one drowned in a swimming pool accident, the other as a result of a methadone overdose after three months of marriage.

In 1989 a biopic of Jerry Lee's early life, *Great Balls Of Fire!*, was released. It was based on a book by Myra about her life with Jerry Lee. Dennis Quaid and Winona Ryder played Jerry Lee and Myra. This film helped to re-establish Jerry Lee in the public eye.

Despite selling millions of records over the course of a lengthy career, Jerry Lee's financial position has been a troubled one; apart from acrimonious and costly divorces which have included countless allegations of drinking, drug-taking and violence, he has had several large-scale battles with the Internal Revenue Service. He has been sued on countless occasions by other creditors and had many of his possessions seized. No matter how much money he earned, he frittered away more. Over the years Jerry Lee also struggled with the many problems associated with heavy drug and alcohol use. He has been arrested on many occasions, on one notorious occasion when he arrived drunk, waving a gun, at Graceland demanding to see Elvis. Over the years Jerry Lee has owned a large collection of guns. On one occasion he shot and wounded one of the musicians in his band during a drunken outburst at his house. It was a similar story with fast cars; he loved driving them and had no scruples about doing so when under the influence of drugs and/or alcohol; he has been involved in numerous accidents. He has been hospitalised on various occasions, sometimes as a result of car accidents, sometimes his drug and alcohol abuse.

Throughout it all, his fixation with conservative religion has continued. He would tell interviewers and anyone else who would listen that you had to be loyal to God or Satan – there was no in between. He despised sinning yet he sinned constantly. He inhabited a world where temptation was everywhere; he gave in and then repented – and then did it all over again, only more so. As he told one interviewer, "I'm a sinner. Soon I'm gonna have to reckon with the chillin' hands of death."

In 1986, Jerry Lee was one of the inaugural inductees into the Rock and Roll Hall of Fame – regardless of record sales, those in the know were only too well aware of his contribution. That said, although he did make some memorable country hits, his greatest achievement in the studio surely remains that unforgettable pair of songs he cut at Sun, 'Whole Lot Of Shakin' Going On' and 'Great Balls Of Fire' which have long since acquired a status that lies somewhere between icon and cliché. Each was subsequently elected to the Grammy Hall of Fame. In 2005, he was given a Lifetime Achievement Award by the Recording Academy (which also grants the Grammy Awards).

In 2007, he received the Rock and Roll Hall of Fame's American Music Masters Award. In October 2009, Jerry Lee opened the Rock and Roll Hall of Fame 25th Anniversary concert at Madison Square Garden in New York. On February 10, 2008, he appeared with John Fogerty and Little Richard on the 50th Grammy Awards Show, performing 'Great Balls Of Fire' in a medley with 'Good Golly Miss Molly'.

Jerry Lee has never seriously contemplated retirement. He has continued to tour, write songs and record and has always been a particularly welcome visitor in Europe. In 2009 he toured there with fellow legends Chuck Berry and Little Richard.

Similarly, he has continued to record sporadically. As his legendary status has grown and the time of his departure from this world drawn closer, more and more current stars have queued up to pay tribute. In 2006 Jerry Lee released the album *Last Man Standing* – a particularly appropriate title for the only survivor of the Million Dollar Quartet session since 2003, when Johnny Cash died. The album featured a whole host of stars eager to share the limelight with the legendary Killer – including Mick Jagger, Willie Nelson, Ringo Starr, Don Henley, Jimmy Page, Eric Clapton, George Jones and BB King. The album earned a gold disc, his tenth, with sales in excess of half a million; no doubt the presence of so many other stars helped. In 2010 he released yet another album, self-deprecatingly entitled *Mean Old Man*. Indefatigable as ever, he continues to keep on keeping on while so many others have fallen by the wayside.

Against the odds, certainly not an obvious candidate for longevity, Jerry Lee has survived into old age. He lives with his family on a ranch in Mississippi not far from where he was born and brought up. Despite his countless achievements, he could be forgiven for musing on what might have been. The scandal of 1958 deprived his career of momentum, a blow from which it never fully recovered. In addition, as a solo piano player, he was a man out of place in a popular music world which has been dominated for years by bands and solo artists. However he can rest assured that his legacy as one of the founding fathers of rock 'n' roll is indisputable. As John Lennon put it, "No group, be it the Beatles, Dylan or the Stones, have ever improved on 'Whole Lot Of Shakin' Going On' On" for my money."

ELVIS PRESLEY

After the Million Dollar Quartet session, and after Christmas with his family, Elvis made the last of his famous trio of appearances on the *Ed Sullivan Show* in January 1957. It was for this show that he was filmed from the waist up. This was perhaps the reason that Sullivan felt able to describe Elvis as a "real decent, fine boy". Perhaps it was also partly due to the fact that he sang 'Peace In The Valley'.

Elvis' stratospheric career trajectory continued in 1957. RCA pumped out singles, including 'All Shook Up', '(Let Me Be Your) Teddy Bear' and 'Jailhouse Rock', all of which topped the charts. Tom Parker adopted a similar approach to movies and after *Love Me Tender* Elvis starred in *Loving You, Jailhouse Rock* and *King Creole*. These early films had some artistic merit, but eventually the films that featured Elvis in the leading role became star vehicles in glorious Technicolor with banal story lines, all turned out on a conveyor belt by establishment moviemakers, most of whom were capable of far better work. The critics never warmed to the films but on the back of them the Elvis Presley industry sold millions of records and tons of merchandise for years to come. The single 'Jailhouse Rock' was one of the early fruits of a collaboration between Elvis and ace songwriters Jerry Leiber and Mike Stoller but the relationship floundered when Leiber & Stoller offered advice to Elvis that wasn't to Tom Parker's liking.

Once he became seriously rich, Elvis invested in an 18-room mansion approximately eight miles south of downtown Memphis called Graceland. It was to be home for him and his parents, and would become one of the most enduring emblems of the Elvis Presley story.

Despite massive national popularity, Elvis still had his detractors. One critic described rock 'n' roll as a disease. Frank Sinatra was outspokenly contemptuous. Despite having attracted some opprobrium for the response he himself had evoked in young female fans a decade before, he described the new music as "brutal, ugly, degenerate, vicious". He asserted that what he referred to as "this rancid-smelling aphrodisiac" was mainly produced by "cretinous goons". By contrast, and despite his comparative inexperience when it came to public relations, when asked to respond, Elvis was remarkably measured and polite. "This is a trend, just the same as he (Sinatra) faced when he started years ago." Ironically the pair appeared on television together, in tuxedos, like old buddies, a few years later.

Regardless of the negative opinions, Elvis continued to draw ecstatic responses from his fans whenever he trod the boards. In consequence Parker soon started to ration his concert appearances. Elvis was achieving so much exposure and income from records, television and films that live concerts were no longer necessary from a commercial point of view. The other problem with live appearances was the mania Elvis generated amongst the fans. As one reporter said, "The trouble with going to see Elvis Presley is that you're liable to get killed."

At the start of 1958, 'Don't' became Elvis' tenth number one seller. In March he was inducted into the US Army which at the time seemed unthinkable (and was probably avoidable) but in the long term seems to have been part of Parker's strategy to reposition Elvis as more acceptable to the great American public. Of course Parker ensured that Elvis' time in the military – not least the day of his induction – was turned into news stories or photo-opportunities.

It was probably Parker who suggested that Elvis donate his Army pay to charity.

There was never any suggestion of Elvis seeking to avoid military service as might have been the case a decade later. Nevertheless, the Army cut Elvis a lot of slack, doubtless because it received plenty of favourable publicity via its new recruit. RCA had stockpiled some recordings which were released on a regular basis while he was busy serving his country, and he was rarely off the charts. Meanwhile, GI 53310761 was introduced to new experiences during his time in the army, including amphetamines and the karate moves he would perform in subsequent live concerts.

Elvis' life was turned upside down in August 1958 when his mother died after a short illness. She was only 46. Elvis, who had enjoyed a close and intense relationship with his mother, was allowed compassionate leave. He was inconsolable, refusing for a time to be parted from the body, and one of the few who was able to provide any meaningful comfort was Sam Phillips. There are those who believe Elvis never really came to terms with his mother's early demise.

In October Elvis was posted to Germany – the only time in his life he would leave the US – where he met and fell for 14-year-old Priscilla Beaulieu whose family were living there at the time. A relationship of sorts developed. Doubtless aware of the furore surrounding Jerry Lee Lewis' disastrous involvement with young girls, in a rather bizarre piece of subterfuge this was kept quiet for a long time. The pair were eventually married in Las Vegas some seven years later although they had lived together at Graceland before this.

Following an honourable discharge from the army in 1960, and after a mere two weeks holiday, Tom Parker did his level best to get his goose right back to the serious business of laying as many golden eggs as possible. In the course of the sixties Elvis continued to make as many formulaic films (nearly 30) and cut as many records as time physically allowed. Some good songs did emerge in the early years of the process, 'It's Now Or Never', 'Can't Help Falling In Love' and 'Are You Lonesome Tonight' being memorable examples. He imbued some of the ballads with real sentimentality and romance; one writer described some of them as "pornographic" rather than merely sexy. However, many of the songs that filled up the soundtrack albums were totally forgettable, written by people far removed from the likes of Bill Monroe or Hank Snow, let alone Leiber and Stoller, and it was often an effort for Elvis to put his heart into performing them. It was a sign of Elvis' powerful appeal that even religious material, such as the album *His Hand In Mine*, sold in substantial quantities. By 1961 he had sold around 75 million records.

However, as the decade wore on, both the quality of the songs and the movies – invariably light romantic tales full of music and tame comedy – deteriorated and the movie–going, record-buying public eventually cooled to Elvis' previously unassailable appeal. The franchise which for years had produced big returns was on the slide. Ironically there was talk of some more serious film roles being offered to Elvis – *Midnight Cowboy, West Side Story, A Star is Born* – which would have provided him with the kind of artistic challenge he needed. However all were stymied by Tom Parker's unreasonable financial demands.

There was another major problem for Elvis and fellow singers who had made it big in the previous decade. The Beatles and the Rolling Stones and countless others had changed the nature of the game. Elvis had been the future once but now he was seen by many as unfashionable and past it. The poor quality of much of his output, and the lazy assumption by his advisors that the public would lap up anything he gave them, led to a dramatic decline in his commercial returns by the late sixties. It surely did not help that Elvis virtually withdrew from live concert performances for more than six years. To many, Elvis appeared to be a spent force.

In an attempt to revive his flagging fortunes a television extravaganza was conceived. It went out in December 1968 and featured Elvis, kitted out in black leathers, looking unbelievably sexy, singing his hits with a backdrop of impressive stage sets in front of a live audience. It was simply called *Elvis* but is often referred to as the "'68 Comeback Special". Though apparently nervous during the making of the show, Elvis comes over as relaxed, throwing himself into some great songs with gusto, almost like the good old pre-military service days. The event served to remind people what an elemental force Elvis was. The viewing figures were spectacular; Elvis was back in an altered guise and what's more he was able to teach many younger rock singers a thing or two about stage presence and putting over a song. Although the show did little to halt the decline in record sales it seemed to give Elvis a new lease of life, as did the birth of Elvis and Priscilla's daughter, Lisa Marie, the same year.

With this came the realisation that soundtrack albums full of third rate material by hack writers were no longer viable. In early 1969 Elvis undertook a series of sessions at American Sound Studios in Memphis and in June the album *From Elvis In Memphis* was released. It featured an eclectic mix of songs – country, soul, rock – that he liked and which had real quality. One standout track, 'In The Ghetto', was an instant classic, and the sessions also produced 'Suspicious Minds', 'Don't Cry Daddy' and 'Kentucky Rain'. 'Suspicious Minds', now widely regarded to be as good as anything he ever recorded, became Elvis' first US number one in seven years.

A return to live concerts was obviously the way forward and Elvis, together with his spectacular clothes and stage show, found a natural home in the larger than life world of Las Vegas. He could have been forgiven for approaching the place with some trepidation in view of his lukewarm reception there in 1956. He needn't have worried. He played to packed houses of more than 2,000 people at the International Hotel and subsequently entered a lucrative contract for annual residencies. The sight of ordered rows of fans in smart clothes was all a far cry from the riots of the mid fifties but the noisy enthusiasm for the King, as people were now routinely calling him, was genuine. Elvis stood before them, resurrected; the final unforgettable phase of his remarkable career was well and truly underway.

Elvis' live concerts became major events in the entertainment world and the venues needed to house them grew bigger and bigger; he played a series of shows at the Houston Astrodome. In 1970 the magic of his live concerts was turned into a successful documentary film, *Elvis: That's The Way It Is,* which featured footage of Elvis in concert and also interviews and clips taken backstage and during rehearsals. Devised by Tom Parker, it was a smart move which emphasised Elvis' greatest strength – his extra special gift for entertaining people in concert. It also exploited the massive audience-reaching power of movies whilst at the same time moving things on from the dreadful films of the sixties. The film also fixed forever in the public mind the enduring image of Elvis in flamboyant white jump suits. Although some of the old raw-edged songs such as 'That's All Right (Mama)' and 'Mystery Train' were included, it was clear that Elvis had shifted decisively towards more mainstream popular music. Songs such as 'Sweet Caroline', 'You've Lost That Lovin' Feeling' and 'Suspicious Minds' were aimed at broadening his appeal in order to attract the greatest possible audience.

Elvis met President Nixon and posed for photographs in front of the American flag. He spoke out against drugs and associated his remarks with some disparaging comments about the Beatles, despite having spent an evening with them in the mid sixties.

Fame brought danger; there were threats against Elvis' life and it was reported that he sometimes had a Derringer secreted in one of his boots onstage. Fame also brought recognition; in Memphis, the road on which Graceland stands was renamed Elvis Presley Boulevard.

In 1971 Elvis became the first singer of rock 'n' roll music to be awarded the Lifetime Achievement Award by the National Academy of Recording Arts and Sciences.

RCA continued to release a large number of records of varying quality. Elvis Presley was now one of the biggest brands in the world which meant he was constantly in demand though the man behind it all often appeared to be lost in the tasteless stampede to exploit his natural gifts. Elvis became a caricature, remote and surrounded by sycophants. Despite numerous promises to visit Europe, he never once toured abroad, nor did he ever give an interview which wasn't carefully stage-managed. At some point, despite his anti-drug remarks to President Nixon and occasionally in the media, he became an increasingly heavy user of prescription drugs. For someone of his wealth and influence there was no difficulty in persuading doctors to provide him with what he wanted. Naively, Elvis felt that this was acceptable in a way that indulging in street drugs would not be. By the early seventies it was apparent that Elvis was also putting on weight and for a time he did his best to shed some pounds before major concert appearances.

In 1973 he performed at one such event in Honolulu, *Aloha From Hawaii*, which was broadcast live to approximately 40 countries across Europe and Asia. Various claims about the size of the viewing audience were subsequently made. Whilst it seems likely that initial claims of 1.5 billion were considerably exaggerated (by Tom Parker), the concert was nonetheless undoubtedly seen by a great many people, perhaps several hundred million. For the show Elvis wore an unforgettable piece of stage gear – a cape with a larger than life American eagle on the back. By stretching out his arms he came to resemble some mythical deity. A double album of the concert was released soon afterwards and sold around five million copies.

Whilst his professional career seemed unassailable, Elvis had mounting problems on a personal level. As the seventies progressed his drug use increased to alarming levels, he continued to put on weight and his marriage fell apart. For years he had been unable to resist the countless offers that came his way from attractive women and this inevitably led to a dramatic cooling of relations with Priscilla. The pair were finally divorced in 1973, after which Elvis embarked on more short-lived relationships, none of which proved successful or enduring.

As his health deteriorated so did his live performances. He sometimes slurred or forgot his words; the once graceful stage movements looked torpid and plodding. Adoring fans still turned out to see him in big numbers but it was noticeable that in line with his more middle-of-the-road and at times grandiose pop music, the audiences increasingly comprised middle-aged, conservative-looking people, predominantly women. In his over-the-top bejewelled outfits, and undisguisable heft, Elvis was in danger of becoming a kind of show business freak, the fabled youth with the sensational voice buried so deep that it was hard to imagine they were one and the same person. Tellingly, his concert itineraries avoided big cities like New York and Los Angeles, where critics with sharpened pens lay in wait, and concentrated on the Midwest and southern states.

Despite emergency hospital attendances and clear evidence that his condition was becoming potentially life threatening, he continued to tour extensively. It appears that Tom Parker put his exploitative lust for money and success above any concerns he might have had for Elvis' wellbeing. On one view of it the strategy worked. Elvis had become one of the most famous, instantly recognisable people in the world; in commercial terms he had become one of the most reliable brands ever.

Amongst an impressive array of top level awards, Elvis was inducted into the Rock and Roll Hall of Fame, the Country Music Hall of Fame, the Gospel Music Hall of Fame and the Rockabilly Hall of Fame, though all of these honours were posthumous. He also received the American Music Awards' Award of Merit in 1987. He won three Grammies – all for gospel songs, his first love. Not surprisingly he did not receive any awards for the many films in which he starred, even though almost all were commercially successful.

Like some noble wild animal displayed for years in a circus, its spirit broken, its health in ruins, Elvis struggled on recording and performing but the end was coming closer. Between tours he passed his time at Graceland reading religious texts and watching Monty Python, and he became famous for giving expensive gifts, many of them cars, to total strangers. Just before the end a book by two of his former bodyguards exposed all that was rotten in his life. It was the final straw. In a drug induced haze Elvis finally gave up the ghost on August 16, 1977. He was 42. He had been due to fly out on yet another tour that very evening.

President Jimmy Carter said, "His music and his personality, fusing the styles of white country and black rhythm and blues, permanently changed the face of American popular culture. His following was immense, and he was a symbol to people the world over of the vitality, rebelliousness, and good humor of his country."

Some 80,000 fans lined the streets to watch his funeral procession. He is buried next to his mother at Graceland which is now the second most visited home in America, after the White House. Worldwide interest in Elvis, his life and his music has continued unabated ever since his death, not least because Priscilla eventually ousted Tom Parker from control of the Presley estate and, in the fullness of time, presided over the establishment of a well-managed legacy worth as much as a billion dollars. Tasteful, lavishly packaged CD box sets of his recordings have now reinstated Elvis as the greatest of all American rock'n'rollers bar none.

Elvis had little contact with the other members of the Million Dollar Quartet after the 1956 session. He quickly moved out of their orbit and into one of his own, so rarefied that only Parker, his family and his personal security – the so-called Memphis Mafia – were allowed in. It is achingly poignant listening to the innocent exuberance of Elvis during the 1956 session; the future seemed so bright but for Elvis it would end in tragedy. Although not in a geographical sense, he had moved a million miles away from the security and familiarity of his roots, into a foreign world where he was treated as a commodity and mercilessly exploited for commercial gain. He was a country boy who was exposed to pressures his psyche could not cope with; and as a result he resorted to the ghastly comforts offered by drugs and junk food.

The Million Dollar Quartet session provides a priceless glimpse of Elvis before all this happened; and even if there is the heart-wrenching sense of what might have been, the session offers an untarnished glimpse of one of the greatest singers of popular music the world has ever known.

JOHNNY CASH

After the Million Dollar Quartet session, Johnny continued to make records he really liked and he continued to achieve considerable success. He recorded Sun's first album, *Johnny Cash With His Hot And Blue Guitar*. He also enjoyed his new found status as one of the top selling country artists of the day in the wake of 'I Walk The Line'. In addition he had the pleasure of touring on a regular basis with some of the established stars of the day, distant heroes until recently, such as Patsy Cline and Hank Snow. Times on the road were often wild with reports of motel rooms being painted black, bombs set off in toilet bowls and chickens being released in hotel corridors. Such shenanigans were probably inevitable given the pressures of the road – 300 shows a year was not unusual.

Johnny's output was extremely varied. In addition to some strong Johnny Cash music, there were also some more unusual choices such as 'Ballad Of A Teenage Queen', a sugary lightweight piece of pop. Released at the end of 1957, it was untypical of both Sun and Johnny Cash, but it was a big hit, one which Johnny promoted heavily on a tour of Canada.

However he was already starting to feel dissatisfied with Sam Phillips and Sun. He wanted to be able to include religious material in his recorded output but Sam, a hard pressed businessman, remained implacably opposed because he just did not believe, probably rightly, that such music would make money. Johnny was also concerned about the royalty rate he received – around 3% compared to about 5% elsewhere – and generally wondered if the crude financial accountings he received from Sam fairly reflected what he was entitled to. He was still wondering about this when he wrote his autobiography, published in 1997.

When he was approached by Don Law about the possibility of switching to Columbia he soon decided he would. Law made it clear that he would be able to record at least some religious music and that he would also receive a larger slice of the financial cake. Along with Carl Perkins, Johnny made the change in 1958. Despite his disaffection with Sam he would, like Carl, always feel indebted to him for having given him his break, and having helped him to establish his distinctive sound.

When Sam realised what was going on, he felt betrayed. He kept Johnny to the terms of his contract and compelled him to record a great deal of material so that he could keep on releasing records for some time to come. Relations between them soured and Johnny was only persuaded to go into the studio by engineer Jack Clement, who said his job was on the line over the issue. The pair became lifelong friends and colleagues despite different approaches to the way songs should be recorded. Ironically, despite Johnny's disenchantment with Sam, some of the material they recorded became very successful. One of his last recordings for Sun was 'Guess Things Happen That

Way', written by Jack, which made number one in the country charts.

A fault line was developing in Johnny's marriage. His wife, Vivian, was essentially a home maker with no particular interest in music beyond hoping that her husband did well in his chosen career. They had two daughters and would soon have two more. The eldest, Rosanne, would go on to become a hugely talented and successful singer-songwriter. The problem was that Johnny had early on discovered the wonders of drugs and their amazing ability to keep him going on tour when his body was exhausted. Within a short time it got to the stage where he was rarely home and when he was there Vivian said he had become a different person as a result of the drugs he was taking.

A move to California – Johnny had ambitions to get into movies – merely made things worse. It meant there was a bigger distance between home and where the musical action usually was. By his own admission Johnny was a negligent father and his daughters suffered as a result of his lengthy absences and also his crazed behaviour on the rare occasions when he was home; but music always came first in his life.

Johnny had been aware of June Carter for some time. She was a member of Mother Maybelle and the Carter Sisters, successors to the legendary Carter Family. She joined his travelling show in the early sixties and there was an immediate mutual attraction. A relationship soon developed, though some of June's time with her new beau was spent getting to his stash of pills before he did, and then destroying them.

Johnny soon put together a touring troupe that included June and her mother and sisters, Carl Perkins, vocal group the Statler Brothers as well as his own backing group the Tennessee Three; this substantial unit stayed together for about 10 years.

Johnny recorded some memorable material with Columbia including 'Don't Take Your Guns To Town' and 'Ring Of Fire'.

He was given a remarkably free rein and was able, musically, to indulge his passion for religion and American history and culture. His popularity meant that his first album of religious material, *Hymns By Johnny Cash*, was a moderate commercial success. Amongst more mainstream material Johnny also released albums about the Old West and everyday characters from the past as on the album *Ride This Train*, which Johnny described as a country opera. He developed an interest in the history of Native Americans and their lengthy struggles against the authorities; for a time he became a sort of unofficial spokesman for their cause. His 1964 album, *Bitter Tears: Ballads Of The American Indian*, was an example of the kind of work that marked him out from most other artists. He was prepared to make a statement on behalf of something he believed in. Reactions were mixed. Those on the liberal left were delighted but many of Johnny's more conservative fans were outraged. In the southern states some DJs simply refused to play songs from it, in particular the single 'The Ballad Of Ira Hayes', about the plight of one man who had helped to raise the American flag after a key victory on the tiny Japanese island of Iwo Jima in 1945, but who died a poor alcoholic on a reservation. The release of such albums helped to build Johnny's reputation as a man of integrity. Years later, Bob Dylan compared him to the North Star: "You can set your ship by him."

By 1968, there were many in the music world who could not see how Johnny could survive into his thirties; his drug intake was gargantuan. Another Hank Williams they said. In 1965 he was arrested at El Paso International airport attempting to smuggle over 1,000 amphetamine pills into America. He was fortunate to get off with a fine and a suspended sentence. He lost a great deal of weight, looked gaunt, was twitchy and restless. He was reckless when it came to cars – usually other people's – and was involved in several accidents, some quite serious, when under the influence of drugs and or drink. He let his fans down at times – failing to turn up or going on stage when his voice was so ravaged that he was incapable of singing properly.

The year 1968 marked a turning point of sorts. After years of misery, Vivian obtained a divorce and Johnny then married June Carter. There was a sense of a new beginning with his drug habit under control. In truth there were countless relapses over subsequent years, with hospital admissions and attempts at family therapy to address Johnny's seemingly unconquerable addiction.

He had played concerts regularly at prisons but was unable to fulfil his ambition of recording a live album in one until he was hooked up with a new producer, Bob Johnston. The result was two memorable albums recorded respectively at Folsom Prison and San Quentin in the late sixties which brilliantly captured the very essence of Johnny Cash doing what he did best – enthralling audiences with his raw spontaneity, straightforward songs and engaging stage presence. By 1969 he was one of the biggest selling artists in the world and won all the key awards including Entertainer of the Year at the annual Country Music Association awards ceremony.

His high profile meant that he was increasingly in demand for film roles on the big screen and on television. He had no particular gift for acting and looked ill at ease and unconvincing in front of the cameras. The producers really just wanted his looks and his voice and offers continued to come for years. More successful was a television variety show with ABC which Johnny fronted from 1969 to 1971. The show featured guests from almost every conceivable style of popular music – Louis Armstrong, the Who, Joni Mitchell, Pete Seeger, Ray Charles, Bob Dylan and many more. Room was also found for more folksy material, some from Johnny's extended family in the shape of Mother Maybelle and the Carter Sisters.

Johnny built up a regular and devoted following in Europe although his only major hit there came in 1971 with the rather anodyne 'A Thing Called Love'.

Johnny got to know Billy Graham and the two became close friends, sharing holidays together sometimes at Johnny's impressive holiday home in Jamaica. Graham was a great admirer of Johnny's work and, naturally enough, his strong Christian beliefs; he felt that with Johnny's help he would be able to get his message across more strongly to younger people. To this end Johnny agreed to appear at some of Billy's world famous crusades for a time. Johnny had previously invested a great deal of his own money taking a film crew and some musicians to Israel and making a film about the life of Christ, *The Gospel Road*, which was neither a commercial nor a critical success.

Although well established as a major figure in the world of entertainment, Johnny's level of commercial success – particularly in terms of record sales – tailed off in the early seventies. He was given a string of producers to work with but none managed to find a sound that sparked the public imagination as in the past. Johnny continued to be in reasonable demand for live concerts – he had many loyal fans – but the decline continued unabated until in 1986 his record contract with CBS was not renewed. He did get another one, with Mercury, but commercial success continued to elude him.

Awards, the crème de la crème, came his way by the truckload. He was inducted into the Nashville Songwriters Hall of Fame (1977), the Country Music Hall of Fame (1980), and the Rock and Roll Hall of Fame (1992). He was one of the recipients of the Kennedy Center Honors in 1996, and in 2001 he was awarded the National Medal of Arts. His fame also gave him entrée to the White House on occasion but Johnny was invariably much happier in the company of some music or fishing buddies.

Johnny hooked up with other ageing stars – Kris Kristofferson, Willie Nelson and Waylon Jennings – to form a country supergroup, the Highwaymen – a much more mature kind of Million Dollar Quartet. For a few years the four managed to work reasonably well as a team, touring regularly and cutting three albums of eclectic material. The fans were happy – four stars for the price of one. After several years though, the novelty wore off, the principals got older and the band faded away.

Just when Johnny appeared to be entering the twilight of his career, artistic salvation and renaissance came in the unlikely form of Rick Rubin. Not long after the artistic nadir of a booking at Butlin's in England's Bognor Regis, Johnny had a face to face meeting with the long-haired, heavily bearded sunspec-wearing Rubin, until then mainly associated with far-out rock bands such as the Beastie Boys and the Red Hot Chili Peppers. The pair might have looked like chalk and cheese but they each knew all about the essentials of good music. Crucially Rubin understood – as most producers had failed to – that for Johnny it was a case of less is more. The debut album, *American Recordings*, featured nothing but Johnny, an acoustic guitar and a bunch of great songs – "not even a pick" as he was pleased to tell people. It was the first in a series of albums which he made with Rubin to general critical approval.

The relationship with Rubin gave Johnny a new lease of life. Unfortunately, by this time his health was in a perilous or poor state. Touring was out of the question from the mid nineties onwards. All the years of drug abuse and hard living had caught up with him. His life became a constant battle against myriad debilitating conditions. Towards the end of his life, despite his very obvious physical problems, he recorded a remarkable video of the song 'Hurt' by Trent Reznor of the band Nine Inch Nails. There was no attempt to disguise his corpse-like appearance and the song seemed to carry a negative message about the pointlessness of life which appeared to fly in the face of his religious faith. It was nonetheless an artistic tour de force, not to mention a monumental physical achievement.

Johnny struggled on for a time but when June, to whom he had been married for 35 years, died unexpectedly in 2003, it was not long before he followed. He died on September 12 that same year. His music encompassed so many styles but its dark energy was hard to define; as he said himself, it was "Johnny Cash music". On a personal level he was a fascinating mixture of radical views, support for the underdog, fierce patriotism and traditional religious beliefs; a conservative rebel. His long time friend Kris Kristofferson described him as "a walking contradiction, partly truth and partly fiction". Johnny himself endorsed this succinct summary.

Following his death there was a huge resurgence of interest in his life and work with major stars such as Bono and Bruce Springsteen queuing up to pay tribute. A biopic of his life up until marriage to June, starring Joaquin Phoenix and Reese Witherspoon, *Walk The Line*, was released in 2005 to general critical acclaim. Almost 10 years after his death interest in his remarkably varied back catalogue remains very strong. He was an American original whose place in history is assured.

10.

The Musical Stage Show

In view of the enduring popularity of the Million Dollar Quartet and the music they created, it was probably inevitable that some lateral-thinking creative mind would see commercial possibilities beyond CDs and television specials. That person was Floyd Mutrux, a man who grew up loving popular music. "The literature of my youth was an AM car radio," he says.

Mutrux has been involved in the film and theatre industry for over 40 years as a writer, director and producer. His many credits include executive producer of *Freebie And The Bean* (1974) and writing and directing *There Goes My Baby* (1994). He directed the 1978 film *American Hot Wax* about the DJ Alan Freed whom many have credited with coining, or at least widely popularising, the term "rock 'n' roll" in the fifties. Freed's career was effectively ended by the payola scandal which involved accusations of corruption in the radio industry. The film received a great deal of critical acclaim but was not a significant commercial success; but as Floyd Mutrux puts it, "rock 'n' roll was in my head". Accordingly he was on the lookout for more ideas for stories of interest from the world of popular music. Various propositions were put to him but in fact the original spark of an idea for *Million Dollar Quartet* came to him in Las Vegas when he attended the opening of *Smokey Joe's Café*, a musical revue showcasing 39 rock 'n' roll songs written by Jerry Leiber and Mike Stoller. He noticed that the audience were lip-syncing the songs as soon as the show started and said to his wife, "It's going to be a hit." Talking recently, he explained further why this moment convinced him that a work based on the music of the past, in particular from the early days of rock 'n' roll, could provide fertile material for a new work. "They came for the music. In my mind memory lane was open for business. Rock 'n' roll bios would have a second life. The literature of my misspent youth wasn't wasted after all."

He began work on a play entitled *Heartbreak Hotel* which featured Tom Parker as the evil villain. Floyd tried the story out in the course of a series of workshops. He liked it but at three hours felt it was too long. In the middle of his play was the Million Dollar Quartet session. It suddenly occurred to him that this could be a stand-alone story, one which also happened to be "the easiest show to do – one set, one night". He planned to call it *Good Rockin' Tonight*. This was also the title of a book co-written by Colin Escott about Sun Records and the birth of rock 'n' roll. Floyd approached him about getting involved in the project in 2001. Colin is one of the leading authorities on Sun Records *et al* and was just the right person to provide the necessary historical detail. He has written various books which are leaders in their field, including the definitive biography of Hank Williams, penned countless sleeve notes and acted as consultant for many television programmes. He won a Grammy for his work on the box-set *The Complete Hank Williams* released by Mercury in 1998.

The pair then set about adjusting and revising drafts. Floyd regards the members of the Million Dollar Quartet, and many other pioneering musical figures, in reverential terms. He describes them as "characters that blazed the trail in post-war pop music", people whose stories "changed us all as listeners and altered the landscape of our subculture, now and forever". The story was based around real events and Floyd was greatly inspired by the fact that the principals were all larger than life characters. As he said of Sam Phillips, "They said that Sam Phillips was so dynamic that when he walked into a room the molecules in the air would change."

One appealing aspect of putting together a musical about the Million Dollar Quartet – from a prosaically practical point of view – was that there was no need to hire writers to come up with a lot of new songs. That said, there was a great deal of time-consuming work involved in acquiring the rights to the songs. In approaching the storyline Colin Escott aimed to squeeze selected events from about a year's worth of Sun's history – some of it fictionalised – into one evening.

The title of Floyd's original play, *Heartbreak Hotel*, made clear right from the start the axiomatic importance to the project, whatever its form, of the presence of the king. An early version of the show was tried out at the Coronet Theatre in Los Angeles. Space was hired for the purpose. At this stage, in 2002, it was nowhere near ready for a paying audience. The theatre had a variety of stages where new works could be tried out. These sessions, or readings, involved actors reading the lines, sitting round a table and perhaps throwing in a few moves to make the piece come alive. Either way, songs would be announced at particular points when they were meant to appear though not necessarily sung. Trusted colleagues and friends were asked to listen and comment. At this stage things were in a very raw, unrefined state. The process of getting from that point to a viable commercial proposition was a long and arduous road.

It happened that the Coronet Theatre was owned by movie and theatre producer Gigi Pritzker, someone with a wealth of experience in film and theatre production. She was at the theatre one day around

2002 when a reading of *Heartbreak Hotel* was taking place. It was her business partner Ted Rawlins who sat in on the reading. Afterwards, he told Gigi about what he had just seen, clearly excited by the possibilities held out by the work. Gigi had not heard of the Million Dollar Quartet but she had certainly heard of Elvis Presley, Jerry Lee Lewis, Johnny Cash and Carl Perkins and quickly realised that they had come across something special. That said, what they saw was a very early version still requiring a great deal of work.

John Cossette, a highly experienced producer responsible for the Grammies, and who had also been in charge of the Olympics in Atlanta in 1996, was a key member of the production team, brought in originally by Floyd Mutrux. The process of developing the show to the point where it was fully prepared for the big stage, and ultimately Broadway – although Broadway only became a possibility much later – took up much of the rest of the decade. Along the way the original storyline was continually revised by Colin Escott as attempts were made to clarify the message of the show and work out how best to put it over. There were also ongoing debates about which songs should be included. It is important for the developmental process of any musical stage show that the work be put on in various settings in order to see how everything looks in a real theatrical context; this provides a taste of how it would all look in a live performance. It is also very helpful to get reactions from trusted associates – not involved in the actual production – prior to a full commercial launch. The creative team applied a critical filter to the work and, as Gigi Pritzker explains, constantly asked questions of particular interpretations: "Does this serve the entertainment and the story and move it forward; how can we pare things down and make this as interesting and exciting and vibrant as it can be?"

She compares the procedure to putting together a building. "First there are the plans, the structure then some questions: is it made of wood, bricks or what? You build on to this structure as you go, music becomes more orchestrated, you figure out costumes. Initially it's just the bare bones of the story and then you slot in where the music is going to be." In the early stages songs were fitted in at appropriate points – perhaps actors would announce that in the final version 'Blue Suede Shoes' would be performed in the middle of a particular scene; sometimes they might read the lyrics or perhaps a recording of the song would be played.

Floyd Mutrux's original intention was that there would be rear screen projections throughout the show featuring documentary style footage which would create a context of time and place – clips from *The Ed Sullivan Show*, *The Louisiana Hayride*, footage of Beale Street and a lot more besides. For him these were important components which would help to recreate, and bring alive for the audience, important elements of the world the music grew out of. However, as the show developed these particular ideas were dropped. This was also the fate of a scene, choreographed by Floyd's wife, Birgitte, in which Elvis and his fictionalised girlfriend Dyanne dance in the studio.

The actual events of December 4, 1956 were not the most important part of the equation. The music was always going to be the star of the show, the crowd pleaser. The producers wanted to create a good story for the stage which would have widespread public appeal. For this reason it soon became clear that hardly any of the songs the quartet originally sang would be candidates for inclusion in the show. Amongst the few originals that have been included are 'Brown Eyed Handsome Man' and 'Down By The Riverside'. The fact is there were too many religious songs and too many obscure Bill Monroe songs in the original session, most of which would be insufficiently commercial for a show aiming to appeal to the broadest possible audience. There was a certain irony in this. When Johnny Cash first approached Sam Phillips in 1955 he too was given the message that the religious songs he wanted to play were not commercial enough.

The challenge, therefore, was to choose songs by the artists from the era in which the Million Dollar Quartet Session took place – but to resist the temptation to include famous songs, which crowds would love, from later stages in their careers. So, for instance, neither 'In The Ghetto' nor 'Suspicious Minds' were possibilities.

The embryonic *Million Dollar Quartet* show was taken to Florida's Seaside Music Theater in Daytona Beach in 2006 and then the Village Theater in Issaquah, Washington, a suburb of Seattle, in 2007. Performances were in front of paying audiences, including the theatre's subscribers. Crucial to the process of honing the piece was feedback from colleagues and audiences; though not the same as a focus group, the technique was nonetheless aimed at letting the creative team see what was likely to work best for the largest number of people.

The general reaction in Florida was positive right from the start, with the musical receiving standing ovations and breaking box office records. The reaction in Seattle was even greater and at this stage the team sensed they just might have a major hit on their hands. Audience response outshone the box office records set by every show in the theatre's 30 year history except *Cats*.

Thereafter the show had a five week run at Chicago's Goodman Theatre, opening on September 27, 2008. This proved to be an ideal arrangement for both parties. The Goodman had a gap in its schedule (and so was, in theatre jargon, "dark") that it was happy to fill. For the producers of *Million Dollar Quartet* it was an opportunity to perform the show in a large theatrical space which gave it a great deal of exposure, all of which helped to raise its profile. From the Goodman, it transferred to the Apollo Theatre in the same city where it became a fully-fledged hit production. It is now in the fifth year of what has proved to be a very successful run

The show received a boost when Cameron Mackintosh, one of the most powerful and influential theatre producers in the world, came to see it. The great man arrived announced, bought a ticket and took in the show as any other member of the public would. Soon afterwards he met Gigi Pritzker and Ted Rawlins and was very complimentary about what he had seen. The Chicago production was co-directed by Eric D Schaeffer who has worked on numerous major shows including *Follies* and *Glory Days* on Broadway and *The Witches Of Eastwick* in London's West End.

Chuck Mead was brought in as a music consultant when the show was put on in Florida. As a member of the successful country/Americana group BR549 he had plenty of experience of how to make a band sound high-energy-good. The fact that he was chosen was indicative of the crucial importance of an authentic musical sound. As Chuck himself put it, "I got this gig because I'm a hillbilly singer by trade.... I guess they hired me because they didn't want it to be a Broadway musical interpretation of rock 'n' roll". From the start he wanted to recreate something of the rough-around-the-edges sound of the original Sun recordings; he was not interested in any kind of smooth, easy listening effect. He used Shure microphones similar to the ones in Sun studio in the fifties and also amplifiers capable of getting close to the authentic kind of sound he was after.

Chuck wanted the musicians hired for the various shows to become tight musical outfits capable of riffing off each other and putting across a band performance – with the whole being greater than the sum of the parts. To this end he got them to play together at real gigs at real music clubs in front of real audiences. When hiring musicians Gigi Pritzker said they preferred those with previous experience of playing live music in the raw. As with the originals many candidates for the principal roles could not read music. As she said, "When we were looking at CVs and saw someone with a massive musical theatre background, the red flags went up. Chuck Mead knows nothing about musical theatre... that was deliberate. His role is to make sure the show was authentic to what it is all about – rock 'n' roll and not musical theatre – a large number of the people coming to see the show simply love early rock 'n' roll." For years during the development of the show there was no written score.

The presence of the stage show in Chicago led to one interesting discovery – the then current whereabouts of Marilyn Evans, the girlfriend Elvis brought with him to Sun in 1956; various writers and journalists had tried unsuccessfully to track her down over the years. As a result of the general publicity surrounding the show, one of Marilyn's friends put two and two together and realised she was the mystery girl from more than half a century before. Marilyn came forward and her identity was established beyond doubt – others had apparently claimed to be her in the past – when she produced a napkin with a scribbled note to her from Elvis. She had never sought publicity following her brief dalliance with him and after the 1956 session soon disappeared from view to follow a more low profile career in the world of dance. She had little recollection of the session beyond the fact that she was wearing an outfit that was all wool.

For most of its period of gestation, the producers of *Million Dollar Quartet* did not see it as a candidate for Broadway, precisely because it was not perceived to be the kind of musical theatre typically associated with the New York scene; the costs involved in putting on a Broadway show were also a deterrent. However everything changed at the Tony Awards ceremony in 2009. John Cossette, through his contacts, managed to secure a couple of spots for the Chicago quartet, fully kitted out in their stage costumes, during the intervals at the awards ceremony which was held at Radio City Music Hall in New York. At this stage the appearance was seen as a good piece of publicity for the show rather than a stepping stone along the road to Broadway.

Getting everybody there, just to play a few songs, was no easy task. All of the understudies had to be used for the Chicago show while the principals were in New York; that was risky because if one of them fell ill it would not be easy to find a replacement. There were also considerable costs involved in terms of transport and accommodation. During the first set the band played it seemed that most of the audience headed for the bathroom. However disaster was averted with the second set; most of the audience was present and the response was overwhelmingly enthusiastic.

Seeing and hearing some of the songs from Million Dollar Quartet being rapturously received in the large theatrical setting of Radio City Music Hall made Gigi Pritzker, Ted Rawlins and John Cossette all think that perhaps the show really was a candidate for Broadway. Events then moved quickly. The next day they were contacted by a representative of the Nederlander organisation, owners of a number of Broadway theatres and concert venues. They indicated a desire to be partners in the project and offered a theatre for *Million Dollar Quartet*. The show opened at the 1,200-seater Nederlander Theater in April 2010 – a considerable step up from theatres the show had played in previously which typically had several hundred seats.

At the Tonys that year *Million Dollar Quartet* was nominated for three awards and won one – Best Performance by a Featured Actor in a Musical, for Levi Kreis as Jerry Lee Lewis; it was quite a journey in only a year. The show has received various other awards and nominations over the years. The run at the Nederlander Theater ended in June 2011. Thereafter it opened Off-Broadway at New World Stages where it ran until June 2012. Between the two venues there were a total of 901 performances. According to Colin Escott there was a good deal of support for the stage show from the Cash estate, Graceland and also the family of Carl Perkins.

A number of celebrity guests have made appearances at the Broadway show including three who were there at the original session: Fluke, the drummer, engineer Jack Clement and the sole survivor of the original quartet, Jerry Lee Lewis. Fluke met up with the cast members backstage after the show and said, "Boys, I've just got one problem – we weren't that good". Both Jack and Jerry Lee performed songs backed by the stage quartet. On the night Jerry Lee made his special guest appearance, former president Bill Clinton brought his family to see the show.

These were remarkable occasions but it was nonetheless poignant to compare these elderly men, displaying the inevitable, unforgiving effects of the passage of time, with the wild and exuberant tearaways of yesteryear. There have been other guest appearances, by Wanda Jackson, "The Queen of Rockabilly", country star Ray Benson (of western swing group Asleep At The Wheel) and Stray Cats bass player Lee Rocker.

According to Gigi Pritzker not many changes were made for the move to Broadway even though the show differs from many of the big budget affairs found there. The tone is more intimate, the set is modest and the musicians play all the songs themselves – there is no orchestra or chorus or other musical backing. As director Eric Schaeffer puts it, "What's always been at the heart of rock 'n'' roll, and the key to this piece, is the raw energy of these guys playing." For Broadway the core was maintained though the costumes were a bit glitzier and there were some changes made to beef up the storyline. Prior to Broadway it turned on whether Johnny Cash would leave Sun. This was changed so that the focus was on Sam Phillips – would he sell out and join RCA, or would he continue to plug away at his small independent label and try to help unknown artists reach a bigger audience as he had done for years?

After the main story has come to an end, the band plays several songs as an encore to send the audience home humming some of their favourite tunes. Before the move to Broadway this took place with the backdrop of the studio set used for the whole show; for Broadway the set was flown out and the band played their songs as if performing at a live concert.

The show also set up shop in London's Noël Coward Theatre in February 2011, opening a run that lasted until January 2012. Some changes were made for London which reflected differences in the American and British sense of humour. The choice of England was no coincidence. Many British fans are very knowledgeable about early rock 'n' roll music – often more so than their American counterparts. Paul McCartney owns Carl Perkins' back catalogue and so receives royalties for some of the songs featured in the show. Notable guests in London were former Rolling Stones bassist Bill Wyman and current guitarist Ronnie Wood, their presence particularly fitting since the Stones were heavily influenced by much of the music of the Million Dollar Quartet and they continued to carry the torch for millions of young people finding their own music and kicking against authority in the process.

A nationwide American tour started in October 2011 in Cleveland, Ohio which is currently booking its third year.

One of the key challenges of running a number of versions of *Million Dollar Quartet* at the same time has been the constant need to cast new people to play the principals. As Gigi Pritzker says, "It's non-stop. At one point we had 65 musicians working on the show between Chicago, London, New York and the tour." For the producers putting together *Million Dollar Quartet*, the process is to some extent more akin to putting together several bands rather than a stage show. As it was in 1956, musical ability is the first priority when recruiting new people – they have to be seriously good players.

Acting ability comes after musicianship. Many of the principals have been played by musicians who have never acted in their lives, though the part of Sam Phillips is always played by an actor. As Colin Escott put it, "We were looking for guys who could channel these performers rather than imitate them. Our guys actually play their own instruments. They are singers/musicians first, rather than actors. We wanted to capture some of the vibrancy of rock 'n' roll at its creation." The creative team were definitely not interested in an evening of legends in concert.

The critical reaction to the show has been mainly positive. Negative comments have usually related to the storyline which is often seen as lightweight and very much secondary to the exuberant music which most critics, regardless of their own musical taste, are seduced by. Indeed the major role played by the music has prompted some commentators to compare the experience of attending the show to watching a tribute band.

American critic Al Bresloff was typical of many when he said, "The musicians make you want to clap your hands and stamp your feet to some of the greatest hits of that era." Charles Spencer, reviewing the London show said, "No one could claim that this is a great, original or ground-breaking piece of work, but anyone who loves rock 'n' roll is almost certain to have a good time." The *New York Times*, a key indicator of critical opinion, had no reservations saying that it was a "buoyant new musical which whips the crowd into a frenzy".

Overall, the show has enjoyed considerable commercial success though not on anything like the scale of established winners such as *Les Miserables* or *The Phantom Of The Opera*.

The term "jukebox musical" (occasionally "deluxe jukebox musical") is often applied to the show and some see this as mildly derogatory. Gigi Pritzker however is not bothered. "We don't really care so long as people come," she says. Floyd Mutrux is less sanguine describing it is a label applied by New York critics which is intended to "categorise music from the street as a lower art form, music coming from a jukebox, something for teenagers, not yet mature enough to have a higher appreciation of theatre". He complains that the label, often applied by critics before the show opens to the public, when it is in development, gives it a "negative vibe".

The very fact that a stage musical has been produced which has evolved and grown in popularity over a decade, and is still pulling in substantial audiences, surely provides proof positive of the enduring appeal of the music produced by the original Million Dollar Quartet in 1956. Whilst it is true that a good number of those who go to see the show do so for reasons which are coloured by nostalgia, no show could survive on that kind of audience alone. There are plenty of young people in the audiences who soon submit to the infectious charm of the popular music from long ago. Even though they might regard it as a good deal less cool than rap, drum and bass, acid jazz or the latest offerings from Adele or Radiohead they nonetheless sense something great, something timeless, part of the continuum that links their music to the music of the past, which gave birth to rock and pop music in its myriad forms. Towards the end of the show the lights go down briefly; when they come back up the musicians have formed themselves into the iconic pose around the piano with a backdrop of the original black and white photograph blown up to life-size. It is a brilliant theatrical moment that takes the breath away. It also serves to remind audiences – of whatever age – that what they have just seen is not some theatrical fantasy tale but the manifestation of a musical revolution brought about by real people through a combination of their natural talent, hard work, a changing social landscape and some good fortune.

What of the future? The producers of the musical, having toured the show in America, Canada and England, have recently taken it to Japan – its appeal is international. How long will it continue? Will there be a film? This will have been discussed by some in the business but there is nothing in the pipeline at the moment.

What is clear beyond doubt though is that the success of the musical stage show over the last decade has demonstrated that the music of the Million Dollar Quartet continues to resonate with large numbers of people old and young and is an established part of the cultural landscape of the world.

Acknowledgements

In view of the amount of time that has passed since the Million Dollar Quartet session took place – almost 66 years – it is hardly surprising that not many people are alive who were actually there. That said, since nobody will ever know for sure who exactly popped in and out of the studio in the course of the afternoon and evening, there might still be people out there with stories to tell.

Of the quartet, only Jerry Lee Lewis is still alive but he is under contract to produce his autobiography and was consequently unavailable. I did speak to both Jack Clement, the engineer on the day, and WS "Fluke" Holland, the drummer for the Carl Perkins session, who played on some of the songs. Both were affable and happy to talk and reminisce but it was clear that for perfectly understandable reasons their recollections of the specific details of the session were hazy to say the least. I am, however, grateful to them for helping to paint a picture of the atmosphere on the day and digging up a few gems from the dim recesses of their memories.

Elvis Presley's girlfriend on the day, Marilyn Evans, disappeared from public view soon after the session, only reappearing in 2008 as a result of publicity associated with the stage show in Chicago. In the course of an interview with a local newspaper she made it clear that she, like the others, had virtually no recollection of the day – beyond what she was wearing.

Accordingly it was a case of trying to glean as much information as possible – and it was often contradictory – from the various accounts of the day in books, magazines, newspapers, liner notes and newspapers. Several back copies of *Now Dig This* and an online newspaper archive threw up some interesting information not found elsewhere.

Colin Escott and Spencer Leigh gave me some useful pointers in the early stages.

For information on the history of the stage musical inspired by the Million Dollar Quartet I am indebted to Floyd Mutrux, the man who had the original idea, and Gigi Pritzker, one of the producers who took the whole project to Broadway and beyond.

In addition I must acknowledge some invaluable assistance from Dave Roe and Dave Gibbons along the way.

Further Reading

Sam Phillips
Crouch, Kevin, and Tanja Crouch. *Sun King. The Life And Times Of Sam Phillips, The Man Behind Sun Records*. London: Piatkus. 2008.

Sun Records
Escott, Colin, with Martin Hawkins. *Good Rockin' Tonight. Sun Records And The Birth Of Rock 'n' Roll*. New York: St Martin's Press. 1991.

Elvis Presley
Guralnick, Peter. *Last Train to Memphis. The Rise Of Elvis Presley*. Little Brown & Co. 1994.
Guralnick, Peter. *Careless Love. The Unmaking Of Elvis Presley*. Little Brown & Co. 1999.

Jerry Lee Lewis
Tosches, Nick. *Hellfire: The Jerry Lee Lewis Story*. London: Penguin. 2007.

Lewis, Myra, with Murray Silver. *Great Balls Of Fire: The True Story Of Jerry Lee Lewis.* London: Virgin Books. 1982.

Carl Perkins
Perkins, Carl, and David McGee. *Go, Cat, Go! The Life And Times Of Carl Perkins, The King Of Rockabilly.* New York: Hyperion. 1996.

Johnny Cash
Cash, Johnny with Patrick Carr. *Cash: The Autobiography Of Johnny Cash.* London: HarperCollins. 2000.
Miller, Stephen. *Johnny Cash: The Life Of An American Icon.* London: Omnibus Press. 2003.